Music in
Biblical Life

ALSO BY JONATHAN L. FRIEDMANN
AND FROM McFARLAND

*Synagogue Song: An Introduction
to Concepts, Theories and Customs* (2012)

*Music, Theology and Worship:
Selected Writings, 1841–1896* (2011)

*Music in Jewish Thought:
Selected Writings, 1890–1920* (2009)

*The Value of Sacred Music: An Anthology
of Essential Writings, 1801–1918* (2009)

MUSIC IN BIBLICAL LIFE

The Roles of Song in Ancient Israel

Jonathan L. Friedmann

McFarland & Company, Inc., Publishers
Jefferson, North Carolina, and London

LIBRARY OF CONGRESS CATALOGUING-IN-PUBLICATION DATA

Friedmann, Jonathan L., 1980–
    Music in biblical life : the roles of song in ancient Israel / Jonathan L. Friedmann.
      p.   cm.
    Includes bibliographical references and index.

    ISBN 978-0-7864-7409-7

    1. Music in the Bible.   I. Title.
ML166.F75 2013
221.8'78—dc23   2012049445

BRITISH LIBRARY CATALOGUING DATA ARE AVAILABLE

© 2013 Jonathan L. Friedmann. All rights reserved

No part of this book may be reproduced or transmitted in any form or by any means, electronic or mechanical, including photocopying or recording, or by any information storage and retrieval system, without permission in writing from the publisher.

Front cover image © 2013 Clipart.com

Manufactured in the United States of America

McFarland & Company, Inc., Publishers
  Box 611, Jefferson, North Carolina 28640
    www.mcfarlandpub.com

Table of Contents

Preface   1
Introduction   5

1. Functional Music   17
2. The Song of the Sea and Group Cohesion: Exodus 15:1–21   31
3. Therapeutic Functions of David's Lyre: 1 Samuel 16:14–23   58
4. Sing unto God: Music in Prophetic Literature   83
5. Music and Public Worship: Singing in the Book of Psalms   114

Conclusion   153
Chapter Notes   165
Bibliography   184
Index   197

Preface

This book uncovers music's role in shaping and defining the self-identity of ancient Israel. Functional music was integrated into Israel's daily life, accompanying activities as diverse as manual labor and royal processionals. At key junctures and in core institutions, musical tones were used to formulate and deliver messages, convey and heighten emotions, assert and strengthen communal bonds, and establish and intensify human-divine contact. The intricate and multi-faceted nature of this music will be demonstrated through a detailed look into four main episodes and genres: the Song of the Sea (Exod. 15), King Saul and David's lyre (1 Sam. 16), the use of music in prophecy, and the Book of Psalms. Specifically, it will be argued that Israel's birth as a free nation was marked by the Song of the Sea, its monarchic system was defined by the archetypical musician-king David, its moral and ethical guidelines were often received through musical prophecy, and its appointed institution for mediating worship was designed and officiated by a class of priestly musicians. Moreover, three of these four areas involve the main leadership categories of biblical society — king, prophet and priest — giving added support to the view that music held a prominent place and played a defining role within that civilization.

In addition to these specific areas of inquiry, the argument will be made that Israel was more musically developed — or at least more musically aware — than neighboring civilizations. Without doubt, the propensity for music has been encoded in the human genome since the dawn of our species. The earliest records of human habitation show evidence of musical activities, from primitive instruments to resonant cave "auditoriums." In most ancient cultures (and most non–Western cultures of the modern world) it was normal for everyone to participate in music-making. In this regard, the musical output of ancient Israel was not outwardly different than that of other Near Eastern populations. The daily lives of all groups included utilitarian songs of varied types: work songs, learning songs, holiday songs, domestic songs, etc. But Alfred Sendrey, in his comprehensive study *Music in Ancient Israel*, contends that the songs of Israel had an ethos absent — or at least not prominent — in other music-cultures. For Israel, singing meant serving God. Sendrey explains: "[song was] a religious creed expressed in sounds, the palpable affirmation of his close connection with the eternal, the union in harmonious sounds of the Creator and His creation."[1]

The term "song" (in various noun and verb forms) occurs three hundred nine times in the Hebrew Bible. More often than not, these references appear in contexts and poems in which the deity is praised. This is resounding confirmation of music's centrality in biblical religion. If the Bible is any indication of attitudes held by the populace, ancient Israel was an utterly religious society. Fortunes, failures, ailments, recoveries, victories, tragedies and all manner of circumstances were attributed to divine intervention. But the religiously minded were not content to simply notice the craftwork and manipulations of God's invisible hand. They wanted to *feel* God's existence. And so they sang.

Singing turns concepts into feelings. If constructed with suitable tones, songs of love, loss, joy, angst, fear and so on tend to evoke corresponding responses. Similarly, a song whose subject is God can, for the believer, inspire a sense of an indwelling divine presence. This does not mean that God is reduced to an emotion. But when music is the conduit to experiencing divinity (as it often was in ancient Israel), God is *perceived* as a feeling.

To be sure, other peoples of the Near East were acquainted with religious song. Inscriptions, scrolls and artworks depicting musical worship have been found in Egypt, Mesopotamia and elsewhere. Yet it was the people of Israel, according to Sendrey, who raised this religious expression to its highest peak. They conceived of singing as a holy act and generated a collection of prayer-songs unprecedented in its expansiveness.

The conception of music as a central element of biblical society will be developed using an interdisciplinary approach, wherein pertinent information from an array of specializations and sources is put into conversation and Bible passages are analyzed through a modern-scientific lens. Rather than relying on a single methodology, this study is rooted in the premise that by applying a variety of contemporary theoretical tools to selected biblical passages, essential functions of music in biblical life can be illuminated. Such an endeavor requires tools from a number of fields—including but not limited to theology, sociology, anthropology, musicology, cognitive science and music therapy—as well as the classification of musical references into four primary functions: cohesive, therapeutic, emotive/spiritual and didactic. The result is a study that identifies reasons for—and not just the existence of—music in biblical life and, most centrally, shows significant ways music informed Israel's understanding of itself.

My interest in the place of music in biblical life has grown from my experience as a synagogue cantor. As a musical clergyman, charged with converting petition and praise into melody, I am acutely aware of the centrality of song in the structured setting of worship and the less formal contexts of classrooms, family celebrations, holiday meals and the like. It seems that music has always been a centerpiece of Jewish religious life, and although its specific sounds are shaped by myriad geographical, denominational and historical influences, Jewish sacred songs of all types exhibit four main functions: communing with the divine, imparting key concepts and ideals, giving voice to personal and collective emotions, and strengthening bonds to community and heritage. More than any other ritual element—and in a deeper way than plainly spoken words—liturgical song is the lifeblood of the Jewish faith and a primary mode through which Jewish identity and affiliation are articulated and sustained.

When I began applying this functional view of sacred music to the Hebrew Bible, it occurred to me that the musical uses prevalent in contemporary practice are also found in verses scattered throughout the biblical text. In addition to fresh insights into the musical character of ancient Israel, this process brought to light significant ways in which musical functions in Jewish and Christian traditions can be traced to the Bible.

Like any study, this book was not written in isolation. Several individuals have contributed to my biblical and musical knowledge over the years, either in classroom, professional or informal settings. Added to this, my fascination with the functional side of religious music has drawn me to the work of many researchers who, though I do not know them personally, have aided my grasp of the intersections of music and psychology, sociology, worship, ethnography, education and other fields. Those who have had a personal influence on my thinking include Cantor William Sharlin, my longtime cantorial mentor, and Bible professors Drs. Joel Gereboff and Marvin Sweeney, both of whom were my instructors and are now my colleagues at the Academy for Jewish Religion, California. I am also indebted to Dr. Jon R. Stone for introducing me to the sociology of religion while I was a graduate student at California State University, Long Beach. I am grateful for the indispensable comments, suggestions, and encouragement of Dr. Kathleen Rochester of Greenwich School of Theology (GST) and Dr. Herrie Van Rooy of North-West University, Potchefstroom, who were my advisors when this study began as my doctoral dissertation. I also wish to thank Peggy Evans, liaison administrator at GST, and my expert proofreader Dr. Ester Petrenko. Above all, I am eternally thankful to my wife Elvia, who makes everything that I do possible.

Introduction

The academic study of music in the Hebrew Bible is a predominantly descriptive enterprise. Since its beginnings, well over a century ago, research in this area has generally fallen into three categories: historical studies of the context and development of music in the Bible[1]; surveys of musical references in the biblical text[2]; and analyses of the types and uses of biblical instruments.[3] Taken as a whole, these efforts demonstrate that the Bible abounds with depictions of the use of music in many aspects of life, from war to celebration.

However, these explorations rarely draw deeper implications about the important functions such musical production likely played. For the most part, they consider music as an aesthetic or secondary feature instead of a potential key element in social formation and expression. Recent work in diverse fields including ethnomusicology, cognitive science and theology has placed music at the center rather than the periphery of human experience. This research indicates that, throughout history and across cultures, music has been used to stimulate communal bonding, assert identities, instill moral lessons, shape moods, intensify emotions, pass on oral histories and a host of other aims. Thus, instead of viewing the Bible's musical references as merely proving an appreciation of the arts in biblical times, it is possible to examine whether — and if so how — this music contributed to broader cultural phenomena.

A thorough picture of music's place in the culture and worldview of ancient Israel requires a systematic approach, in which musical depictions serve as the basis for further inquiry. While the precise sound of this music is irretrievably lost to history, evidence of its significance is found in a range of biblical literary genres, including narratives, poetry, proverbs and prophetic musings. Through a combination of textual analysis and social-theoretical investigation, a more comprehensive understanding of the Hebrew Bible's music-culture can be achieved.

Though scholars have expended much effort in categorizing biblical passages mentioning instruments and singing, there is a need for a detailed assessment of how music-making helped to shape and articulate personal and collective values, ideals and emotions. While not identical, daily life in biblical times was virtually as complex as our own,[4] and many of the applications of music known today can also be identified in the Hebrew Bible.

A study of this kind requires both a close reading of selected musical episodes in the Bible, and an evaluation of research into how music operates in contemporary settings, with due recognition that there are differences in historical and cultural placements. Much more than a superfluous or embellishing element, music has historically been an indispensable part of the human experience. That this is true in the biblical context can be gleaned from exploring passages through a modern lens.

This book rests on the claim that musical accounts in the Hebrew Bible convey the wider import of music in biblical life. The picture of Israel's music-culture comes into focus by asking: How was music integral to social, intellectual and spiritual life in biblical times? This question gives rise to several others: What role did music play in group instruction and cohesion? How was music used to encourage personal and communal wellbeing? What role did music play in the prophetic experience? What does the Book of Psalms reveal about the purpose of musical production in biblical worship?

Our awareness of the roles music played in Bible times will be informed by five main objectives.

- First, to isolate and assess biblical passages illustrating the important place of music in biblical life. The broader cultural-religious import of these representative verses will be learned through examining their textual and historical contexts and through insights culled from modern disciplines.
- Second and more specifically, to determine the social functions of music in the Hebrew Bible, looking at accounts of communal worship, both spontaneous and structured.

Introduction

- Third, to analyze ancient Israel's apprehension of music's therapeutic qualities using David's musical sessions with Saul as a focal point.
- Fourth, to investigate the link between music, prophetic experiences and the public reception of prophetic messages.
- Fifth, to explore music's role in achieving central goals of worship, such as moral and theological instruction, articulation of identity, and experience of the divine.

This study is grounded in the assertion that applying contemporary theoretical tools to select passages can illuminate essential functions of music in biblical life. Such an endeavor requires an interdisciplinary approach. Musical accounts will be assessed using tools and sources from a number of fields, including but not limited to theology, sociology, anthropology, musicology, cognitive science and music therapy. This will involve, among other things, the classification of numerous musical references into four primary functions: cohesive, therapeutic, emotive/spiritual and didactic. The examination will also draw upon several pertinent theories, notably Émile Durkheim's appraisal of ceremonial ritual (1912), Rudolf Otto's understanding of the numinous experience (1923), and Daniel J. Levitin's view of music's use in shaping culture and identity (2008). Of course, as an interdisciplinary study, there will be points of intersection among these theorists, as well as insights derived from other sources; but these thinkers will provide clear perspective with which to address biblical accounts.

Rather than devoting attention to every verse that alludes to music — an effort that is as unnecessary as it is onerous — I will be examining four representative biblical episodes and genres: the Song of the Sea (Exod. 15), King Saul and David's harp (1 Sam. 16), the general use of music in prophecy, and the Book of Psalms. More than other biblical examples, these four areas show the extent to which music helped inform the self-identity of Israel. Most fundamentally, they indicate how musical tones aided the formulation and delivery of messages, conveyed and heightened emotions, asserted and strengthened communal bonds, and established and intensified human-divine contact. In the Temple service and the individualized utterances of prophetic poetry, song proved an effective means of transmitting ideas and stirring souls; and both the crossing of the Red Sea — a key transformative moment in Israel's history — and the kingship of David — the model monarch and national hero — were filled with music. Thus, the Song of the Sea, monarchy, prophecy and priesthood together demonstrate music's integration into the social structure of ancient Israel. Furthermore, three of these four areas involve the main leadership categories in the Hebrew Bible — king, prophet and priest — giving added support to the view that music held a prominent place and played a defining role within that civilization. It can therefore be said that Israel was a musical people both because they were highly developed in that art, and because they utilized music to shape and express who they were as a nation.

Assessing the Text

Before embarking on this musical journey, it behooves us to consider these words of warning from musicologist Joachim Braun: "Of all pre–Christian cultures, none has a music history as burdened by one-sided and subjective perspectives and prejudices as that of ancient Israel/Palestine. Research into other high cultures of the ancient world has never been as plagued by a neglect of scientific principles or by unscientific arguments as is the case with this region."[5] Especially problematic for Braun is the over-reliance on the Bible itself — a document of biased construction and mythological content. He observes a sort of fetishism around what the Bible states regarding musical instruments, events and practices. This fixation has contributed to a neglect of cultural entities and tendencies present within contemporaneous societies, and the elevation of biblical musical descriptions — no matter how legendary — to the status of history. Indeed, only in the past few decades has the emergence of archaeological and iconographic evidence begun to recast what was previously presumed from biblical accounts.

But such an overhaul does not require excavation or anthropology; it can be made on literary grounds. Since at least the nineteenth century, textual critics have questioned the veracity of numerous biblical episodes, including a few involving music. Most significant for our purposes are the verses sung at the Red Sea (Song of the Sea) and the musical activities of King David, both of which are folk traditions rather than historical facts. For reasons I will explain later, I have nonetheless chosen to focus

Introduction

on these musical examples, along with similarly problematic texts of the prophets and psalms. Suffice it to say, even if we acknowledge the suspect nature of these passages, we can appreciate their content and inclusion in the biblical canon as a reflection of ancient Israel's music-culture. It takes a musically literate people to revere such stories and accept them as plausible.

The issue with the Song of the Sea is multifold. The exodus story, as presented in the books of Exodus and Numbers, has long been doubted. A recently published survey by Sherwin T. Wine outlines four "tests" that scholars have posed.[6] First is the evidence test. To date, there is essentially no evidence from non-biblical sources that Egypt ever experienced a mass migration of Israelite slaves, or that the Egyptians held such slaves in any sizable number. Second is the probability test. Egypt was in control of the land to which the Israelites reportedly marched, making their escape futile at best. Third is the realism test. A deified and protected leader like Pharaoh would not pay personal visits to rebellious slaves, no matter how severe the plague. Fourth is the motivation test. The story's credibility is tarnished by its transparent agenda to show the superiority of the God of Israel over the Egyptian deities.

In light of these broad objections, it would seem that details of the exodus, like the Song of the Sea, are but the imagined particulars of a mythic tale. Indeed, scholars have argued that the Song, which appears in Exodus 15, is actually the product of a cultic custom of the First Jerusalem Temple.[7] It is unclear exactly how old the roots of this tradition might be; but it is likely that it originated in a worship context and was backdated to Moses, Miriam and the Israelites. "So far as further back in time is concerned," writes John Arthur Smith, "the song's interpolation in the exodus narrative is itself probably a consequence of its having acquired an established place in cultic worship, perhaps in connection with a Passover liturgy, by the time of the final redaction of the Pentateuch in the early post-exilic period (that is, after 539 B.C.E.)."[8] Along these lines, the Talmud states that Levitical choirs sang the Song during afternoon sacrifices on the Sabbath.[9] This is a late source — roughly 600 C.E. — but its description is probably accurate for the last fifty years or so of the Second Temple. This might account for the text's implicit responsorial form, which was a favored method of singing in the Temple.

Similar issues exist with the portrayal of David as a musical king.

Tradition paints David as a gifted lyre player, singer and writer of song lyrics. This last conception is especially doubtful. David's was an illiterate age, and David — along with his son and fellow warrior king Solomon — was almost certainly incapable of writing.[10] This did not prevent the editors from attributing large quantities of text to the king, including seventy-three psalms—a decision prompted by the rabbinic criterion that every book in the canon be ascribed to a legitimate "prophetic secretary."[11] Thus, it seems, the popular image of David as the "sweet singer of Israel" is more legend than reality.

Added to this, there are a few scholars (sometimes called "minimalists") who posit that Moses and David never existed, or that their lives were far different — and far less impressive — than what the Bible recounts.[12] Though unconventional, this view is not as arbitrary or sensational as it might at first seem. It is based on a stunning lack of archeological evidence. However, the impact of the stories— whether read in antiquity or the present — has never depended on the existence or non-existence of the biblical figures. From a cultural standpoint, they are genuine characters. Ahad Ha'am articulates this distinction in his 1904 essay "Moses," which deserves quoting at length:

> I care not whether this man Moses really existed; whether his life and his activity really corresponded to our traditional account of him; whether he was really the savior of Israel and gave his people the Law in the form in which it is preserved; and so forth. I have one short and simple answer for all these conundrums. This Moses, I say, this man of old time, whose existence and character you are trying to elucidate, matters to nobody but scholars like you. We have another Moses of our own, whose image has been enshrined in the hearts of the Jewish people for generations, and whose influence on our national life has never ceased from ancient times till the present day. The existence of this Moses, as a historical fact, depends in no way on your investigations. For even if you succeeded in demonstrating conclusively that the man Moses never existed, or that he was not such a man as we supposed, you would not thereby detract one jot from the historical reality of the ideal Moses— the Moses who has been our leader not only for forty years in the wilderness of Sinai, but for thousands of years in all the wildernesses in which we have wandered since the Exodus.[13]

Despite these and other obstacles, it is possible to positively assess the musical significance of the Moses and David traditions. Even if we take the extreme view that neither man even existed, the musical light their stories shed is not irreparably distorted. Rather, if we claim — as Ha'am does — that the value of biblical stories rests more in their cultural import than their historicity, then the stories offer a reliable look into how ancient Israel perceived the role and power of music. It is for this reason that this book accepts the premises and particulars of its central topics: the Song of the Sea, David's lyre, prophecy and the Book of Psalms. Any of these subjects can be criticized on textual and/or archaeological grounds. But, at the very least, they reveal a society that valued music enough to include it in seminal stories, messages, customs and poetry.

On the one hand, the analyses that follow might not satisfy Braun's desire for a purely historical investigation of music in biblical times. It is not my aim to challenge the reality of a given passage or provide an alternate scenario. For the most part, the text will be treated as a coherent story sprinkled with pertinent musical details — factual or otherwise. On the other hand, this is a cultural-sociological study that seeks broader implications of cherished texts. It is my position that what the Bible says about music is a true representation of the musical world in which the authors lived. Thus, a story like the Song of the Sea is valid not because it records a moment in time, but because it shows how music was understood, utilized and performed in biblical society. The principle is this: a text need not be literally true to be culturally true.

Cultural Accuracy

This point is especially apt when we consider the amount of musical references in the Hebrew Bible. The Hebrew Bible consists of thirty-nine individual books. The composition and collection of this material spans a period of over a thousand years. Within each stage and literary genre of this expansive anthology, allusions are made to music performance. As expected, these references are more abundant in a songbook like Psalms than a storybook like Genesis, which contains just two incidental citations (4:21; 31:27). But Genesis and the other four books of the Torah do provide important insights into the nature of music in the wider biblical canon.

Introduction

Musical scenes in the Torah are scattered and few. The Five Books are mainly concerned with imparting wisdom and behavioral guidelines, explicating the nature of the divine, and unraveling the early history of the Jewish people. It is only when music intersects with one of these streams—either as a secondary element or a way of advancing the story—that it receives coverage in the text. Yet this was not the full extent of ancient Israel's musical output. On the contrary, because the Torah's agenda yielded such a limited window into everyday life, its musical episodes can be seen as snapshots of a much larger phenomenon.

There are only a dozen musical occurrences in the Torah. But if we take these sparse references as indicators of cultural norms, we find that the Israelites used music to celebrate (Gen. 31:27), express devotion (Exod. 15:1–21; 32:18), announce special events (Exod. 19:16, 20:18; Lev. 23:24, 25:9; Num. 29:1), deliver messages (Num. 10:1–10, 31:6), accompany labor (Num. 21:17), give moral instruction and transmit historical knowledge (Deut. 32:1–43, 33:1–29). From this summary alone, it is clear that music was not merely an afterthought or embellishment, but a tool for achieving specific aims.

Going a step further, each of these examples can be classified as universal. Human societies of all types and levels of development incorporate music of celebration, worship, announcement, communication, work and education. One can also presume that ancient Israel, like other musical people, had thriving traditions of domestic and secular music. Admittedly, the text does not point explicitly to these forms; the Torah's religious emphasis made their mention superfluous and irrelevant. However, it is almost always the case that advanced development in public and sacred music is matched with equally evolved private and nonreligious music. Thus, the same Israelites who blared trumpets on the battlefield also sang lullabies by the cradle; and the same people who gathered to sing divine praise also sang the street songs of the day.

All of this makes the Torah a potentially rich source of investigation for ethnomusicologists, who study the social and cultural aspects of music in global contexts. Of course, because the music itself was not transcribed and has not been passed on orally in any reliable fashion, the sound component cannot be confidently duplicated. So, from a purely musical standpoint—where elements such as tonal range, stylistic variants and performance techniques are of paramount import—Torah passages are of meager value. But from the vantage point of music and culture, the text paints a vivid picture of a society in which music was interwoven into other non-musical activities. In this way, the Torah can be cited as ancient support for the ethnomusicological claim that music is a constant companion to human life and is most often functional in design and intent.

This view expands as we look at other sections of the Hebrew Bible. Notwithstanding the varying number of musical occurrences in the individual biblical books—more a reflection of genre than of society—it is remarkable that only eight books lack direct mention of songs or instruments. These include two narrative scrolls, Ruth and Esther, and the prophetic accounts of Obadiah, Jonah, Micah, Nahum, Haggai and Malachi. Since these books are such a rarity in the biblical canon, we might venture a guess as to what accounts for their apparent music-less-ness.

In the case of Ruth and Esther, the absence of musical material is a consequence of the stories themselves. Music simply did not factor into these narratives. Outside of devotional passages—like Psalms and the prayers of Deborah, David, etc.—music was not a central concern of the biblical authors. Rather, music production generally appears as part of a larger event. For instance, instruments might be mentioned in the description of a coronation ceremony or during the course of a military celebration. Along these lines, Esther may contain at least a hint of music, though it is by no means explicit. Following the Jews' victory over Haman and his forces, "The city of Shushan shouted and was glad" (8:15). Shouting in this context is probably a synonym for singing, and the Bible regularly depicts music making as an expression of gladness. We can also presume that music accompanied the striptease, beauty pageant and drunken revelries portrayed in the book.

A similarly subtle musical clue is present in most of the music-less prophetic books. Though, as noted, they have no clear musical imagery, there is a long line of singing prophets in the Hebrew Bible. Whenever prophecy exhibits poetic structure, it can be assumed that it was delivered with some type of speech-melody, if not true singing. This would apply in whole or in part to the prophecies of Obadiah, Jonah, Micah and Nahum. Only Haggai and Malachi are bereft of such poetry.

The Hebrew Bible preserves a record of ancient Israel's musical proclivities. These references can be frequent and direct or scattered and implied. But the fact that they are found in nearly every biblical book suggests an obvious conclusion: Israel was a musical civilization. For this reason, our "Bible as literature" approach is more than justified.

That being said, this book is not an exercise in willful ignorance. Historical criticism, archeological insights and other social scientific arguments are offered when relevant. At the same time, each musical subject is taken seriously and, for the most part, on its own terms. The references are gauged as exceptional cultural artifacts and are examined as windows into biblical life. Whether or not the passages should be read literally is a debate for another volume. The claim here is that the way music is utilized in the Hebrew Bible is indicative of a musically aware, advanced and active society. And because music is featured in central biblical episodes and institutions, it can be claimed that it played a sizable part in shaping and defining the character of ancient Israel.

A Silent Source

Another glaring issue in the study of music in the Bible is the complete absence of audible evidence. Musical examinations, whether of a technical, ethnographic or aesthetic kind, usually require sonic material — that is, the music itself. It goes without saying that music is an aural phenomenon and that its full appreciation depends on the experience of sounds. But we have no hearable record of music from biblical times, only textual references and a handful of artifacts. Any attempt to recreate that music — however sophisticated — is ultimately an imaginative endeavor.

There was a time when this mystery was believed to be solvable. Prior to the mid-twentieth century, most scholars of Jewish culture agreed that a distinct national substance united all the music of the Jews, no matter how geographically or stylistically diverse. Just as Jewish history was seen as a continuous flow from biblical to modern times, Jewish music was thought to contain features — however subtle — reaching back to at least the Second Jerusalem Temple. This idealistic view was an inspiration for Abraham Z. Idelsohn's monumental anthology, *Thesaurus of Hebrew-Oriental Melodies* (1914–1932), the first volume of which collects songs of Yemenite Jewry — a historically isolated group once believed to possess a musical language rooted in the first century C.E. Idelsohn and others took it upon themselves to locate and purify these ancient elements, and to demonstrate their presence in the music of far-flung Jewish populations.

More recent scholarship has all but abandoned this goal. Sentimental longings for an Ur-tradition have been replaced by a sobering realization that Jewish music did not originate in a vacuum. Because Jewish communities have always interacted with their environment, their music is tied to that of their non–Jewish neighbors. As ethnomusicologist Mark Slobin puts it, the "mirage of Jewish music evaporates as you gaze at it, replaced by the vision of a group of Jews singing whatever they like, from any local source."[14] Musical mixing is usually identified as a Diaspora phenomenon: centuries of migration and exposure have left an ineradicable audible imprint. Some bemoan this hybridity, claiming it obscures a pure and glorious Temple sound. But history shows that similar musical borrowing shaped the music of both Jerusalem Temples.

Ancient Israel was a small and vulnerable nation at the crossroads of the political, economic and cultural life of the Fertile Crescent. Surrounded and sometimes controlled by larger empires of the region, Israel was susceptible to external influences—political, economic, theological, gastronomical and otherwise. Whether the foreigners were occupiers, rival powers, allied populations, or simply passing through, they inevitably left their mark. The resulting adaptations and transformations—readily seen in texts and holidays—are evident in Israel's worship songs.

This does not mean that Israel's music was helplessly malleable or without distinctive qualities. Performed and supervised by a proud and protective priestly class, there was most certainly a sturdy musical mainstream. This would be akin to other relatively homogenous musical systems we find throughout Jewish history, such as the *maqamot* of Aleppo and choral material of the German Reform. However, while recognizable signatures typify such mainstreams, many of these conventions originated among non–Jews. This was the case in ancient times as well.

Writings and artifacts support the proposition that Temple music included sounds of outside origin. The Book of Psalms—the Levitical hymnbook—contains chapters whose content and structure reflect contemporaneous religious poetry. For example, the psalmic formula "O, how long" (Pss. 6:4; 74:10; 80:5) is found in petitions to the Mesopotamian goddess Ishtar; and Psalm 104 was adapted from the "Hymn of Aten," a devotional song for the sun god of Pharaoh Akhenaten. Archaeomusicologists have also identified instrument types and performance styles common throughout the region. From these clues, we can presume that musical scales, motifs and perhaps even melodies were shared between different groups.

Surely, Israel was not only a receptive player in this cultural transmission. The exchange of musical information proceeded in both directions. What this does tell us is that the notion of a pristine Temple sound, once promoted in academic circles, is untenably romantic. Gradual change occurred in both Temples, spurred on in part by foreign influences. So, even if we could hear Jerusalem's ancient music, its composite character would parallel that of Diaspora traditions.

But appreciating the role music played in biblical life does not necessarily depend on how the music sounded. If we take the broad view that music in those days was functional, or *Gebrauchsmusik*, it is the activities it accompanied and role it played that are of central interest. Being able to hear the music would add little of essential importance apart from a more complete sensual experience. As it is, we must settle for what the Bible states concerning musical perceptions and uses. This is drawn from five main categories of textual information: song lyrics, performance contexts, modes of presentation, instrument names and miscellaneous musical terms. Together, this is sufficient data from which to draw inferences and conclusions about music in biblical life.

Chapter 1

Functional Music

The Bible takes many aspects of daily life for granted. Its foremost purpose is to reveal and describe God's character, desires and involvement in the world, and most accounts of events and individuals support this aim. One of the necessary outcomes of this "theocentric bias"[1] is a general neglect of mundane thoughts and activities in favor of teachings and episodes with wider historical, spiritual and ethical significance. Nevertheless, scholars have managed to paint a fairly comprehensive portrait of biblical life using a three-fold premise: life in antiquity was essentially as complex as it is today; Israel shared much in common with its neighbors; and Bible references to everyday living, however brief or incidental, are indicative of a larger reality.[2]

Working with these ground rules and supporting evidence —culled from biblical and extra-biblical texts, archaeological and iconographic findings from Israel and surrounding civilizations, and ethnographic research — Paul J. King and Lawrence E. Stager amassed a thorough book reconstructing the "lifeways and attitudes" of ancient Israel "from the courtyards of commoners to the courts of kings."[3] Their investigation offers insights into seventeen facets (or "ways") of daily existence: family; child-rearing; gender; marriage; social; age; sex; food; work; dress; leisure; building; learning; religion; death; order; and power. A variety of customs, patterns, taboos, perspectives and guidelines are laid out in each of these areas to demonstrate the complexity of life in ancient Israel on interpersonal, local and national levels.

Most crucial for our study is the recognition that music seems to have played an integral part in virtually all of the above-mentioned categories.[4] Yet, like other details in the Bible, musical depictions are most numerous and intricate when they appear in connection with divinity and/or in overtly religious contexts, such as the communal worship, music therapy, prophetic experiences and Temple ritual that will be explored in the chapters that follow. Secular settings and situations are given far less attention, and so piecing together "everyday music" or "music ways" relies to some extent on elaboration and generalization. In this sense, writing about the music-culture of ancient Israel requires a degree of viewing the past as— or at least in light of— the present.[5] But such research should not be dismissed as mere speculation. By applying tools and information from relevant disciplines, such as Near Eastern studies, anthropology and sociology, it is possible to gain an understanding of music's functions in biblical times. Indeed, this approach is rooted in a position articulated by Tikva Frymer-Kensky, that an interdisciplinary analysis of biblical literature can uncover "cross-cultural patterns and provide models that can help reconstruct life in ancient Israel."[6]

A case can be made that this process of reconstruction — and the assumptions and generalities it entails— is more justified when dealing with music than in other areas. For one thing, music has been intertwined with the human experience since its very beginnings. Researchers have found that Paleolithic paintings are generally clustered on the most resonant parts of cave walls, suggesting that ritualistic singing was connected with these images.[7] Among the carved bones and ivory of the Upper Paleolithic period are a number of musical whistles and flutes, the earliest of which is a 35,000-year-old vulture wing flute with five perforated finger holes.[8] Steven Mithen even posits that while Neanderthals lacked the neural circuitry for language, they did have a protomusical form of communication that incorporated sound and gesture, influenced emotional states and behavior, and was rhythmic, melodic and temporally controlled — that is, "a prelinguistic musical mode of thought and action."[9] Music's apparent ubiquity in human life persists in modern times, and volumes of quantitative and qualitative data in fields including sociology, ethnography, anthropology, psychology, philosophy, history, theology, linguistics and cognitive science demonstrate the utilitarian role of music in a remarkable array of activities and interactions.

It is, then, not surprising that the Hebrew Bible contains examples of music in a host of settings, like family gatherings (Gen. 31:27), work

1. Functional Music

(Num. 21:17), merriment (Judg. 11:34–35), military processionals (1 Sam. 18:6), banquets (Isa. 5:12; Isa. 24:8–9), harvesting (Isa. 16:10; Jer. 48:33) and teaching (Neh. 8:3), as well as in the more obvious arena of formal divine worship. Taken together, biblical accounts of secular and sacred music confirm two basic cross-cultural observations regarding music production: song and dance are woven naturally into the fabric of societies both large and small,[10] and all known cultures use music in rites and ceremonies.[11] In this way, the people of the Bible can be seen as representative of humanity as a whole.

While it would be a stretch to say that Israel's conventions of sound and performance match those of any modern culture — or that aesthetic preferences remained static throughout its long history and in all strata of society — it is reasonable to claim a broad relationship between ancient Israel's music-culture and that of other ancient and modern peoples. This is mainly because the music of Israel, like the majority of the world's music, was functional: music designed and presented as an aid to other non-musical activities, as opposed to music for its own sake.

The purpose of this chapter is twofold: to bring the Bible into the larger discussion of music and human experience and to illustrate how passages featuring music have relevance for sacred song in contemporary worship settings. This will be accomplished through an examination of two main areas. The first seeks to affirm the familiar (and controversial) notion that music is a universal language, though not in the sense that it takes the same forms or is understood the same way in all cultures and subcultures. Rather, while musical expression seems as diverse as humanity itself, the major functions of music are essentially identical across the globe.

This will bring us to the second part, which carves out music's place within the larger cultural and religious relevance of the Bible. Just as modern readers of the Bible find truth and immediacy in the stories, worldview, rulings, spiritual insights and practical wisdom housed in the text, its musical references can shed profound light on music's spiritual and theological value. These general discussions will provide a framework for approaching the topics contained in this book — namely, that music was tightly woven into the fabric of biblical life, and that music's perceived religious benefits were much the same in that ancient setting as they are today.

A Universal Language?

An understanding of the Bible's musical references as illustrative of music in general rests on the assertion that music of all times and places exhibits certain universal qualities. Of course, such sweeping claims are always open to criticism, as they run the risk of blurring distinctions between the peoples of the world, the culturally specific nature of their music, and the socialized responses they have to certain sounds. Indeed, the field of ethnomusicology emerged partly in response to the conviction current in the nineteenth century that certain intervals, rhythms and so forth comprise a "universal language," understood the same across the globe, even as verbal languages, social structures, dress, food, mythologies and other cultural features display endless variation. Typical of this viewpoint is the following except from a review of William Gardiner's book, *The Music of Nature* (1832), printed in an 1839 issue of *The Christian Examiner*:

> Music properly is the only language which is pathetic. Poetry is so only by the tones in which it is read, or in which we imagine that it should be read. Music is quicker understood than words. Words are arbitrary, and require to be learned before they mean anything; only fellow countrymen can talk together. But music is a universal language; the same tones touch the same feelings the world over. Spoken languages address the understanding; when they would interest the feelings, they pass at once into the province of music; then it matters not so much what is said, as in what tones it is said. When an emotion would utter itself, words are nothing, tones are everything. We instinctively recognize the peculiar notes of joy and anguish, triumph and despair, consolation, pity, and entreaty; they need no words to interpret them.[12]

This sort of reasoning was dismissed by early ethnomusicologists, who began exploring world music in the latter decades of the nineteenth century. Noting the romanticism and ignorance — willful or otherwise — that fueled ideas of worldwide musical norms and human responses, several researchers took the contrary view that music is a "non-universal language." An early (albeit ethnocentric) formulation of this approach came from Berthold Seemann, who spoke at an 1870 meeting of the Anthropological Society of London:

> I make bold to doubt whether, even amongst the nations of Western Europe, intimately connected, as they are, by close and frequent inter-

course, the music of the one is interpreted in the same sense by the others. By traveling eastwards we find that there is certainly a different language of music. Songs of joy, and even dance-accompaniments, are no longer, as with us, in the major keys, but always in the minor. Proceed still further eastwards, to the Indies, and you have to endure, in listening to the people's music, a monotony almost unbearable to European modes of thought. Continue your journey amongst the great Mongolian races, and the bulk of what you have to listen to is positively painful to your ear; and your greatest puzzle is how what is so painful to you should give positive pleasure to them. Again, cross over to America, and you find the aborigines uttering musical sounds, doubt full of meaning to them, but altogether unintelligible to us, and to our habits of thinking without any ending.[13]

George Herzog makes the case that music is not universally understood, but exists in many and variegated "dialects."[14] Thus, instead of being subject to an overarching (and ultimately flawed) set of values, standards and expectations, each of its manifestations should be studied individually and on its own terms. Others have noted that no single conception of what constitutes music is applicable cross-culturally, and so a definition that satisfies Western principles might fail when applied to a non–Western society.[15] Arriving at a useful definition of music is further complicated by the fact that ideas about musical sounds change over time, as most music-cultures interact with the outside world, respond to internal and external pressures, and contain subgroups with divergent tastes and preferences.[16] Nevertheless, since the 1960s there has been a growing recognition among scholars that despite the enormous assortment of musical meanings and expressions, the music of people everywhere is similar in terms of function and presentation, though not sound or form. As such, what can be called "universal" about music is not its constituent elements—tonality, rhythm, timbre, etc.—but the behaviors associated with it.[17]

Alan P. Merriam lists nine non-mutually exclusive functions of music present throughout the world: emotional expression; communication; symbolic representation; physical stimulation; validation of institutions; preservation of heritage; integration of society; aesthetic enjoyment; and entertainment.[18] Bruno Nettl adds that cultures use comparable means to achieve these musical functions.[19] First, all cultures have singing and many have instruments (rudimentary or advanced).

Second, singing usually involves words. Third, all peoples associate music with dance. Fourth, music usually involves internal repetition and variation. Fifth, the rhythmic structure of music is based on note length and dynamic stresses. Sixth, musical creativity within a culture or subculture is subject to constraints regarding proper and improper sounds, though the group may tolerate occasional departures. The observations of Merriam and Nettl show that music is presented and operates in common ways across the globe, whether or not any isolated sound pattern conveys the same meaning or emotion from one group to the next.

Interestingly, a similar understanding of the functions of music underlies the thinking of Henry Wadsworth Longfellow, who popularized the notion of music as "the universal language of mankind." Unlike scholars of the past and many who quote his words today, Longfellow does not mean that music is a universal language in the sense of being perceived identically by all, but rather that it is used in universal ways. When read in its original context, an essay entitled "Ancient Spanish Ballads," this eloquent saying conveys, among other things, that music provides rhythmic and emotional support for laborers.

> The muleteer of Spain carols with the early lark, amid the stormy mountains of his native land. The vintager of Sicily has his evening hymn; the fisherman of Naples his boat song; the gondolier of Venice his midnight serenade. The goatherd of Switzerland and the Tyrol, the Carpathian boor, the Scotch Highlander, the English ploughboy, singing as he drives his team afield, peasant, serf, slave, all, all have their ballads and traditionary songs. Music is the universal language of mankind, poetry their universal pastime and delight.[20]

It is fitting that Longfellow uses work songs to illustrate the common functions of music. Work songs are among the most basic types of musical production, and exemplify music's ability to ease the burden of everyday tasks.[21] Moreover, work songs are prime examples of collective functional music. In addition to their practical purpose of coordinating the group's efforts and adding a degree of pleasure to tiresome or even painful toils, such songs can, like other verbal forms, express shared values, beliefs and hopes. And because these songs tend to be highly rhythmic, collaborative and repetitive, they often give shape and significance to the group itself.[22]

The attainment of social solidarity is also a major goal of religion.

Like music, religion is enormously diverse, and no single definition or set of characteristics satisfies each system. Anthropologists place the world's religions into several categories, including animism, ancestor cult, polytheism and monotheism, but recognize that the unique convictions, rituals and myths each group espouses limit the usefulness of such classifications.[23] Nonetheless, several purposes are shared by all religions and help account for their pervasiveness. Religions offer people tools to deal with the uncertainties of existence, provide meaning for their lives, give answers to what might otherwise be unexplainable and, as mentioned above, help foster unity. While no particular belief or practice is shared or deemed valid by every group, these aims, like those achieved by music, are, for lack of a better term, universal.

The crucial role music and religion play in asserting, maintaining and strengthening a sense of communal identity and affiliation is a point that will be addressed throughout this study. In the thoroughly religious worldview of ancient Israel, where all aspects of life were believed dependent upon and judged by the divine, communal musical expressions of devotion were the norm. Such acts—whether of a spontaneous kind like the Song of the Sea or highly ritualized like the ceremonial music of the Jerusalem Temple—worked vertically, connecting the people to their God, and horizontally, connecting the participants to one another. It was, in short, a way in which the people of Israel defined who they were. Thus, as with observable cultures today, it is safe to say that Israel's music was socially meaningful largely because it was a medium through which people recognized themselves and the boundaries that separated them from others.[24]

Worship Music

The convergence of prayer, the most pervasive feature of religion,[25] and music production, among the most pervasive elements of human culture,[26] makes music and religion a natural partnership. All known cultures associate music with the supernatural and accompany religious activities with music.[27] In ancient Israel, the combination of music and religion pervaded the general population and the three major institutions of the day: monarchy, prophecy and priesthood. Each of these interrelated segments of society was infused with divine-consciousness, and, to a greater or lesser extent, used music to stipulate and reinforce the ideology, aspirations, sentiments and rules that defined them.

Again, for such an argument to be made, it is not necessary to know what the music sounded like, but to be aware of the many aims it served. Though an incredible diversity of music is produced by the world's cultures, the purpose of these sounds is remarkably consistent from place to place. This is confirmed not only in the well-documented societies of today, but also in the biblical text, where musical allusions merge to depict a civilization that grasped and took full advantage of music's practical applications. Functional music was utilized in both secular and sacred contexts, but, as stated above, the Bible's religious orientation makes references to sacred singing and playing much more pronounced. Yet, even in the worship setting, details of performance are in most cases secondary to the physical ritual and the textual component of the prayer. Still, as this study will show, there is evidence to support the claim that music was a central aspect of life in biblical times.

At key junctures and in core institutions, musical tones helped to formulate and deliver messages, convey and heighten emotions, assert and strengthen communal bonds, and establish and intensify human-divine contact. To be sure, some situations and settings relied more heavily on musical expression than others. For instance, music's role was more formally integrated into the Temple service than the individualized utterances of prophetic poetry; but in both cases, song proved an effective means of transmitting ideas and stirring souls. It should also not be overlooked that the crossing of the Red Sea, a pinnacle and transformative moment in Israel's history, and the kingship of David, the model monarch and national hero, were both filled with music. Taken together, the Song of the Sea, monarchy, prophecy and priesthood demonstrate music's integration into the social fabric of ancient Israel.

These examples, along with references to singing and instruments during family feasts and other informal occasions, make the Hebrew Bible a potentially rich source of investigation for ethnomusicologists, who engage in "the study of social and cultural aspects of music and dance in local and global contexts."[28] Of course, because the music itself was not transcribed and has not been passed on orally in any reliable fashion, the sound elements of such a musical inquiry is rendered all

1. Functional Music

but impossible — save for the hints gleaned from archaeological reconstruction and regional music from later periods. From a purely musical standpoint — where features such as tonal range, stylistic variants and performance techniques are of paramount import — biblical passages are of little value. However, from the vantage point of music and culture, the biblical text paints a vivid (though not systematic) picture of a society in which music was interwoven into other non-musical activities. In this way, the Bible can be cited as ancient support for the dual observation that music is an ever-present accompaniment to human life and is most often functional in design and intent.

It is in this spirit that musical depictions in the Hebrew Bible can be viewed as applicable to our own day. Just as the constraints of time and space do not hinder the application of biblical insights to modern life, the musical environment of ancient Israel has much to offer current-day musicians, researchers and others interested in the place of music in human experience. Not only have the fundamental uses of music remained more or less constant since that time, but the spirit of performance — conveyed in exuberant dancing, playing and poetry — serves to justify musical worship in Judaism and Christianity. It is, after all, no accident that many psalms are still sung in houses of worship, or that passages from other biblical prayers long ago secured a revered place in the liturgical traditions of both faiths. The enduring legacy of ancient Israel's music-culture is obvious: though musical styles and worship venues have undergone dynamic changes over the centuries, biblically informed songs have remained a steady presence.

An appreciation of music in the Hebrew Bible can contribute to a greater understanding of music in general and worship music in particular. So far in this chapter, the focus has been social-scientific — that is, grouping ancient Israel with the world's music-cultures. Israel exhibited many of the same musical traits as other known societies, at least as far as uses and prevalence. And though it can be asserted that the Israelites were more musically advanced than their neighbors (and some cultures of today), and so may not be a proper basis from which to draw generalizations, it should be remembered that music has always been intertwined with human activities, even as the degree of this infusion differs from group to group.

As mentioned, most readily apparent in the Hebrew Bible is the integration of music, theology and worship. This relationship is present in the majority of the Bible's musical depictions, and the authors clearly perceived religious expression as music's primary purpose, whether that was an accurate reflection of society or a by-product of the book's religious emphasis. For most readers of the Bible, it is the connection of music and devotional practice that makes its musical citations relevant for religious life. It is, in fact, possible to use these verses as authoritative backing for the incorporation of song in modern services.

Finding biblical justification for worship music is not a novel or even difficult undertaking. One needs only to look at the influence of the Psalter on Jewish and Christian services—where it is a source of sung texts and a model for later liturgy—to see the direct way the Bible has helped shape and inform religious devotion of subsequent generations. A succinct appraisal of this essential continuity is found in an essay published by Jacob Beimel in 1934. It appeared in the short-lived magazine *Jewish Music* (1934–1935), which featured brief articles and musical transcriptions by Beimel and other renowned experts of synagogue song, including Abraham W. Binder, Adolph Katchko and Abraham Z. Idelsohn. Beimel travels through a number of biblical references in an effort to draw connections between sacred music practices of ancient Israel and those of modern Jews and Christians. His is a representative study, touching upon ideas and arguments made in writings before and since.[29] A few of his eloquent passages are quoted in more recent studies on the subject.[30]

Beimel begins his exposition with a statement concerning the age-old link between music and religion: "The human soul, which expresses itself in religious beliefs and customs, finds a medium for the utterance of its varied impressions in music also. Moreover, even its nourishment, the human soul itself receives from these two attributes, religion and music. There exists, therefore, in the human mind, from time immemorial, a strong and inseparable bond between Divinity and the Art of Music."[31] He notes that this bond is equally present in "the pagan world and among nations with polytheistic beliefs," and in "nations confessing a monotheistic religion, of whatever beliefs and customs it may consist...."[32]

Following this introductory comment, the essay narrows in on Judeo-Christian belief and ritual, tracing a line from biblical to modern-day musical worship. A number of Beimel's observations relate directly to the main chapters in this study. For instance, he writes that Israel's assumption of the "predilection of God for music" was manifested in the prophets' vocation, which frequently relied on the art form for the purpose of inviting contact with God and relaying these communications to others.[33] He pays special attention to the prophet Elisha who, "after some hesitation, was willing to prophesy, provided a musician would be called to play before him," and describes the scene in 1 Samuel 10:5–6 where Saul meets a band of prophets ascending from a high place accompanied by instruments.[34] Beimel also writes of the healing effect of David's lyre on King Saul (1 Sam. 16:14–23)—a healing that, according to him, "could only be achieved by the one means in which Divinity found its greatest favor, namely by music"—and of the "poetical and musical genius of David" epitomized in the Book of Psalms.[35]

Beimel concludes that the Jewish—and, by extension, Christian—conception of the "relationship between Divinity and the art of music is as old as Israel."[36] As discussed, this observation is confirmed by anthropological studies, and can be broadened to read that the "relationship between Divinity and the art of music is as old as humanity." As evidence of this persistent partnership, Beimel offers three sayings from Jewish mystics of the eighteenth century, each celebrating the spiritual efficacy of sacred sounds: "The gates of song precede the gates of repentance" (Rabbi Pinchos of Koretz); "The temple of song is nearest to the source of holiness" (Rabbi Nachman of Breslov); "There are gates in heaven which can be opened by song alone" (anonymous kabbalistic saying). These quotations are not mere hyperbolae. Like the array of biblical verses that unequivocally disclose the intersection of music and God's presence, these mystic pronouncements—poetic though they may be—speak to a palpable phenomenon felt by worshipers through the ages and across denominational divides.

Another classic overview of biblical support for sacred song is "The Bible Authority for Church Music" (1874), a brief article written by Wilbur Fisk Crafts. The essay begins by asking the reader to "trace in [the Bible's] pages the history of music. The first inspiration God gave to man was a musical inspiration. First of arts was music; first of artists was Jubal...."[37] This is followed with an observation well supported in scientific literature[38]: "Before men learned how to write, they learned to sing; as the baby crows with a musical song before ever his lips have learned to form 'papa' and 'mamma.'" In Crafts's analysis, this natural tendency towards song is more than just a precursor to the complex patterns of speech; it is a divine gift to be used for promoting interpersonal harmony and bringing people into communion with the divine. "There is nothing that so warms the heart as singing," he writes, "nothing that so breaks down the barriers of pride and caste, nothing that so cures quarrels, nothing that is such a highway from earth to the very throne and heart of God."[39]

The remainder of the essay centers around two biblical examples that will be covered at length in this book: the Song of the Sea and the verses of Psalms. In particular, Crafts highlights the similar impetus behind the outpouring of musical praise following the Red Sea crossing and a line from Psalm 68 — a song of praise extolling God's victory over enemies: "Sing to God, chant hymns to His name" (v. 5). Drawing a link between these passages, in which the actors cannot help but sing divine praise, Crafts writes: "if you want a church that shall have in it the power of the church of David, teach it to sing; if you want a church that shall have in it the spirit and enthusiasm of the apostolic church, teach it to sing; if you want a church that shall prepare for the Church of Mount Zion above, teach it to sing."[40]

Despite these and other thoughtful expositions, scholarship delineating biblical support for worship music is meager relative to the plentiful writings on other aspects of the Bible's relevance for today, whether of a spiritual, moral, "self-help" or other kind. This owes in part to the virtually seamless continuity of musical prayer from biblical times to the present. There has never been an age when worship was completely devoid of song, and only in a few groups, like the Quakers before 1860 and silent monastic orders, has there been a concerted effort to subdue the natural urge to set divine petition and praise to music.[41] Furthermore, the experience of music is immediate and intimate, and so defies easy assessment by purely rational measurements.[42] Music is effortlessly and often strongly felt, but does not always lend itself to deep reflection. As a result, while there may be little controversy in claiming that the Bible advocates devotional music, there is also little appreciation of precisely which features of contemporary musical worship are based in or supported by the biblical text.

1. Functional Music

Even so, such evidence is far from elusive. As a brief demonstration, each of the main chapters of this study illuminates at least one quality essential to worship. To be sure, reducing these complex and multifaceted topics to a single feature is not a fair reflection of their profundity—which will be given more detailed treatment in the coming pages—and each of the chapters can potentially speak to a range of attributes central to sacred song. Nevertheless, for the sake of illustration, it will suffice to entertain this single-focused approach.

From the Song of the Sea, we learn the importance of singing in building and affirming communal bonds. The therapeutic quality of David's lyre shows us music's potential to evoke and heighten a desired mood. The prophetic episodes demonstrate the power of musical sounds to connect us with something beyond ourselves. The Psalms illustrate the efficacy of tones in delivering liturgical content. While it should be stressed that these are not the exclusive traits in the Hebrew Bible that pertain to worship music, when taken together, they establish a firm rationale for the singing of prayer-songs. Today as in biblical times, these forces of song—community building, emotional pull, transcendence and communication—reveal a powerful and inherent relationship between musical and religious experiences. Likewise, by going back and examining these ancient examples through a modern lens, it is possible to flesh out and draw connections between the Bible's musical references, and arrive at a detailed depiction of Israel's music-culture.

Summary

The Bible's mention of music at family feasts, community festivals, national events, royal processionals, religious devotion and other occasions—however brief or incidental they may appear—reflects a broad recognition that music, both vocal and instrumental, was apt for establishing moods, imparting ideals, asserting convictions, encouraging cooperation and solidifying communal ties. Though we cannot reconstruct the music of biblical times, there is sufficient textual evidence that Israel made thorough use of musical sounds. Music appears in numerous and varied contexts, ranging from worship to work, and it is widely held that most (if not all) of biblical poetry was originally sung or chanted in accentuated "speech-melody." Most crucially, though music is not the Bible's main area of interest and technical aspects of sound and performance are rarely touched upon, the fact that references to singing and playing appear in nearly every biblical book suggests that it was an integral rather than anomalous feature of everyday life.

At the same time, the Bible is a theocentric text, both in terms of its worldview and the information and interpretations it chooses to present. As such, the bulk of biblical passages alluding to music — and virtually all verses containing significant musical detail — are religious in nature, whether involving formal or informal worship or some other form of holy encounter. Yet, as with other known cultures that include music of religious and secular kinds, the wealth of sacred music examples in the Bible — especially when added with the scattered allusions to song and dance in more mundane situations— points to the musical richness and complexity of ancient Israel. And because the uses of music in the Bible conform to the universal musical functions found in modern cultures— a reality apparent when comparing the merits of worship music in those days with the present — we can apply what is known today about music's importance in human society to the text, and, in so doing, construct a more thorough picture of music in biblical life.

Chapter 2

The Song of the Sea and Group Cohesion: Exodus 15:1–21

The Red Sea crossing is the climax of the liberation narrative in the Book of Exodus. The story travels through four main sections: the enslavement of Israel and advent of Moses (1:1–2:25), the call and commissioning of Moses (3:1–7:13), the plagues and Passover rite (7:4–13:16), and the miracle at the sea (13:17–14:31). In response to their deliverance, Moses and the Israelites burst forth in exalted song, praising God for enabling their miraculous escape from the pursuing Egyptian army (15:1–18). Known as the Song of the Sea, this lyric poem is among the oldest texts in the Bible.[1] It recounts in enthusiastic terms the drowning of Pharaoh's forces (vv. 4–12), God's guidance of Israel to the Promised Land (vv. 13–17), and His eternal rule (v. 18). Not mentioned, however, are key elements of the escape account, such as the splitting of the sea, the walls of water, and the crossing to dry land (14:26–29). But the Song was not a ballad; it was a triumphant hymn offered at the "shore of freedom's sea."[2] Rather than a recapitulation of a historical event, it was a musical celebration of God's redemptive power.

The exodus from Egypt has been described as the creation story of the Israelites, with the emergence from the sea symbolizing a national rebirth.[3] Viewed in this way, the Song of the Sea was not only a fitting response to a miraculous episode, but also the first proclamation of a newly freed nation. Additionally, the singing of the Song was the first corporate worship experience in the Bible, as well as its first instance of devotional music. It provided a model for subsequent biblical hymns in terms of both content and presentation.

The account of the Song is musically significant for two main reasons. First, it presents singing as a spontaneous and natural response to a seminal event in sacred history. At the precise moment when the Israelites realized the immensity of their deliverance, they turned to music, the "tonal analogue of emotive life."[4] Instead of remaining silent in awe and wonder, the Israelites used song — heightened speech — to express their gratitude. Only through the marriage of words and music could their deepest sentiments aspire toward heaven. Second, the passage shows song as a vehicle of identity assertion. In dramatic fashion, they emerged from bondage as a singing community. This imagery was not lost on the rabbis, who added that "Even the sucklings dropped their mothers' breasts to join in singing, yea even the embryos in the womb joined the melody."[5] Music and words combined as the mode by which the Israelites expressed their new identities as a free, God-fearing people. This is particularly important as music often serves as a powerful identifier. This is equally true for strong groups that celebrate their grandeur through song, and for historically marginalized or persecuted people, who use song to bring members together and fortify their sense of self and common purpose.[6]

Using the Song of the Sea as an illustration, this chapter explores the cohesive role of music in biblical life. The first section offers a general overview of the practical uses of music in the Hebrew Bible, with special emphasis on the social functions of singing and instrumental playing. Section two looks at sociologist Émile Durkheim's analysis of the impact of ceremony on group solidarity, and how music can amplify this effect. This provides the background for the third and final section: a more thorough examination of the Song of the Sea, the Bible's clearest depiction of cohesion through music. This analysis will show that, beginning with the Red Sea crossing, Israel regularly utilized music as a way of articulating and asserting its collective identity.

Music and Society

Music in ancient Israel was almost entirely of a utilitarian kind, or *Gebrauchsmusik*. Both vocal and instrumental music figured prominently in a variety of biblical settings and occasions. In addition to its

2. The Song of the Sea and Group Cohesion

more obvious place in religious devotion, music was a part of family gatherings (Gen. 31:27), well digging (Num. 21:17), merrymaking (Judg. 11:34–35), military marches (1 Sam. 18:6), banquets (Isa. 5:12; 24:8–9), harvesting (Isa. 16:10; Jer. 48:33) and a slew of other activities. Prior to King David and the establishment of Levitical orchestras and choirs (1 Chron. 15:16–24), music appears to have been distinctly popular and non-artistic.[7] Music-making was the domain of non-professionals, and less concern was given to aesthetic qualities than to practical functions. Rather than a set of skills reserved for a trained class of performers, as was the case in Temple worship, singing and playing were organically interwoven into ordinary life.

Among the most comprehensive lists of musical references in the Bible is Shlomo Hofman's *Miqra'ey Musica* (*Occurrences of Music*).[8] Hofman categorized over 900 instances of singing, songs or musical instruments in the biblical text, and excluded several additional verses that likely allude to music, but are too ambiguous to be certain. The sheer number of citations suggests the vibrant music culture of ancient Israel, as well as the probability that other musical styles and genres not mentioned in the Bible were also in use. In fact, there is evidence that Jewish communities in Yemen and Iraq preserved song-forms (though probably not actual melodies) that reach back to biblical times, such as textual chant and lullabies.[9]

It is also revealing that depictions of music in the Hebrew Bible lack technical detail. Outside of the Book of Psalms, which supplies the names of composers and instruments, stage directions, and other musical clues, there is a scarcity of information regarding the nature of musical sounds and performance. Most indications of music's daily functions come from brief and cursory remarks in legal, narrative and anecdotal sources; passing mention of music is typically made within larger scenes of weddings, funerals, pilgrimages and so on.[10] Yet, as Alfred Sendrey explains, this does not negate music's importance, but rather shows that music was in such wide and common use that further details were not needed: "The biblical authors took it for granted that the people were thoroughly familiar with musical matters, so that they considered it unnecessary to indulge in long descriptions and minute details."[11] The very absence of in-depth accounts seems to confirm the ubiquitous presence of musical sounds in biblical life.

An example of this is the first reference to music in the Bible, which occurs in a compressed passage in Genesis listing the descendants of Cain and the growth of human civilization (Gen. 4:17–22). As in many ancient cultures, the Bible links the invention of music with a single personage.[12] His name is Jubal, "the father of all those who play the lyre and pipe" (v. 21). This short verse is the only place Jubal appears in the biblical text; we have no other accounts of his personality or the music that he made. It is therefore possible that Jubal is a survival from a longer saga about the birth of civilization, which may have been the basis for the verses in Genesis.[13]

Regardless, Jubal's significance can be gleaned from the context in which he is found. In the same passage, we read that his brother, Jabal, was the first to raise cattle (v. 20), and his half-brother, Tubal-cain, "forged all implements of copper and iron" (v. 22). Mention of music's invention alongside the origins of cattle raising and tool forging suggests an early recognition of the vital role of music in society. The Bible seems to imply that herding, metal forging and music making are the three fundamental pursuits upon which humanity depends. Viewed historically and culturally, musical tones not only enhance the experience of a range of activities, but also facilitate the retention and transmission of collective memories, oral histories, wisdom and sacred stories. Thus, while Jabal can be seen as the ancestor of food production and Tubal-cain as the ancestor of technology, Jubal is in many ways the ancestor of knowledge.

The uniquely musical character of ancient Israel is attested in both biblical and external sources. Though music is found in worship practices elsewhere in the ancient Near East,[14] it apparently reached high levels of expressiveness and sophistication in the hands of the people of Israel. There is evidence that surrounding cultures were impressed by — and even coveted — Israel's music. For instance, an Assyrian bas-relief depicting King Sennacharib's victory over King Hezekiah describes ransom and tribute including Judean musicians.[15] The Arch of Titus in Rome similarly shows two silver trumpets being taken to Rome as loot from the conquest of Jerusalem.[16] Psalm 137 recounts the Babylonians' demand that their Hebrew captives "Sing us one of the songs of Zion" (v. 3). To seek musicians and instruments as tribute and to show interest in the folk songs of a defeated people is indeed unusual. At the very least, it suggests that the Israel's music had achieved renown in the region, and was a source of curiosity or wonder for other, perhaps less musically developed, people.

Three factors are particularly helpful for explaining the prevalence of music in the Hebrew Bible: iconoclasm, ceremonial occasions and group orientation. While it is true that no civilization has been completely without music,[17] its significance in biblical life was especially pronounced. Some scholars link the flourishing of vocal and instrumental music in biblical society to the prohibition against idol worship.[18] They point to the Second Commandment as the Bible's central statement regarding artistic imagination: "You shall not make for yourself a sculptured image, or any likeness of what is in the heavens above, or on the earth below, or in the waters under the earth. You shall not bow down to them or serve them" (Exod. 20:4–5). While this proscription did not suppress all figural representation, it did substantially limit visual arts to *menorahs*, altars, garments and other ritual accessories (Exod. 31:4; 2 Chr. 2:6). These ancient restrictions have reverberated throughout Jewish history, which in most periods and locations has favored poetic and musical creativity over the pictorial or plastic arts.[19]

P. T. Forsyth sums up the negative impact of iconoclasm on the appreciation and development of physical arts: "The second commandment passes the death sentence on Hebrew art. In killing idolatry, it killed plastic imagination. At least it placed it under such a disadvantage that it could hardly live and certainly could not grow."[20] Though Forsyth does not draw specific connections between the minimizing of visual images and the growth of linguistic and musical arts, it can be inferred from his comments that the Israelites and their Jewish descendants, needing a creative outlet, turned to these more abstract artistic forms.

The ceremonial culture of ancient Israel also contributed to its musical output. Anthropologists have concluded that public ceremonies almost always have a musical component.[21] Defined broadly, ceremony is a sequence of socialized and symbolic activities, separated from the routines of everyday life.[22] Ceremonies are imbued with and guided by specific sets of ideas, and are used to commemorate important occasions, such as rites of passage, times of day and sacred dates. These ritual activities tie participants to the event itself, and to the flow of history in which similar events have already occurred and will occur again. Especially when marked by music, ceremonies stir emotional and intellectual associations, accentuating the importance of the moment and a sense of community. And because ritual songs are specific to certain times and places, they act as a "powerful retrieval cue" for individual and group memories.[23]

Numerous biblical verses associate music with ceremonial observances, including weddings (Jer. 7:34), funerals (Job 30:31), banquets (Isa. 5:12), royal celebrations (1 Kgs. 1:39–40) and religious festivals (2 Chr. 30:21); and effectively all Temple music was an accessory to the sacrificial rite.[24] These musical examples are bereft of precise detail, but taken collectively, they paint a picture of a society in which ceremonies were regularly served by music. Although there is no indication whether the same melodies or motifs were used for each repetition of a particular ceremony, the use of specific music to mark and distinguish between occasions is a regular pattern of human culture, and was carried into early Jewish practices of biblical cantillation and modal liturgical chant.[25]

The group orientation of ancient Israel likewise added to its musical character. Israel's collectivity is stressed throughout the Hebrew Bible.[26] From the period of tribal leagues, when Israel was a loose confederation of tribes, through the institution of monarchies and the nation-state, community was the essential background for the individual.[27] This found expression in theological concepts, such as chosenness (Gen. 17:7; Exod. 19:5; Deut. 14:2) and collective responsibility (Deut. 21:8; Num. 25:8–9; Josh. 7:1–5).

The music making process similarly depends on a number of actors working together: creators, performers, dancers, audience members, etc. Music is at its core a group activity, lending itself to cooperation and corporate expression, and has long been considered the most social of the arts.[28] It is thus fitting that most of the Bible's musical references occur in social contexts. While group association substantially defined the people of Israel, the many collective acts in which they engaged — ranging from public ritual to manual labor — encouraged and benefited from musical accompaniment. In short, their inclination toward music was partly an extension of their community orientation.

As a predominantly social activity, music surely added enjoyment to communal gatherings and intensified the emotional content of public events, both cheerful and solemn. For instance, we find mention of

2. The Song of the Sea and Group Cohesion

drinking songs, "They hum snatches of song to the tune of a lute ... they drink straight from the wine bottle" (Amos 6:5), and public rejoicing, "David and all the House of Israel danced before the Lord ... with lyres, harps, timbrels, sistrums, and cymbals" (2 Sam. 6:5). But music was neither confined to nor chiefly designed for recreation or entertainment. Rather, it accomplished essential and practical functions. Key among these was the fostering and strengthening of group cohesion. Music's capacity to bolster collective identity is well documented in ethnomusicological literature.[29] Philip V. Bohlman notes that group-specific songs aid the generation and maintenance of boundaries demarcating the community,[30] while Martin Stokes affirms music's role in defining a community's identity and place.[31] Though these observations are derived from contemporary, observable group phenomena, there are clues in the Hebrew Bible that music was a potent vehicle of social cohesion.

The Book of Psalms provides several examples of music's cohesive effect. Much of the psalms were scribed in corporate language—that is, first personal plural. For example, a number of communal complaints were composed in response to war, pestilence, exile, famine and other calamities (e.g., Pss. 44; 74; 79; 80; 83; 89). These laments typically follow a five-step progression: plea to God, complaint about the community's condition, confession of sin, appeal for divine help, and a conclusion of praise, vows or acknowledgement of God's help.[32] Communal thanksgiving psalms were also sung, though these are less prevalent in the Psalter (e.g., Pss. 66; 67; 68; 124). A representative example is Psalm 68, which praises God's victory over His foes and His choice of Jerusalem as the place of His rule. Additionally, many psalms written in personal language seem to convey collective aims, so that the "I" of the psalmist should be read as "we."[33] Perhaps because most (if not all) of the psalms were intended for public worship, they relied heavily on stereotyped and accessible language, which could be appropriated by the masses. Even psalms addressing specific events or ascribed to historical figures frequently incorporated general themes and expressions that resonated with a range of experiences.[34]

Both in content and performance setting, the psalms were socially directed. They stemmed from and spoke to the shared history and sentiments of the people, and were performed and listened to by unified groups—choirs, orchestras and audience. Furthermore, their presentation in the elevated speech of musical tones helped to consolidate the hearts and minds of the people. In the original context of Temple worship, as in modern settings of church and synagogue, psalm singing forged a "bond of unity between social levels of people and between private and public life," and encouraged "achievement of communal attention and order."[35] This unifying result can be seen, to a greater or lesser extent, in all forms of communal music.

Durkheim and Ceremonial Song

Émile Durkheim (1858–1917) recognized the essential place of cohesion in shaping and reinforcing both personal identity and social consciousness. Defined simply, cohesion is the degree to which participants in a social system are bound to and support its norms, values, beliefs and structures.[36] In groups formed around consanguinity and kinship, like the Israelite slaves, consensus regarding goals, convictions and behaviors arises from a mixture of socialization and common experience.[37] There is a degree of cohesion in all collectivities big or small. But in kinship-based systems where the unit of organization is the extended family, clan, lineage or the moiety, the distinction between the individual and society is minimal, and members naturally come to have very similar consciences.[38] As Durkheim maintains, each member "becomes, with those whom he resembles, part of the same collective."[39] Cohesion of this sort is the "result of resemblances."[40]

Durkheim termed this phenomenon mechanical solidarity, or solidarity by similarities.[41] This type of cohesion involves a group of individuals who play similar roles and whose status is equally valued, save for the few in leadership positions, like Moses, Aaron and Miriam.[42] This contrasts with industrial societies—characterized by role differentiation and division of labor—where cohesiveness is achieved through the interdependence of specialized parts rather than homogeneity. In Durkhiem's assessment, this sense of togetherness—or better, of working together—stems from the performance of multiple and integrated tasks necessary for society's functioning. Using a biological analogy, Durkheim calls this "organic solidarity":

[It is] constituted, not by a repetition of similar, homogeneous segments, but by a system of different organs each of which has a special role, and which are themselves formed of differentiated parts.... They are not juxtaposed linearly as the rings of an earthworm, nor entwined one with another, but coordinated and subordinated one to another around the same central organ which exercises a moderating action over the rest of the organism.[43]

In addition to the practical role of cooperation in work and communal organization, Durkheim cites religion as a fundamental ingredient of solidarity within "primitive" and modern societies. Religion, in his view, is a phenomenon intimately connected to the deep structures of social life.[44] As a systematic expression of society's deepest moral sentiments and ideals, religion is a unifying and vitalizing force, reaffirming already strong ties in close-knit groups, and balancing competing interests in societies where individualism dominates.[45] Indeed, it is largely through religion that codes of morality, which are crucial for the society's well being, are specified and articulated.[46] Of course, religion can also be a source of contention, especially in modern pluralistic settings where denominations and sects vie for membership and cultural influence. Even so, Durkheim argues that religion generally supports society by reinforcing a set of common rules, aims and controls. In most religious communities, this unifying process is established and reinforced through public ritual.

Durkheim appraises ceremonial rites as the "chief mechanism of religion."[47] In his influential study, *The Elementary Forms of Religious Life* (1912), he defines religion as a system of beliefs and practices that "unite[s] its adherents in a single moral community called a church."[48] He is careful to distinguish religion from magic, pointing out that, while magic "does not bind its followers to one another and unite them in a single group living the same life," religion is never found without a church.[49] Such "churches," according to Durkheim, are assemblages of individuals bound together by shared beliefs, unified standards of character and practice, and common conceptions of the sacred and its relation to the profane. Furthermore, he asserts that the best way of achieving and maintaining this imperative bond is through the performance of ritual.

Most centrally, Durkheim understands the sacred to be a force emanating from a group. This is evidenced by the fact that things typically deemed sacred — scriptures, devotional texts, sounds, ritual objects, behaviors, etc.— are closely associated with public rites and rituals. It is through these collective representations that societies become aware of themselves; they capture and sustain group feelings, experiences and ideas. In no small way, the group is defined and revitalized by the dynamic energy produced when its members gather together.

In contemporary worship, this effect is an underlying reason for unison prayer, which works to integrate individuals into a single entity. A variety of ethnographic studies highlight the role of corporate liturgical recitation in promoting communal bonding.[50] The act of praying together, sometimes regardless of the words being recited, can forge and maintain group cohesion. This is particularly true for intensely emotional group prayer experiences. According to Durkheim, individuals engaged in emotionally charged rituals tend to lose track of their separate identities, and become absorbed in the group. Worshipers gathered in a religious assembly are frequently drawn out of "egoistic self-absorption" and into a "self-transcending experience of social solidarity."[51] Durkheim explains the process: "Vital energies become overstimulated, passions more powerful, sensations stronger; there are even some that are produced only at this moment. Man does not recognize himself; he feels he is transformed…"[52] People gathered around symbolic objects, sounds, or activities produce an external force or constraint that reduces self-awareness and stimulates group-consciousness— a phenomenon Durkheim terms "collective effervescence."

Because such effervescence is dependent on intensely felt emotions, music is almost always a part of religious services. As a corporate act, unison prayer naturally produces some degree of togetherness; but this feeling is increased when the prayer is sung. Music can capture and make visceral moods implicit in a text, producing a range of associations. Recent studies have shown that people who experience a piece of music together, either as performers or as audience members, have remarkably similar responses.[53] In the religious arena, this is particularly true of congregational song, during which individual voices blend in a unified sound, creating an audible representation of the group. Singing works to consolidate the intellectual and emotional energies of the community, generating or enhancing a sense of affiliation and unity. A group engaged in song tends to experience common physical responses as well: changes in pulse rate, respiration, adrenalin flow and so on.[54]

On a fundamental level, then, music can help awaken and solidify social ties. For this reason, Durkheim argued that collective rituals, like congregational singing, form the ultimate basis of religious communities.[55] The emotional energy produced during musical worship works to draw people together in unity and cement their existence as a group. Given music's capacity to inspire these "bonding emotions," it is not surprising that every society has occasions that utilize music for unifying members.[56] Music frequently serves as a solidarity point around which members gather.

The Song of the Sea

Durkheim's observations are particularly apt for explaining the cohesive role of the Song of the Sea, the Bible's primary example of congregational singing.[57] The Song's laudatory verses give voice to the group's feelings of relief and delight in the aftermath of God's defeat of the Egyptian army. It begins with three verses of introduction proclaiming God's protection and deliverance of the Israelites, the Israelites' duty to enshrine and exalt their deity, and identifies God as a warrior (Exod. 15:1–3). Importantly, though all of this is phrased in the first person singular, it is prefaced with a collective description: "Then Moses and the Israelites sang this song to the Lord. They said" (v. 1). It therefore follows that they sang in the collective "I," emphasizing their unity and the shared nature of their experiences and emotions. The next set of verses describes the drowning of the Egyptian chariots and soldiers (vv. 4–12). God's supreme power is repeatedly praised, as in these words that later became part of Jewish morning and evening liturgies: "Who is like You, O Lord, among the celestials; Who is like You, majestic in holiness, awesome in holiness, working wonders!" (v. 11). The following section tells of God's guidance of Israel to the Promised Land, the defeat of its inhabitants—Philistines, Edomites, Moabites and Canaanites—and His establishment of the Temple (vv. 13–17). These are future events, and there is debate among scholars whether these verses are the product of later expansion and editing.[58] Whatever the case, they are presented as past occurrences, or, perhaps more accurately, as foregone conclusions. With the defeat of Egypt, God is enthroned as the eternal "cosmic victor," and thus the conquest He foretells is, in a sense, already done.[59] The Song concludes with a coda exclaiming God's eternal reign (v. 18), and a verse led by Miriam reiterating God's triumph over Pharaoh's forces (v. 21).

The designation of the Song as an archetype of congregational music is justified for at least four reasons. First, it was a communal outpouring. Moses and the Israelites sang the prayer together (v. 1), and it is followed by a short refrain sung by Miriam and the women (vv. 20–21). Despite the brevity of Miriam's words, some scholars contend that she was the author of the entire poem, or that her version of the Song has been lost.[60] Regardless, the text reports that everyone, male and female, was involved in rejoicing and singing words of praise — an extraordinary occurrence, as the group may have numbered two million or more.[61]

Second, the Song was sung in commemoration of a divine act. In every epoch, song and chant have been a mode of communicating gratitude and adoration to God. This type of expression is especially pronounced in the aftermath of momentous events, or in recognition of past accomplishments. The Song of the Sea was a spontaneous victory song. Other biblical examples of this type include those sung by individuals, like Deborah (Judg. 5) and David (2 Sam. 22), and communal hymns found in the Psalter (e.g., Ps. 68). Later traditions of Judaism and Christianity adapted and developed songs of praise for worship services. While not of a spontaneous nature, they likewise capture the spirit of the moment — a holy day or other sacred occasion — and focus the congregation's attention on the divine.

Third, the Song was delivered on holy ground. The Red Sea was the site of a miracle. The splitting of the waters, defeat of Pharaoh's soldiers, and deliverance from generations of slavery were all cause for wonderment. No longer frightened by the Egyptians, the Israelites' mood turned to awe: "when Israel saw the wondrous power which the Lord had wielded against the Egyptians, the people feared the Lord" (Exod. 14:31). With their song of praise, they marked the dry land as a sort of temporary sanctuary — a place for divine worship. In like manner, congregational singing elevates the sacred atmosphere of houses of worship. Such places are not necessarily built on the location or in honor of a miraculous episode; but their principal aim is to inspire a sense of the divine presence, a goal substantially aided by music.

Fourth, the Song introduced linguistic and structural elements that influenced later hymns. These include its basic form, consisting of a summons to praise followed by reasons for giving praise, and delineation of divine attributes: triumphant, glorious, faithful, etc. Certain of its phrases took on a popular character. Two in particular became formulaic in later songs of praise: the introduction, "sing to the Lord," which appears in a number of biblical verses (e.g., 1 Chr. 16:23; Jer. 20:13; Ps. 98:5), and the conclusion, "The Lord will reign for ever and ever," which also occurs elsewhere (e.g., Pss. 10:6; 146:10). These aspects of the Song proved effective during its original performance, and were adopted by prophets, psalmists and later liturgical poets seeking to inspire communities with song and prayer.

These four elements of the Song of the Sea—communal outpouring, commemoration, sacred setting and language—make it an exemplar of congregational music. It was simultaneously a hymn of praise and a means by which the Israelites asserted their new identity as a free and blessed nation. As Durkheim would attest, this powerful, shared experience generated and circulated an "effervescent vitalism," which encouraged, maintained and expressed social solidarity.[62]

In addition to the somewhat general characteristics listed above, there are three more specific aspects of the Song that further elucidate the cohesive effect: its function as a national anthem, responsorial form and dance accompaniment. Following Durkheim, these unique features helped "to bring individuals together, to increase contacts between them, and to make those contacts more intimate."[63] As details of one of the Bible's many corporate songs, they demonstrate some of the assorted and complex ways music advanced group solidarity in ancient Israel.

National Anthem

One of the most powerful genres of group song is the national anthem. In modern usage, anthems became widespread during the nineteenth century, though a few have older origins.[64] The designation of national anthem is given to songs either by official government decree or through the consensus of the people. These songs blend tones and texts to convey the (idealized) character or self-perception of a nation, and express and reaffirm shared beliefs, norms and values. As such, they can engender communal stability and identity, and express social sentiments that would otherwise remain fleeting or precarious.[65] This is evidenced in the comments of one nineteenth-century scholar, who found the "profoundly religious nature" of the Germans reflected in their anthem, "God Save the Emperor."[66] Wagner reported similarly, "the whole of the British character lay in the first two bars of 'Rule Britannia.'"[67] And a statesman famously said, "Let who will make the laws of a people; let me make their national songs."[68]

Zdzisław Mach adds that most national anthems contain condensed and romanticized accounts of a nation's heritage, traditions, and the "heroic periods of its mythic creation or its fight for sovereignty," which combine with nationalistic music to articulate a coherent ideological image.[69] For this reason, Mach explains that radical changes in power usually bring with them changes to anthems and other national symbols deemed incompatible with the new state's ideology. Likewise, emblems, flags and anthems—the "most obvious symbols of national identity"[70]—are often contested or even desecrated by citizens who do not agree with the state.[71] Because anthems communicate a particular idea of national identity, they are potent symbols around which patriots rally and detractors voice their concerns. They can bolster intra-group solidarity within opposing factions.

Though the Song of the Sea was first sung in the wake of a miraculous victory, and thus recounted an event in the immediate past, its subject matter and later usage give support to the idea that it was Israel's national anthem.[72] Not only was it the first religious song of Israel, but also its first song of nationhood. Like many anthems, it was born out of and stirred emotions connected to a paramount and heroic event. The text is rich in imagery and poetic flare, giving dramatic and memorable expression to the Red Sea episode. It starkly interrupts the narration that precedes it, announcing in laudatory tones God's defeat of Egypt and the birth of a nation. The special character of the Song is also displayed in the way it appears in the Torah scroll, where its verses are arranged metrically like bricks in a wall instead of in the standard parallel columns. This unique layout recalls, perhaps, the Israelites' experience

2. The Song of the Sea and Group Cohesion

as brick-laying slaves, and draws special emphasis to this central text.[73] At its core, the Song was a sonic representation of the nation itself, fusing the group around essential and defining aspects of history and theology.

It is also interesting to note that most modern national anthems are either in the style of a military song or a hymn.[74] The Song's original melody is lost to history, but the text indicates it was a song of praise and victory — that is, a martial hymn. A hint of this musical character is present in the special tune used for chanting the text in the synagogue. Just as the text's appearance departs from the surrounding verses, its melody is not bound by the usual system of biblical chant, which utilizes prescribed musical patterns indicated by a system of textual accents called *te'amim* (tastes). It exists instead as an independent tune that in sound and structure signals a departure from the cantillation, and resembles the martial notes of a trumpet-call.[75] Known simply as the *Shirah* (Song), this tune, among the oldest in the synagogue, has at least imagined roots in the time of the exodus.[76] Its musical presentation offers one possible way the Song of the Sea could have served to coalesce the populace into a convergence of emotional fervor and feelings of national pride. The music amplified themes of victory and praise, and elicited responses similar to the marches and hymns of modern national anthems.

Donald Thiessen isolates phrases in the Song that correspond to the military character of some national anthems: "went down into the depths like a stone" (v. 5); "shatters the foe" (v. 6); "consumes them like straw" (v.7); "the blast of Your nostrils" (v. 8); "floods stood straight like a wall" (v. 8); "They sank like lead" (v. 10); "The earth swallowed them up" (v. 12); "All the dwellers of are aghast" (v. 15); and "they are still as stone" (v. 16).[77] These stirring images combine with praise language — "The Lord is my strength and might" (v. 2), "Who is like You, O Lord, among the mighty" (v. 11), etc. — to embolden the formerly enslaved nation. As a martial and religious song, it inspired collective feelings of triumph, honor and self-confidence, and assured the faithful — in those days and in future generations — that they were favored in the eye of the sovereign and steadfast God.

The exodus was and remains a central national myth. It is at the same time a riveting chapter of sacred history and a cogent "theory of who and what Israel is."[78] The story told in Exodus 1–15 — spanning the settlement in Egypt and rise of Moses to the ten plagues and Red Sea crossing—sets forth one of Israel's chief socio-theological claims: just as the one God heard the Israelites' cry and freed them from bondage, so does He continue to play a redemptive role in every generation. In dozens of biblical passages, God is referred to or identifies Himself as "the Lord Your God, who brought you out of Egypt." This epithet is used variously to remind Israel of its allegiance to God (Lev. 22:33), announce God's faithfulness (Deut. 9:26) and to recall collective memories (Josh. 24:16). It is also central to the biblical command to observe the Feast of Passover (Deut. 16: 1). In light of this, the Song of the Sea, which marks the triumphant end of the story, is both an expression of gratitude for God's saving power and a proclamation of peoplehood.

It is not inconsequential that this moment, signaling the new beginning of the nation, was acknowledged with participatory song. Like a national anthem, the Song gave the group a "vivid notion and experience of active cooperation and kindled [its] feeling of belonging to the same ethnic community."[79] This musical outpouring—partly national and partly theological—generated social momentum that continues to this day.

Responsorial Singing

Most commentators since antiquity concur that the Song of the Sea was sung responsorially.[80] This type of song, also known as call-and-response, follows a musical "back and forth," with the leader or lead group singing a phrase and a second group singing a response. The second phrase is usually a direct commentary or elaboration on the first, corresponding to the conversational pattern of human communication. This manner of singing is highly participatory, depending entirely upon the interaction of two parties. While the biblical account does not specify exactly how the Song was sung, the text's form and the indication that it was simultaneously spontaneous and communal suggest that it was a call-and-response.

The best—albeit indirect—textual evidence to support this view comes in the verses following the Song, which depict Miriam leading the women in song and dance (vv. 19–21). In addition to the short refrain preserved in the Bible—"Sing to the Lord for He has triumphed gloriously; Horse and driver He has hurled into the sea" (v. 21)—it has been argued that Miriam either led the women in a repetition of Moses' song, or sang verses that were interwoven into his song.[81] In much the same way Moses could have led the men, or a combination of men and women, in responsorial singing.[82]

John Arthur Smith has identified several modes of responsorial singing in the Hebrew Bible.[83] Using biblical canticles, including the Song of the Sea, Deborah's song (Judg. 5), David's lament and thanksgiving (2 Sam. 22) and Isaiah's hymn of praise (Isa. 12), Smith concludes that call-and-response was conducted in the following ways: the congregation repeating each unit of the leader; the congregation repeating a standard refrain after each verse of the leader; the congregation completing the second half of the unit started by the leader; the leader singing the incipit of each unit and the congregation repeating the incipit and completing the unit; and the leader singing the entire song with the congregation repeating.

The Talmud records the opinion of Rabbi Nehemiah, who taught that Moses and the Israelites proclaimed the song "like men who recite the *Shema* [declaration of monotheism] in the synagogue service ... for [Moses] first opens, and the rest reply following him."[84] This implies that Moses sang the first half of each verse, and the people answered him with the second half. Another possible method is offered by William C. Stafford, who envisions the Israelites divided into two great choirs, one of men led by Moses and Aaron, and one of women led by Miriam: "Whilst the former sung the canticle, the latter would appear to have answered them by repeating the first stanza, accompanying their singing with the sound of tabrets, or timbrels, and with dancing."[85]

Herbert Lockyer, Jr. imagines a third possibility, with the Song alternating between three groupings: everyone present, men and women.[86] Most instructive is Lockyer's placement of Miriam's song (vv. 20–21) as a refrain dividing larger portions of the text:

Sung by All:
I will sing to the Lord, for He has triumphed gloriously;
Horse and driver he has hurled into the sea (v. 1).

Sung by Men:
The Lord is my strength and might;
He is become my deliverance.
This is my God and I will enshrine Him;

The God of my father and I will exalt Him.
The Lord, the warrior — Lord is His name (vv. 2–3).

Sung by Miriam and the Women:

Sing to the Lord, for he has triumphed gloriously;
Horse and driver He has hurled into the sea (vv. 20–21).

Sung by All:

Pharaoh's chariots and his army He cast into the sea;
And the pick of his officers are drowned in the Red Sea.
The depths covered them;
They went down into the depths like a stone.
Your right hand, O Lord, glorious in power,
Your Right hand, O Lord, shatters the foe!
In Your great triumph You break Your opponents;
You send forth your fury, it consumes them like straw.
At the blast of Your nostrils the waters piled up,
The floods stood straight like a wall;
The deeps froze in the heart of the sea (vv. 4–8).

Sung by Miriam and the Women:

Sing to the Lord, for he has triumphed gloriously;
Horse and driver He has hurled into the sea (vv. 20–21).

Sung by All:

The foe said,
"I will pursue, I will overtake, I will divide the spoil;
My desire shall have its fill of them.
I will bare my sword — my hand shall subdue them."
You made Your wind blow, the sea covered them;
They sank like lead in the majestic waters.
Who is like You, O God, among the celestials;
Who is like You, majestic in holiness,
Awesome in splendor, working wonders!
You put out your right hand, the earth swallowed them.
In Your love You lead the people You redeemed;
In Your strength You guide them to Your holy abode (vv. 9–13).

Sung by Miriam and the Women:

Sing to the Lord, for he has triumphed gloriously;
Horse and driver He has hurled into the sea (vv. 20–21).

Sung by All:

The peoples hear, they tremble;
Agony grips the dwellers in Philistia.

Now are clans of Edom dismayed;
The tribes of Moab — trembling grips them;
All the dwellers in Canaan are aghast.
Terror and dread descend upon them;
Through the might of Your arm they are still as stone —
Till Your people cross over, O Lord,
Till Your people cross whom You have ransomed.
You will bring them and plant them in Your own mountain,
The place You made to dwell in, O Lord,
The sanctuary, O Lord, which Your hands established (vv. 14–17).

Grand Chorus Sung by All:
The Lord will reign for ever and ever (v. 18).

Although the Song is the Bible's first occurrence of responsorial singing, it can be assumed that call-and-response was already in common use among the Israelites. Whatever the specific groupings may have been, the text displays imagery, meter, word choice and other devices indicative of a mature genre. It is also probable that the character of the Israelites' music was informed by Egyptian practice. The Bible records that the Israelites resided in Egypt for 430 years (Exod. 12:40–41), from the time of Joseph to the escape, and rabbinic sources propose that 210 of those years were spent in slavery.[87] It would have been impossible for the Israelites to avoid the influence of the host culture, especially because, during the many generations of slavery, their own customs and practices would have been severely restricted. In addition to being in Egypt for such a long duration, there were few Israelites, even in the early years, who knew of life outside that foreign civilization. According to the Bible, there were only seventy Israelites in Egypt during Joseph's lifetime (Exod. 1:5); but by the time of the Red Sea crossing, there were "600,000 men, aside from children" (Exod. 12:37), and over two million with women and children added.[88] This point is recapitulated in Deuteronomy 10:22: "With seventy souls your fathers went down into Egypt, and now the Lord your God has made you as numerous as the stars." The Israelites grew from a family to a nation while living in an alien land, and retaining distinctive or uncorrupted traits—outside of basic identifiers, such as class, racial features and basic monotheism—would have been an exceedingly difficult task.

Cultural borrowing, an inevitable consequence of years of subservient existence in foreign territory, certainly left its mark upon — and may have even spurred on — Israel's musical development. Music in Egypt was closely connected with religion. As would later be the case in the Jerusalem Temple, there was a class of Egyptian priests who functioned as musicians. They sang and played instruments resembling the harps, flutes, lyres, trumpets and drums mentioned in the Bible.[89] Moreover, while little trace is left of Egyptian music, there is evidence that responsorial singing was employed.[90] Israel's spontaneous responsorial hymn at the Red Sea can therefore be understood, at least in part, as an adaptation from Egyptian practice.

Importantly, too, the process of assimilating cultural influences while remaining a distinct group is a defining feature of Jewish Diaspora communities. The music of the Jews, no matter where they reside, exhibits close ties to the traditions of their non-Jewish neighbors.[91] It is not difficult to imagine similar adaptation occurring in ancient Egypt, where the Israelites — particularly during the slavery years — had only faint memories of their homeland customs, and were probably consumed by the dominating host culture. According to the rabbis, only the tribe of Levi maintained strict adherence to the Israelite religion in Egypt, while the rest took on Egyptian ways.[92]

The slave experience itself may have also contributed to the development of responsorial singing. This sort of song is ideally suited for communal labor. As a form of rhythmic accompaniment, it helps to ensure that all laborers work at the same pace; and as a mode of dialogue, it stresses the interconnectedness of members and focuses their attention on the group. These benefits of responsorial song were present among black slaves in America. Call-and-response was a regular part of field labor, and typically involved a gifted leader who would sing an improvised or embellished phrase to which the others would respond in unison chorus. Such singing contributed to the formation of cohesive groups out of individuals whose backgrounds were in various parts of Africa.[93] And the lyrical content, often infused with religious overtones and hope for future redemption, was a way for the group to assert its self-worth and "claims about its own humanity."[94] Though arising in a vastly different time and place, these slave songs shed light on the likely purposes of responsorial singing for Israelite slaves — perhaps the most important of which was the boosting of morale and solidarity beneath the shadow of the pyramid.

The Song of the Sea was not a ritual in the sense of being connected to a reoccurring event or following a prescribed order. However, the call-and-response model it provided was carried into the rituals of ancient Israel, occurring wherever assemblies gathered to take part in religious ceremonies.[95] It reached its fullest expression in the Second Jerusalem Temple where antiphonal psalm singing, alternating between two or more choirs, was the preferred species of choral art. Responsorial singing continued through the days of bondage, the Red Sea crossing and the Jerusalem Temple, in each period promoting shared affiliation, conviction and purpose.

Dance

The Song of the Sea also inspired solidarity through its accompanying dance. The Exodus account relates that Miriam the prophetess "took a timbrel in her hand, and all the women went out after her in dance with timbrels" (Exod. 15:20). This description is followed by a short verse of simple text: "Sing to the Lord, for He has triumphed gloriously; horse and driver he has hurled into the sea" (v. 21). The verse, sung perhaps to successive melodies that returned to a few central pitches, lends itself to constant repetition, and when added to the evidently infectious beat would have led (or at least contributed) to an ecstatic state.[96] This is consistent with the flavor of festive dance music in Eastern traditions dating back to antiquity, which utilize simple, direct music to ensure immediate stimulation.[97] Subtleties of tone and structure are left aside in favor of more accessible and intuitive styles that encourage outbursts of energy and emotional release.

Women's dancing at victory celebrations was customary in ancient Israel and in neighboring societies.[98] Celebratory dances are reported elsewhere in the Bible (Judg. 11:34; 1 Sam 18:6) and vestiges of the practice are found in Arab villages and in communities throughout the Mediterranean region.[99] Group dancing was integral in signaling military victories and welcoming heroes home from battle. Yet, beyond the immediate purposes of extolling and receiving soldiers, these dances bolstered unity of sentiment among the women, amplified feelings of communal pride and accomplishment, and strengthened bonds throughout the group.

Miriam and the women most likely performed a circle dance.[100] Such a dance would have required the coordinated movements of all involved. This is important to note, as feelings of solidarity are strongest when dances are done in unison.[101] Synchronized movements generate entrainment, a process by which the self-awareness of individual participants dissipates in the mass activity.[102] The energy and emotions exerted in and stimulated by the dance merge the participants — and, to a lesser extent, those around them — into a unified whole. It is quite plausible that the Song of the Sea, with its group singing, rhythmic drumming and coordinated dancing, amplified the Israelites' sense of shared purpose and meaning. Throughout human history, values and cultural heritage have been created, expressed and transmitted through the combination of music and movement.[103]

The impact of dance on group sentiment is particularly pronounced in religious contexts, where dance and music combine to evoke "peak experiences." To be sure, dancing can potentially inspire a wide range of feelings, from the most solemn to the most playful. But when the aim of dance is to intensify emotions connected to divine praise, it has the unique ability to bring a person or group into a new experience of itself and the transcendent. Religiously inspired dance enables participants to step into "a new dimension of existence" and "develop a new essence."[104] The self seems to dissipate in the rhythm of the movement.[105] However, although this feeling of transcendence entails a break from ordinary time and space, it generally does not cause a separation between the individual and the group. Instead, as anthropologist Herbert Spencer notes, "The element of religious ecstasy, the shifting boundaries, the transformation of time itself reflect an act of communion, rather than of detachment."[106] Swept into a state of euphoria, the dancer makes intimate communion both with the divine and with fellow participants.

To better picture how Miriam and the women likely achieved this state, it is instructive to look at a contemporary account of a Native American circle dance. George Horse Pasture describes how dance transported him to a deeper experience of community and the sacred — the dual effect of dancing in the exodus story. It is, indeed, beneficial to

2. The Song of the Sea and Group Cohesion

imagine Pasture's words as a first-hand report of an Israelite dancer at the Red Sea:

> As I adjust the space between the people in front and in back of me, I am part of a widening circle of dancers.... As the perspiration begins, I dance my best, continuing to enter clockwise in ever-tightening circles.... Soon, the chemistry, the ambience, and the magic are just right. While vigorously dancing, an irrefutable awareness arises that I am close to the center, the essence of life. As the world dissolves in color and music around me, a warm spiritual feeling spreads throughout the heart and body, and the song and dance carry me away from the heat and earth. Another zone of awareness, a detachment is entered: my feet, body, and arms move automatically to the rhythm of life. My fellow dancers are a part of me and I a part of them.[107]

Women playing drums was also a familiar scene in the ancient Near East, and remnants of the practice are found in isolated Jewish communities in North Africa and the Middle East.[108] Along with Miriam's dance, the Bible includes several instances of the practice (e.g., Jgs. 11:34; 1 Sam. 18:6; Jer. 31:4; Ps. 68:26). Each case employs a generic term for drum (*toph*), which is usually called a timbrel in English translations and is the only membranophone mentioned in the Bible.[109] The text does not provide information as to the size or shape of this drum, but it is generally agreed that it had a round, wooden frame with two membranes, resembling a modern tambourine without the metal jingles attached to its sides.[110] It does not appear in connection with Temple music, but seems to have been played regularly at cultic celebrations and feast day observances.[111]

As a rhythmic group activity, drumming further promotes unified movement and energy. It requires that attention be centered on the combined effort; everyone must keep time together in order to create interlocking patterns. In modern settings, such as a drum circle, drumming acts as a catalyst for engendering intense feelings of bonding.[112] For Miriam and the women, the rhythm of the timbrels helped drive the dance and support and accentuate the exuberant song. Even for those not involved in the drumming or dance, these expressions of joy generated a fervent sense of electricity that coursed through the group. This magnified the collective feelings of relief, merriment, devotion, awe and national pride that consumed the Israelites after crossing the Red Sea.

Spontaneous Prayer-Song

Prior to the establishment of the Temple service, worship music in ancient Israel arose in much the same way as the Song of the Sea. It did not spring forth as part of a pre-ordained occasion, nor did it utilize stipulated words, structured choreography or formulaic sounds. It was a spontaneous outburst of singing, drumming and dancing following a dramatic and miraculous experience. The three basic features of impulsivity, response to an event and outpouring of emotions are common to early biblical depictions of prayer-song. From the Red Sea crossing until the establishment of Temple worship, musical prayers did not usually follow a set pattern of performance or come about exclusively (or even predominantly) in connection with a set holiday or other scheduled event. One of the most striking examples of this kind is found in the Second Book of Samuel, when David brings the Holy Ark to Jerusalem: "David and all the House of Israel danced before the Lord to the sound of all kinds of cypress wood instruments, with lyres, harps, timbrels, sistrums, and cymbals" (6:5).

Such scenes of open expression, emotional abandon and lay participation gradually gave way to the formal, stylized service of the Temple. In that ordered setting, the music and the reason for its performance were governed by the time of day and date on the calendar, and religious expression was designed and managed by a class of trained priests. It can be presumed that this shift produced music aimed more at arousing emotions than providing an outlet for already intense feelings. Additionally, music took on an intellectual component, with the various instruments and practices representing themes and concepts tied to the liturgical system. For example, the blowing of trumpets was intended to show God's power and authority, while cantillation, the chanting of Scripture, symbolized the sanctity of the text.[113] These and other musical-liturgical devices were part and parcel of this decorum-conscious setting, removed from the ecstatic aftermaths of victory and deliverance. But this does not mean that ritual music lacked profundity or spiritual efficacy. On the contrary, the development and perpetuation of the musical service is a testament to its ability to inspire awe, dramatize worship and draw people to a sense of the divine presence. As one scholar explains, "Worship in the temple must have been thrilling and colorful

2. The Song of the Sea and Group Cohesion

to the eye and ear, but in its latter days the music became part of a ritual which seems to have left little room for spontaneity."[114]

Chapter 50 of Ecclesiasticus (or Sirach), an apocryphal book from the second century B.C.E., describes the structured ritual and carefully executed musical accompaniment of the Second Temple, including this scene of a wine offering:

> Finishing the service at the altars, and arranging the offering to the Most High, the Almighty, [the High Priest Simon son of Onias] held out his hand for a cup and poured the drink offering of the blood of the grape; he poured it out at the foot of the altar, a pleasing odor to the Most High, the king of all. Then the sons of Aaron shouted; they blew their trumpets of hammered metal; they sounded a mighty fanfare as a reminder before the Most High. Then the singers praised Him with their voices in sweet and full-toned melody [vv. 14–19].

This account is paralleled in the Mishnah's description of the final part of the daily service:

> They gave him the wine for the drink-offering, and the Prefect stood by each horn of the altar with a towel in his hand, and two priests stood at the table of the fat pieces with two silver trumpets in their hands. They blew a prolonged, a quavering and a prolonged blast. Then they came and stood by Ben Arza, the one on his right and the other on his left. When he stooped and poured out the drink-offering the Prefect waved the towel and Ben Arza clashed the cymbals and the Levites broke forth into singing. When they reached a break in the singing they blew upon the trumpet and at every blowing of the trumpet a prostration. This was the rite of the daily whole-offering.... This was the singing which the Levites used to sing in the temple.[115]

Structured rituals such as these differ in location, form and sentiment from the impromptu outpouring of Moses and the Israelites. Whilst I have argued that the Song of the Sea can be regarded as a model of congregational singing, it is not congregational in the liturgical sense of being stipulated, rehearsed or formulaic. Moreover, the inclusion of women in the celebration after Egypt's defeat is an element apparently excluded from later ritualized forms. As prayer-song took on a more statutory character, it also became increasingly male-dominated. Earlier spontaneous acclamations and celebrations regularly came from the lips of women. Primary examples include Miriam's participation in the Song of the Sea (Exod. 15:21), Deborah's song of victory (Judg. 5) and Hannah's thanksgiving song (1 Sam. 2:1–10). But women's voices are conspicuously absent from liturgical performance. Though Ezra 2:65 and Nehemiah 7:67 mention male and female singers as part of the community returning from the exile, it is unclear if they were involved in Temple or secular music. This difficulty owes to the fact that only male singers are explicitly shown as Temple singers (Neh. 10:29; 12:28, 29, 42). And although the Chronicler states that Heman's fourteen sons and three daughters were "under the charge of their father for the singing in the House of the Lord, to the accompaniment of cymbals, harps and lyres" (1 Chr. 25:5–6), only the brothers are named and assigned to the service of the Temple (1 Chr. 23:13–31).

The probable barring of women from Temple performance is further suggested by the absence of the timbrel from the Levitical orchestra on one hand, and its close association with women's singing and dancing on the other. The timbrel seems to have been primarily a "women's instrument." This is attested not only in the song of Miriam and the women (Exod. 15:20) but also in the dance of Jephthah's daughter (Judg. 11:34), the women's celebration of David and Saul's military victory (1 Sam. 18:6) and elsewhere. In Egyptian sources we find an instrument of similar description played exclusively by women and eunuchs[116]; and to this day the timbrel is held up as a symbol of Miriam's prophet status and women's spirituality more generally.[117]

Still, it would be a mistake to think that religious spontaneity for men and women disappeared in the mature days of Israel's worship. Though ritualized public prayer was the sanctioned mode of religious expression and one of the Bible's main areas of concern — as seen in the Latter Prophets, the Psalter, First and Second Chronicles, etc. — it is unlikely that other forms were completely abandoned outside of the official sanctuary. In every age individuals have turned to God in times of joy, sorrow, gratitude and uncertainty, whether or not the urge coincides with a set time or place of prayer. For many, singing in such moments is a natural impulse, as if melody generates wings on which words travel heavenward. The preservation of spontaneity in a religious culture that favors liturgical worship is demonstrated in various periods and locales, including the Hassidic sects of Judaism, which use music as a way to attain religious fervour,[118] and the Ethiopian Orthodox Church, which maintains links to the distant past.[119]

2. The Song of the Sea and Group Cohesion

Summary

The range of music's impact is seen in the Song of the Sea, the Bible's first and arguably most influential communal song of praise. Arising in response to the miraculous escape from Pharaoh's forces, the Song's performance helped capture shared feelings of gratitude and awe, and generate what Durkheim terms collective effervescence: the perceptible energy of a group engaged in a ceremonial activity. Through a combination of music, words and movements, the newly freed slaves transcended whatever individualism they may have had, and proclaimed their identity as a victorious and favored nation. In this profound sense, music was the mode through which they marked themselves as an autonomous people.

As a case study in music in the Bible, the Song confirms that music making was much more than a casual or isolated activity. Music helped stipulate, encourage and celebrate behaviors, emotions, beliefs, values and ideals that characterized the society as a whole. As the Bible's first instance of musical praise, the Song established an indelible relationship of music and worship that reappears in myriad later passages.

On a deeper level, the Song of the Sea is the origin story of a musical people. Building on the notion implied in the Jubal legend of music as a cornerstone of civilization, the performance of the Song shows how the Israelites, reborn after centuries of slavery, discovered and asserted who they were through music. Not only is the foundation of their worldview laid out in the text—conceptions of God and their relationship to Him, a sense of shared purpose and historical awareness, and so forth—but their presentation was a complete musical experience, involving solo and group singing, instruments (percussion), dancing and the involvement of both men and women. In this profound way, the Song was a holistic activity, laying the foundation for how the Israelites would come to see themselves both on intellectual/ideological and spiritual/artistic levels. They would not separate self-identifying words and music, but utilize them as mutually reinforcing elements of their national identity.

Chapter 3

Therapeutic Functions of David's Lyre: 1 Samuel 16:14–23

The meeting between David and Saul in 1 Samuel 16:14–23 is frequently cited as a biblical example of music therapy.[1] The passage shows King Saul driven to madness by an evil spirit. Concerned for his well-being, Saul's courtiers urge that he invite a skilled musician to his bedside. The young man who answers the call is David, whose playing of the lyre (*kinnor*) succeeds in calming the anguished king. According to the narrative, David's music has three distinct effects upon Saul (v. 23). First, it helps him "find relief," demonstrating the ability of music to impact one's state of mind. Second, it makes Saul "feel better," exhibiting the healing power of music. Third, it causes the evil spirit to "leave him," indicating that the music is imbued with a perceived supernatural force. For his musical skills, David is made a member of Saul's court, available to play for the king whenever he feels diminished.

At first glance, this brief episode appears to be an isolated incident. It stands out as the Bible's sole instance of what can be called a music therapy session; nowhere else do we find the controlled use of musical tones revitalizing someone in a troubled state. In the context of the storyline, the main purpose of this encounter is to move the plot along and not to demonstrate music's healing properties. David's skillful playing gains him entrance into Saul's court, initiates a close relationship between the two men, and sets David on the path toward kingship. Still, the account subtly points to the prevalence of musical healing practices in the biblical world. For one thing, the courtiers do not hesitate to recommend a musical treatment for Saul; their search for a musician is an automatic response to their master's condition. Music is also the only healing method proposed, and the author felt no need to justify or elaborate upon the efficacy of such music. Furthermore, the servants specifically seek "someone skilled at playing the lyre" (v. 16), which suggests widespread usage of that instrument for therapeutic aims. This function is recognized by present-day music therapists, who use lyres and harps to treat a number of ailments.[2]

With David's healing music as its focal point, this chapter draws inferences about the implementation of music therapy in ancient Israel. It begins with a brief overview of the general uses of therapeutic music from ancient times to the present, giving special attention to the relationship of music, healing and religion. Section two consists of a profile of David as musician, highlighting the important ways music figured into his personality, helped facilitate his rise to power and informed his career as king. The third section presents a historical and theological analysis of the *kinnor*, the lyre David used to treat Saul, with emphasis on its perceived joyous and divine qualities. The fourth section offers the possibility that David treated King Saul with a technique related to the iso principle, which matches music to the patient's mood and gradually introduces changes in harmony, dynamics and so on in order to bring him/her to a desired state. Underlying these discussions is the extent to which Israel — the House of David — defined itself through David's kingship, and how the prominence of music in his biography helped shape Israel's self-perception as a musical people.

Healing Music

Music therapy generally refers to the planned and controlled use of music to modify non-musical behaviors and bring about therapeutic change.[3] As an official allied health profession, music therapy is relatively new; but music's capacity to impact one's physical, psychological, social and spiritual domains is among its original purposes. Virtually all cultures, in one way or another, have utilized music for stimulating positive changes in people experiencing undesirable, unhealthful and uncomfortable conditions.[4]

The roots of music therapy reach back to antiquity. Musical healing is an almost universal component of the world's shamanic traditions.[5]

Greek mythology includes legends of Orpheus and Apollo curing diseases with song.[6] Since the second century B.C.E., Chinese medicine has relied on music in the treatment of maladies.[7] Indian *ragas* have long been used to positively influence mental and physical health.[8] These are but a sampling of the countless ancient healing traditions that comprise the historical underpinnings of the Western field of music therapy, which had its inception during the two World Wars.[9] Since then, the clinical practice of musical healing has proven effective in combating a remarkable array of conditions. Physiological and psychological benefits of music have been reported for patients in coronary care and in surgical and neonatal intensive care units.[10] Music is used in the treatment of various types of anxiety and mental handicaps,[11] and in caring for the elderly.[12] The extent of music's use in therapeutic settings far exceeds the scope of this study. But even from this cursory list, it is amply clear that cultures ancient and modern have been drawn to music as an agent for changing moods, ameliorating ailments, recharging spirits, redirecting energies and channeling emotions.

It is perhaps not surprising that the "quasi-magical efficacy" of music has for millennia carried religious implications.[13] For the earliest humans, divine worship, magic, healing and music were all part of the same activity.[14] Music's inherent palliative effects have been linked equally to the physical, psychological and spiritual domains.[15] While music therapy is not an explicit part of most contemporary forms of Judaism and Christianity, signs of the relationship of music and healing are found in many worship services. Curt Sachs traces this aspect of Jewish and Christian worship to the musical practices of indigenous religions: "Where the medicine man (*shaman*) performs religious ceremonies, the music approaches the liturgical intonation. And from the chants of the witch doctor it has descended by a long chain of heredity to the liturgy of the higher religion: it lives on in the *Saman* of the Hindu as in the *Leinen* of the Jews and the *Lectio* of the Christian churches."[16]

A more recent study by Dale A. Matthews and Connie Clark emphasizes the health benefits of congregational singing in Western faith traditions.[17] Singing requires deeper breathing than other forms of exercise, opening up the respiratory tubes and sinuses, and increasing aerobic capacity. This results in greater oxygen intake which can, in turn, aid the heart and circulation, decrease muscle tension, lower heart rate, decrease blood pressure and reduce stress.[18] In the congregational setting, the positive effects of singing with one's mind, body and spirit stimulate an added sense of engagement with a transcendent force. "Sacred music," Matthews and Clark conclude, "seems to soak into our very bones, carrying the message of God's glory and God's love deep into our being."[19]

Some of the most intriguing remarks on the religious nature of music therapy come from the pen of medieval Jewish philosopher and physician Moses Maimonides (1135–1204). In general, Maimonides is opposed to listening to vocal and instrumental music as a sign of mourning for the destruction of the Second Temple, and for the potential of secular music to lead to frivolity and debauchery. However, he does allow for "dignified" music at festive occasions of a religious nature, such as weddings, and permits songs of praise to God (without instrumental accompaniment).[20] Though he warns against the potentially tarnishing impact of music, Maimonides, being a pragmatist, promotes the use of musical tones for therapeutic aims. He asserts that fitness of mind and body are both necessary for obtaining wisdom and striving for knowledge of God, and recognizes that certain types of music can help one achieve this goal.

In one document, Maimonides states that the soul is aided by listening to beautiful music, like "a bride with her accompanying musical instruments."[21] Elsewhere, he prescribes that a person suffering from melancholy should stroll through pleasant gardens and listen to vocal and instrumental music.[22] In another medical treatise, he offers an hour-by-hour regimen for the depressed Egyptian Sultan Al Malik Al Afdal. Using the story of David and Saul as a guide, Maimonides recommends that the royal singer chant songs accompanied by the lyre: the musician should perform for an hour, and then "lower his voice gradually, loosen his strings, soften his melody until the Sultan falls into a deep sleep, and then cease completely."[23] The purpose of all of this, according to Maimonides, is to restore mental and physical health so that the soul can continue striving for knowledge of God without impediment.[24]

Lewis Rowell observes that the historical and cross-cultural examination of music therapy yields three major functions.[25] The first is regulation, which involves the arousing or soothing of certain emotions in order to achieve a state of equilibrium. The second is the stimulation of pleasurable sensations, which brighten one's mood or disposition. The third is catharsis or the purging of emotional conflict. As these options suggest, no single type or use of music is appropriate for all conditions; specific musical sounds address specific needs. All three of these functions can potentially accomplish the Maimonidean aim of "endow[ing] the soul with a good nature" and sending it on an unobstructed path toward the divine.[26] In the case of David and Saul, it is the third function, catharsis, which best describes the expelling of the evil spirit with the lyre. This function of music was, in fact, a traditional cure for spirit possession "common to all ancient societies confronted by demons."[27]

David the Musician

The musical encounter between Saul and David is situated in the story of David's rise to power, which spans from 1 Samuel 14 to 2 Samuel 5. Like other narratives in the books of Samuel, it reads like a "historical novel" rather than a chronicle. David emerges as a complex and very human character. At times, he is an outlaw, a deserter and a Philistine mercenary,[28] and at other times a pure soul (1 Sam. 16:12), loyal friend (1 Sam. 18:1) and faithful servant of God (2 Sam. 25–28). He is both an "innocent man of destiny" and a "cunning schemer,"[29] both a pious king and "tough practitioner of *Realpolitik*."[30] For all of this, David stands as one of the most multifaceted characters in the Bible, exhibiting a range of traits and talents. Especially intriguing for our purposes is the degree to which David's rise and kingship relied on his musical skills.

David is first introduced when God sends the prophet Samuel to find a replacement for King Saul, who has lost divine favor. "Fill your horn with oil and set out," God tells Samuel. "I am sending you to Jesse the Bethlehemite, for I have decided on one of his sons to be king" (1 Sam. 16:1). Samuel meets seven of Jesse's sons at a sacrificial feast, none of whom is God's choice. Samuel asks if any sons are absent, and Jesse replies that there is one more who is "tending the flock" (v. 11). This missing son is David, the youngest and least esteemed of the eight brothers. As soon as David arrives at the feast, Samuel is commanded to "Rise and anoint him, for he is the one" (v. 12). This unlikely selection continues the biblical motif of the younger being preferred to the elder: Abel to Cain (Gen. 4:2–5), Isaac to Ishmael (Gen 21:9–13), Jacob to Esau

(Gen. 27:28–40) and Joseph to Reuben (Gen. 37:3–11). Suitability, not seniority, is the decisive factor.

Though David receives divine blessing, it is his skill as a musician that enables his spectacular rise from lowly shepherd to exalted king. The spirit of God "gripped" David on the day of his anointment (1 Sam. 16:13). In the following verse, we read that the divine spirit has departed from Saul, implying that the movement of God's blessing from Saul to David also includes the transfer of divine spirit. As a consequence, Saul is filled with the evil spirit of God, which terrifies him. Desperate to alleviate his torment, Saul orders his courtiers to "find someone who can play [the *kinnor*-lyre] well and bring him to me" (v. 18). One of the royal attendants announces, "I have observed the son of Jesse, a Bethlehemite who is skilled in music; he is a stalwart fellow and a warrior, sensible in speech, and handsome in appearance, and the Lord is with him" (v. 18). David's music soothes the anguished king, and he is made an arms-bearer so that he is available to play whenever the evil spirit returns. David eases the madness that consumes Saul at odd moments; his "musical medicine" provides much-needed, though temporary, relief.[31]

At this point, Saul is not yet aware that David has been appointed to replace him, and his introduction to the young man is purely a musical matter. David poses no initial threat to Saul's power and the relations between the two are most promising. David is Saul's loyal servant and musical rescuer. Though their rivalry is inevitable (1 Sam. 18, 19), for the moment David is the recipient of Saul's warm affection. It is significant that this intimate relationship is initiated through music. David's musical adeptness is the sole and immediate cause for his invitation to the court, and the sound of his lyre forges an instant bond between the two men of vastly different ages and social statuses.

As an aside, it is worth noting that while initially David's music has a therapeutic effect, eventually it becomes a source of contention as the relationship of David and Saul grows in complexity. Perhaps because Saul is at first so engrossed with David's power of musical persuasion and the divine favor and force it entailed, his escalating hostility toward David is exacerbated rather than eased by the once-therapeutic playing. It is no stretch to imagine the increasingly paranoid king regarding the emotional sway of David's lyre as a medium of subversive manipulation.

This understanding does much to explain the scenes in 1 Samuel 18:10–11 and 19:9–10, where Saul, again consumed by an evil spirit, throws a spear toward David as he tries to soothe the king with his lyre. The music, intended to provide relief, becomes "an irritant and catalyst to evil actions."[32]

Alfred Sendrey stresses the centrality of David's musicianship in his rise to royalty:

> It is questionable whether David would ever have become king of his people and fulfilled his historical role, if his artistry had not opened him the way to the suffering king Saul. The meteor-like rise of David from the simplest life to highest honors would have probably never materialized without his musicianship. The erstwhile shepherd boy as future extolled hero and ruler of his nation — the leading spirit, whose activity was to become decisive for the religious and intellectual history of Israel — all this turned out to be the immediate consequence of his artistry.[33]

Read as a detached episode, Sendrey's comments are correct. Yet, the scene described in 1 Samuel 16:14–23 is actually the second of three separate accounts of David's election. The first is the above-mentioned anointment, in which Samuel evaluates the sons of Jesse and singles David out for divine appointment (1 Sam. 16:1–13). The third account centers on David's victory over Goliath (1 Sam. 17:1–18:5). Though the latter follows the stories depicting the anointment and Saul's musical treatment, it re-introduces David as if he is previously unknown. He is described only as a shepherd — no allusion is made to his music skills — and upon his return to Jerusalem after slaying the giant, Saul asks him, "Whose son are you, my boy?" (1 Sam. 17:58). These three mutually exclusive accounts present entry points for David's course to kingship. Each foreshadows the honor that would be bestowed upon him, and emphasizes characteristics that would define him in his own day and in later traditions.[34]

For all of their discontinuity, these three accounts do have strong uniting elements. This is especially apparent when comparing the confrontation of David and Goliath and the "battle" between Saul's madness and David's lyre. On the surface, these narratives have little in common and leave the reader with the impression of different authorship. Among the questions raised in positioning these entry accounts side-by-side, there are two that point to their origin as distinct storylines: If David was already serving as Saul's personal musician, what was he doing back home in Bethlehem? And why does Saul profess he does not know who David is?[35] Notwithstanding these and other chronological issues, the combative nature of each account does paint a consistent picture of David as warrior: in one with music as his weapon and in the other with a slingshot. In both cases, David is seemingly outmatched by his opponent; he is a young man of low station who confronts profound evil in the guise of a king's psychosis and an imposing giant. Although David is described as possessing exceptional skill in music and military arts, his abilities alone are not enough to defeat these forces. Saul's healing and Goliath's defeat are attributed to divine power present in and working through the personage of David (1 Sam. 16:18; 17:45).[36]

While aspects of any one of these events could have accounted for David's "meteor-like rise," his close connection to Saul is ultimately owed to music, "the most intimate and affecting of all the arts."[37] And it is the story of the lyre that offers the most insight into David's personality. This does not mean that the other election stories present a one-dimensional young man. The anointment provides some physical descriptions—"ruddy-cheeked, bright-eyed, and handsome" (1 Sam. 16:12)—which convey young David's purity and virtue. In addition, much like Moses (Exod. 3:1), David is identified as a shepherd who tends the flock and, by implication, is suited to tend the people (cf. Ps. 78:70–71). "Shepherd" was a common epithet of kings in the ancient Near East, and an early sign of his aptitude for leadership.[38]

The story of David and Goliath also shows David as a shepherd, and through the unfolding drama reveals him as a pious warrior and orator—crucial attributes for his success as leader. David's eloquence, bravery and devotion come to the fore in a speech he delivers before the battle: "You will come against me with sword and spear and javelin; but I come against you in the name of the Lord of Hosts, the God of the ranks of Israel, whom you have denied. This very day, the Lord will deliver you to my hand" (1 Sam. 17:45).

But it is the musical encounter that gives us the most thorough characterization of the future king. David is recommended to Saul because he is "skilled in music" (1 Sam. 16:18), and in the same verse we learn that he is loyal, sensible in speech, handsome, godly and skilled in warfare. Four of these qualities are found in the other two accounts: good looks, piety, articulateness and battle expertise. However, only 1 Samuel 16:18 highlights David's loyalty and musical adeptness. It is also important that these six traits are given as a succinct list without any action to support them, as if making a case for David's ability to succeed as king. These attributes are fleshed out in the narrative that follows, and considerably account for why David is considered Israel's "greatest king" and "most beloved hero."[39]

Most of these qualities translate to clear advantages for a leader. Loyalty breeds trust and respect, powerful words inspire crowds, good looks enhance charisma, piety brings divine support and military skills ensure stability and power. Less obvious is the role of music in leadership. A national leader's artistic side might at first seem secondary or tangential to the more immediately applicable talents as communicator, warrior and so forth. But, as Thiessen observes,[40] exceptional musicians can exude a certain magnetism that draws people in and wins them over. This certainly aids David in gaining access to Saul's court. Even more notable is music's role in other fields in which David excels: oration, warfare and religious devotion.

David is not merely a gifted communicator, but the "sweet singer of Israel" (2 Sam. 23:1). His talent for the lyre is matched by his vocal abilities. He offers beautiful songs in varying circumstances throughout his life. For example, 2 Samuel 1:19–27 contains David's heartfelt dirge over the deaths of Saul — who by that time was his crazed nemesis — and Saul's son Jonathan — who was his dearest friend. The lament song is not only an exquisite example of biblical poetry, but also an expression of David's loyalty — one of the virtues mentioned in 1 Samuel 16:18. Rather than a religious or nationalistic song, it is an intimate and emotional outpouring for two men whose lives deeply impacted David's. Particularly moving is the verse praising the pair's military prowess, "They were swifter than eagles, they were stronger than lions!" (v. 23) and the words sung expressly for Jonathan, "I grieve for you, my brother Jonathan, you were most dear to me. Your love was wonderful to me, more than the love of a woman" (v. 26).

Song also accompanies David in battle. In 2 Samuel 22:2–51, he sings an extended song of praise "after the Lord had saved him from the hands of all his enemies and from the hands of Saul" (v. 1). Always mindful of God and the abilities He bestowed upon him, David sings of the following themes: divine praise (vv. 2–4); his existential plight (vv. 4–7); God's appearance (vv. 8–16); God's revenge (vv. 17–20); reward for righteousness (vv. 21–25); God's requital (vv. 26–28); God's help in battle (vv. 29–37); victory (vv. 38–43); David's rule over the nations (vv. 44–46); and a concluding praise (vv. 47–55). The same song, with slight variations, is found in Psalm 18. Its opening verses are especially powerful (2–4): "O Lord, my crag, my fastness, my deliverer! O God, the rock wherein I take shelter: My Shield, my mighty champion, my fortress and refuge! My savior, You who rescue me from violence! All praise! I called on the Lord, and I was delivered from my enemies." With this victory song, David establishes himself not only as a devoted servant of God, intrepid warrior, brilliant strategist, empire builder and dynastic founder, but also as the musician-king *par excellence.*

It is under David's rule, too, that music becomes an official part of Israel's religious life. Though the relationship of music and prayer was well in place before David's time, prayer-songs were spontaneous rather than institutional. They were sung in response to specific circumstances, either by a group, like the Song of the Sea (Exod. 15:1–21), or individuals, like Deborah (Judg. 5:1–31) and Hannah (1 Sam. 2:1–10). With David the music of religious devotion is made a regular part of the national religion: "David ordered the officers of the Levites to install their kinsmen, the singers, with musical instruments, harps, lyres, cymbals, joyfully making their voices heard" (1 Chr. 15:16). Among the reportedly 38,000 Levites under David's charge, 4,000 are appointed as musicians (1 Chr. 23:5). This special class is crucial for the development and preservation of Israel's musical heritage — fixed scales, tunes, instrumental techniques, etc.— as well as for the transmission of history, core beliefs, moral standards and other key aspects of the nation's religion and society. Just as David uses music to express emotions, articulate religious concepts and profess God's presence, he carefully organizes guilds of singers and players to perform psalms that espouse Israel's feelings, doctrines, ethics and religious character. Knowing of music's capacity for instruction and inspiration, the musical king helps engender and fortify a national consciousness through song.

Numerous other biblical passages relate David's musical expertise. In addition to singing and playing the lyre, David is a sacred dancer. As the Holy Ark is transferred to Jerusalem, David and the people of Israel dance before God to the music of all sorts of instruments (2 Sam. 6:5). David is, then, portrayed as an expert in the three forms of musical art known to Israel: instrument playing, singing and dancing.[41] He is also identified as an inventor of instruments (Neh. 12:36; 1 Chr. 23:5; 2 Chr. 29:26) and as an archetypical musician (Am. 6:5). David's eloquent singing and legendary playing earned him a place in Jewish tradition as the author of the entire Book of Psalms, "including in it the work of the elders Adam, Malkizedek, Abraham, Moses, Heman, Jeduthun, Asaph, and the three sons of Korah."[42] Another source states, "All praises which are stated in the Book of Psalms, David uttered each one of them."[43] His connection to Psalmody is even more pronounced in the large Psalm scroll from Qumran, which claims that he wrote 3,600 psalms and an additional 450 songs.[44] David is extolled as a model of musical perfection in Jewish, Christian and Muslim sources, and is touted as a symbol of divinely inspired music-making.[45] Nineteenth-century Jewish poet Naftali Herz Imber sums up David's high musical stature:

> King David, to whom is ascribed the authorship of the Psalms, was more than a poet, singer, or artist, and deserves the title of "father of Hebrew music." Himself a gifted poet and composer, he was also a good organizer — a talent so seldom found in an idealistic nature. David was the first to uplift music as an art. He ordered the Levites should no longer be porters and carriers, but only singers, and players of instruments.... The elevation to that dignity was an immense step in the development of the divine art. Musical notes, and the invention of a variety of instruments, were the outcome of that elevation.[46]

Kinnor (Lyre)

The instrument used in 1 Samuel 16:14–23 deserves special attention. Upon recognizing Saul's diminished state, the courtiers immediately suggest that he be visited by someone expert in playing the *kinnor* (lyre) (1 Sam. 16:16). This almost instinctive recommendation points to a well-established practice of playing the instrument for therapeutic ends. There was evidently something inherent to the instrument that made it particularly effective in eliciting positive changes in mood. However, though this effect is obvious from the meeting of David and Saul, the exact qualities of the instrument remain a topic of conjecture.

While musical instruments were an important part of the cultural makeup of ancient Israel, the Bible provides no clear indication as to their sizes or shapes, nor does it describe techniques for playing them. Sixteen instruments or instrument groupings are mentioned by name, appearing in numerous sacred and secular settings. These references are typically brief and vague, and rarely allude to the sounds produced. Still, they bespeak an environment rich in instruments representing the four main divisions: idiophones, membranophones, aerophones and chordophones.

For centuries, scholars have grappled with the dearth of information about biblical instruments. The Romans were among the first to examine the names of the instruments, hoping to find in them some deeper meaning and symbolism.[47] Similar efforts were attempted in Mishnaic and Talmudic tractates, as well as in the writings of the church fathers.[48] Fortunately, archaeological evidence has shown a basic consistency of musical instruments in the ancient Near East. Variant forms of instrument types, such as flutes, lyres and frame drums, appear in Egyptian, Babylonian, Assyrian, Greek and Roman pictorial representations, furnishing us with a "working basis for drawing reasonable conclusions about the instruments of the ancient Hebrews."[49] Further clues have also been gleaned from a few discoveries of actual remains in neighboring cultures.[50]

The *kinnor* is subject to many of the issues surrounding the positive identification of instruments in ancient Israel. While research into the origins and characteristics of the *kinnor* is too complex and voluminous to summarize here, an overview of this scholarship sheds sufficient light on both the challenges and general areas of inquiry related to this and other biblical instruments. Most crucially, no authentic pictures of the instrument have been found among the ruins of Israel.[51] The earliest known rendering appears on a coin from the period of the Bar Kokhba revolt (132–136 C.E.), but because of the coin's late date, it is questionable whether it contains an accurate depiction of a *kinnor* from biblical times. When viewing such images, it may be tempting to fall back on the notion of the "eternal East." The region tended to be conservative in its customs and institutions, and its ceremonial practices underwent slow change through the centuries.[52] But this does not necessarily relate to artifacts, such as musical instruments, which were subject to more frequent and drastic modifications and embellishments.[53] The basic types may have persisted for long periods, but their features were not static.

Scholars have also explored the etymology of the term *kinnor*, suggesting that it may have derived from the name of a similar instrument. Possible sources include the Egyptian *kn-an-aul*,[54] Syrian *kenara*,[55] and Arabic-Persian *kunar*.[56] Sachs is skeptical about such speculations, concluding that the apparent connection between the names does not prove which instrument came first, and the term's origin may simply be unknowable.[57] Added to this, *kinnor* may have been used in connection with more than one instrument, or may be a general term for instruments in the string family.[58]

The biblical scribes did not record anything about the shape or component parts of the instrument. This omission has generated a number of theories and educated guesses about the instrument's dimensions and the number of strings it may have had. Macy Nulman has compiled several of these propositions from antiquity to modern times.[59] Rabbi Judah (135–219) asserts that it had seven strings,[60] while Josephus writes that it had ten.[61] Abraham Ibn Ezra (1089–1164) posits that it had the shape of a candelabrum (commentary on Daniel 3:5), and Abraham Portaleone, a sixteenth-century scholar, claims that it resembled a modern harp with forty-seven strings.[62] Joel Brill-Loewe (1760–1802) contends that it had six strings and was similar in shape to the Greek letter delta, whereas Abraham Z. Idelsohn (1882–1938) speculates that the strings of the instrument varied in number from three to twenty-two. This diversity of opinion reflects the uncertainty about the instrument and the freedom of interpretation this uncertainty affords.

Nonetheless, all of these interpretations agree that the *kinnor* was some version of a lyre — identification confirmed in the archaeological record.[63] No other stringed instruments besides lyres and harps have been found in the areas that formerly comprised Canaan, Israel and Palestine. To date, at least thirty representations of lyres have surfaced in the region, which can be divided into four broad categories: large asymmetrical lyres with diverging arms and rectangular resonators; small symmetrical lyres with rounded or rectangular resonators; asymmetrical lyres with parallel side arms and rectangular resonators; and symmetrical lyres with horn-shaped side arms and rounded resonators.[64] In each case, the instrument is comprised of a body, two arms and a yoke.

There is also some discrepancy regarding how sounds were produced on the *kinnor*. Bowed instruments were not yet invented, leaving the likelihood that the *kinnor* was played either by hand or with a small stick known as a plectrum.[65] Josephus claims that it was played with a plectrum[66] — a technique described by Carl Heinrich Cornill[67]: "The man picks the strings with the fingers of his left hand while he strikes them with a so-called plectrum, a small stick held in his right hand." It has also been suggested that the *kinnor* was played with a plectrum when it accompanied singing, but was plucked with the fingers when performed alone.[68] Alfred Sendrey and Mildred Norton describe the effect of this technique: "it could be very eloquent when played alone, with the fingers of both hands sweeping the strings freely."[69] This was presumably the way David played for Saul. There is no mention of him singing, which would have required a plectrum, and playing the instrument by hand would have produced softer, more soothing tones.[70]

Because David and the Levites played the *kinnor*, it is considered the foremost and noblest instrument of ancient Israel.[71] The Talmud records that there were at least nine *kinnors* in the Temple at a given time.[72] It is also the first instrument mentioned in the Bible, coupled with the pipe (*uggab*) in the Jubal account, and is therefore an emblematic string instrument. Given its special status, there is little doubt that the *kinnor* was the preferred instrument in elite circles; but it appears in humbler settings as well. The instrument is cited forty-two times in the Hebrew Bible, serving a range of exalted and earthly purposes. These include divine worship (1 Chr. 15:16; Ps. 43:4; 98:5; 149:3; 150:3), prophecy (1 Sam. 10:5), secular festivals (Gen. 31:27; Isa. 24:8) and prostitution (Isa. 23:16).

In these instances and others, the *kinnor* is associated with gaiety. Sendrey calls the instrument "a dispenser of joy at merry banquets, at popular feasts, and at celebrations of victories and coronations."[73] Its sounds were sweet and pleasant (Ps. 81:3), and served as conduits of gladness and delight (Ps. 45:9). The connection to joy is further expressed in Isaiah, where the "merriment of lyres" is stilled as punishment for the people's transgressions (24:8). Psalm 137:2 recounts how the captives at the rivers of Babylon silenced the instrument as a sign of sadness. And the single verse linking the instrument to lamentation, "So my lyre is given to mourning ..." (Job 30:31), is not meant as a literal depiction of musical accompaniment, but as a poetic metaphor suggesting that at times of deep sorrow even the joyous tones of the *kinnor* turn melancholy.

The link between the *kinnor* and joy is illustrative of the broader relationship of music and emotions. Music's ability to stimulate moods or feelings is known throughout the world's cultures. More accurately, music triggers states of consciousness that are analogous to those produced by extra-musical means.[74] This is why musical tones, pieces and instruments are often described in terms of their emotional effect. To be sure, the feelings conjured by music are largely dependent on associations. For a given listener, certain music will generate subjective non-musical images, sentiments and memories. A piece can be linked to one's past, stirring feelings and thoughts of a particular time, place or relationship. Musical conventions, such as a modulation or turn of phrase, may arouse specific emotions for listeners familiar with these devices. Music closely tied to a holiday or event can bring entire communities into shared sentiments connected with that day.

As these examples show, music's impact is personally and/or culturally specific; the reactions it evokes stem from previous knowledge or experience. Because music-inspired emotions are strongly dependent on one's past and cultural conditioning, some scholars argue that any claim of a direct connection is ultimately invalid.[75] But debates over whether emotions are intrinsic to musical tones or result from subjective factors do not diminish the fact that music moves us, often in ways more powerful and immediate than other forms of expression. It is, then, safe to assume that biblical instruments, like instruments in our own day, were designed to elicit or came to be associated with specific emotional responses. The timbre of an instrument, along with the tunes or patterns played upon it, exploited musical expectations of the people, and inspired a range of feelings.

This explains the identification of the *kinnor* as an instrument of joy, and religious joy in particular. In the biblical perspective, observes D. Miall Edwards, "Religion is conceived of as touching the deepest springs of emotion, including the feeling of exultant gladness which often finds outward expression in such actions as leaping, shouting, and singing."[76] Several verses show joy as a direct outcome of fellowship with God. The emotion is stirred by divine attributes, such as His lovingkindness (Pss. 21:6, 7; 31:7), salvation (Ps. 21:1; Isa. 25:9; Hab. 3:18), judgment (Ps. 48:11), comfort (Jer. 15:15), and sovereignty (Pss. 93:1; 96:10; 97:1). Not surprisingly, a number of these passages include musical outpourings, in which the *kinnor* is often involved. For example, Psalm 33, which describes joy coming from trust in God, includes these words: "Praise the Lord with the lyre ... play sweetly with shouts of joy" (vv. 2–3). This idea is repeated in Psalm 71: "I will acclaim You to the music of the lyre for Your faithfulness, O my God" (v. 22). Psalm 43 is especially clear in linking God to joy, and joy to the music of the *kinnor*: "God, my delight, my joy ... I [will] praise You with the lyre" (v. 4).

These psalm verses depict players using the instrument to express their delight in God's presence. The exuberance they feel cannot be adequately articulated in words alone; the sound of the *kinnor* is needed to capture and convey the magnitude of the moment. The playing of the instrument for this purpose was likely repeated to the point of being standard, and so its sound became synonymous with divine joy. It was probably played both in response to elation and merriment already felt, and in order to arouse these emotions in the listener. The instrument stirred "the life enhancing, vital, pleasurable joy of connection, love, and celebration."[77]

The joyful effects of the *kinnor* are seen in the story of David and Saul. Saul is described as haunted by an evil spirit — a condition suggesting some form of spiritual malady.[78] Bible critics have described his state as melancholia, paranoid schizophrenia and bipolar syndrome.[79] Robert Henry Pfeiffer diagnoses Saul as having "Fits of acute mental depression with violent explosions of anger."[80] In light of these medical explanations, David would have functioned like a modern-day music therapist. His gentle playing refreshed and uplifted the bedridden king. This shift in state is consistent with the instrument's joyous qualities. Saul's depression is alleviated through the musical conjuring of the opposite emotion. More generally, the episode describes the vivid and often all-consuming impact of music on the listener, whether sick or well. Whatever thoughts or feelings may be affecting one's disposition can be altered or swept away by musical tones.[81]

Yet, this is not only a case of musical intervention, but also of divine intervention. God's healing presence is invoked through David's playing, causing the evil spirit to depart from him (1 Sam. 16:23). The biblical author regarded Saul's illness strictly as a spiritual matter; it is depicted in theological rather than psychological terms. As such, only a divine remedy could cure him. It is as if God Himself is present in the notes, radiating an irrepressible sense of joy. As one scholar puts it, "Through music God plays His power, and the power is vested in the music."[82]

Other biblical instruments are also shown to evoke the divine presence. Most notable is the *shofar* (ram's horn), the only instrument of ancient Israel that remains in use to this day. Though it is not particularly musical (it produces only two or three tones), the *shofar* held a special place in biblical times. Among its many purposes, it announced holidays (Ps. 81:4), accompanied processionals (2 Sam. 6:15; 1 Chr. 15:28) and signaled warfare (Josh. 6:4; Judg. 3:27; 7:16, 20). But the blowing of the *shofar* was not just used for practical ends, like marking events or calling assemblies, but also as a means of transmitting God's power. For instance, Numbers 29:1–6 commands that Israel celebrate the new moon of the seventh month by blowing the *shofar* over burnt, meal and sin offerings. A similar practice was known among other ancient peoples, who blew horns to chase away evil spirits at new moon ceremonies.[83] Joshua 6:20 describes the *shofar*'s role in the fall of Jericho: "When the people heard the sound of the horns, the people raised a mighty shout and the wall collapsed." Widespread in the ancient Near East was a belief that loud sounds could invoke deities.[84] When human shouting was not powerful enough, they resorted to musical instruments. Most cultures availed themselves of percussion instruments for this end, but Israel used the *shofar*, "the sound of which was closest to the human shrieking voice."[85] In the battle of Jericho, the thundering tones of the *shofar* brought on the mighty hand of God. In Talmudic literature, the *kinnor* is ascribed powers identical to those of the horn blasts at Jericho: "R. Amni said that the noise of the lyre strings (played by Jews rebelling against the Persians) about Caesarea-Mazaca burst the walls of Laodicea."[86] Though this account of the *kinnor* differs from its soothing effect in First Samuel, it nevertheless highlights the instrument's function as a divine conduit. Like the calls of the *shofar*, the sounds of the *kinnor* were infused with a sacred force.

Still, the *kinnor* does not completely alleviate the hate fomenting in

Saul's tormented heart. On two subsequent occasions, Saul attempts to kill David while he plays his lyre (1 Sam. 18:10; 19:9). The text explains that the evil spirit returns to Saul, filling him with a jealous rage so strong that it cannot be overcome by the sweet tones of the *kinnor*. Music, even when infused with divine force, does not exert absolute power over one's innermost thoughts and feelings. This, too, has parallel in modern music therapy, which serves mainly as an aid — not an end — to the healing process. Music helps patients to improve or maintain their health, but "cannot remove a depression by applying certain musical means or [permanently] ease a handicap with specific music."[87] Music can be a valuable ally to medicine, but rarely cures on its own.

The Iso Principle

First Samuel relates that at various times, David would "take his lyre and play it; Saul would find relief and feel better, and the evil spirit would leave him" (16:23). It is not clear, however, how long these therapeutic sessions lasted, or whether Saul's shift in mood came quickly or emerged over a longer duration. While the text is careful to mention that Saul received musical healing, it is not concerned with explaining how this healing was achieved. This minimal description may itself be a clue that music therapy — and specifically lyre playing — was a standard method for treating people like Saul, and so the author found it unnecessary to provide further details. It is also possible that since the main purpose of this story is to show how David became intimately involved in Saul's life, what specifically took place in the king's chambers is irrelevant to the larger narrative. Either way, the reader is left to speculate about how the music sounded and what technique(s) David employed.

As noted, Saul either suffered from a mental illness, such as manic depression, or from an ailment brought on by supernatural forces. This madness came to the surface several times in Saul's later years (e.g., 1 Sam. 19–20), and he ultimately succumbed to its negative pull. Whether of demonic or psychological origin, the condition took possession of his personality. From a biblical standpoint, Saul's suffering was a punitive measure for violating divine rules. This conforms to a major line of thinking in the Hebrew Bible, which deems pain, disease and other hardships as punishment for disobeying God.[88] This rigid position is challenged in several places, such as the Book of Job and various lament prayers; but the consequences of Saul's actions fit neatly into this black and white system of justice. Saul's major shortcomings surfaced in the events surrounding two battles: one with the Philistines and one with the Amalekites. In both instances, the king's failure to trust in God and follow His plan resulted in the departure of the divine spirit and an evil spirit taking its place.

The first battle was waged between Israel and an overpowering Philistine army. Fearing for their lives, Saul and his men "hid in caves, among thorns, among rocks, in tunnels, and in cisterns" (1 Sam. 13:6). Saul waited seven days for Samuel to arrive in Gilgal and when he failed to appear, he initiated a burnt offering to win God's favor. When the sacrifice concluded, Samuel arrived and condemned Saul's lack of confidence in God: "You acted foolishly in not keeping the commandments that the Lord your God laid upon you! Otherwise the Lord would have established your dynasty over Israel forever. But now your dynasty will not endure" (1 Sam. 13:13–14). Saul's major transgression was his doubt concerning God's promise that He would "never abandon His people" (1 Sam. 12:22). His compromised trust led him to conduct a sacrifice; he reverted to an outward practice when inward faith and commitment were required.

A short while later, Samuel instructed Saul and his men to kill all the Amalekites: "Spare no one, but kill alike men and women, infants and sucklings, oxen and sheep, camels and asses!" (1 Sam. 15:3). The Bible regards the Amalekites as "vicious adversaries of Israel" and therefore deserving of annihilation.[89] Saul forewarned the Kenites, who were living among the Amalekites, and proceeded to attack and defeat the Amalekites. Saul made sure that all the men, women, children, babies and poor quality livestock were killed, but "spared the choicest of the sheep and oxen" (v. 13) and "captured King Agag of Amalek" (v. 20). When Samuel discovered that Saul had not killed them all, he was enraged and launched into a bitter diatribe, concluding with the words: "Because you rejected the Lord's command, He has rejected you as king" (v. 23).

In the ensuing verses, we learn of the anguish that consumed the disfavored king, and of his need for musical treatment. Though an imperfect comparison, traditional societies utilize at least five kinds of healing music, according to a classification developed by A. E. Meremi.[90] His results derive from practices current in African tribal societies which, like ancient Israel, tend to attribute human ailments to supernatural forces. Meremi's five types of therapeutic music are: axiolytic, meant to free one from fear and/or anxiety; tensiolytic, intended to relieve one of mental and physical pain associated with labor; algolytic, devised to alleviate physical pain in general; patholytic, for one experiencing grief, bereavement, or heavy loss; and psycholytic, meant to loosen a person from the grip of evil powers. The latter use would have been most appropriate for Saul's affliction: David was engaged specifically to combat the evil spirit that beset the king. Yet, while the designation is instructive in providing a label for the sort of music David used, it does not explain what the music sounded like or provide clues as to the method by which it was administered.

It has also been asserted that David functioned as a kind of "magician-exorcist," who used musical tones to charm the evil spirit from Saul's consciousness.[91] On its surface, this depiction runs counter to the canonical consensus that magical powers and methods were not to be used for God's service (e.g., Deut. 18:9–11; Lev. 19:26–31; Exod. 22:17–18; Isa. 8:19; Ezek. 22:25–29). Outside of Israel, it was commonplace for individuals to manipulate natural objects or recite formulae in order to force their gods to act for the good of the one who initiated the action, or the harm of that person's opponent.[92] Such practices were rooted in the belief that humans could harness and hold sway over deities—a concept antithetical to the theology of ancient Israel. David's playing is, however, analogous to magic on one important level: it channels God's healing energy and delivers it to Saul.

This view finds resonance in ethnographic studies showing the effects of music in spiritual trance.[93] Music has figured prominently in rituals designed to induce spirit possessions and exorcise malignant spirits. Several prominent scholars have framed David's healing music in this way. For instance, Curt Sachs writes that music "drove the demons out of Saul's soul when David played for him."[94] Don C. Benjamin likewise pictures David as "a shaman whose music treats Saul for spirit possession."[95] But Gilbert Rouget is of the opinion that Saul's musical treatment should not be considered an exorcism, since it involved no classical incarnation.[96] Instead, he asserts that the music merely helped to re-establish a perception of the divine presence or more precisely, enabled Saul to stop obsessing about what he viewed as God's absence. This is based on the premise that Saul's diagnosis as a spiritual ailment reflects a primitive understanding of psychology. For Rouget and others, Saul's trauma was purely psychological, and David's playing merely had a soothing (not an otherworldly) effect.[97]

Even so, the depiction of Saul's condition as divine punishment does emphasize its severity. There is no doubt that his torment was deeply rooted, and whatever therapeutic remedy was used would have had to confront the many layers of his distress. There is, then, reason to assume that David's playing had a slow and measured rather than an immediate effect upon Saul. This gradual approach is the usual course of treatment for modern music therapists, who apply a sequence of interventions leading to specific changes in the client. Whether used for treating psychological, physical, developmental, educational or interpersonal disorders, music therapy, like therapy in general, is an incremental process, taking place over time and involving progressive change and growth. As one practitioner explains, it "demands a commitment of time and energy from both the client and the therapist; it is not a simple, instant cure or a magical panacea."[98]

The Bible states that David visited Saul "whenever the evil spirit of God" came upon him (1 Sam. 16:23), suggesting an ongoing program. The fact that Saul made sure to keep David near him is likewise indicative of continuous and/or regularly scheduled therapy sessions. These indications give the impression that David's lyre playing, though divinely infused, could not provide the troubled king a spontaneous or rapid remedy. Instead, it is possible that David utilized a process similar to what is now called the iso principle. The iso principle is derived from the Greek term isomorphic, meaning "same shape." It states that a person should be eased into the therapeutic process with music that evokes a similar mood state. Someone who is anxious, for instance, would first be exposed to frenzied music. The therapist would then introduce slight variations in musical properties like tempo, dynamics and harmony, which over time lead the patient to a desired state. At its most potent, this vectoring power not only shifts the person's mood by degree (e.g., decreasing anger), but also transforms the mood state itself (e.g., turning anger into joy).[99] In music that embodies the iso principle, there is never a surprise, pause or abrupt change, but an easy and barely noticeable series of alterations that build toward a specified outcome. Ravel's "Bolero" is sometimes cited as a piece reflective of the iso principle.[100] It starts off slowly and quietly, but with each repetition, increases in speed, becomes more rhythmically and harmonically complex, and escalates in intensity and expressiveness. As the music travels through these alterations, the listener's mindset changes accordingly.

The origin of the iso principle is generally traced to the work of Esther Gatewood, who recognized the need for music that elicits gradual change in the patient's state.[101] It received fuller development in the 1940s with researchers like Ira Altshuler,[102] and has become a standard technique of music therapy in the United States.[103] Yet although the principle did not gain official status as a therapeutic method until the twentieth century, it is in fact a modern, scientific incarnation of a natural and intuitive technique of musical healing.[104] There is evidence that ancient tribes used similar methods, matching the person's initial mood to appropriate drumming, singing and dancing, and then altering the performance to bring him/her to an agreeable state.[105] Some therapists working with indigenous populations do in fact use music of those cultures in facilitating the iso principle.[106] This shows at least the possibility that a similar approach was known in ancient Israel.

Any attempt at reconstructing the music therapy session in First Samuel is speculative. But it is not difficult to imagine David using this basic method to ease the disturbed king. As a skilled and sensitive musician, he was surely aware of and able to exploit the interplay of music and emotions. Indeed, throughout the ages, musicians and non-musicians alike have relied on music to vent their emotions and transition to more positive states. Without giving the technique much thought — let alone a clinical name — they choose to sing, play or listen to music that joins their mood instead of expecting abrupt changes brought by music contrary to their current condition.

A hypothetical example from modern, everyday life illustrates the intuitive nature of this approach. A man suffering from work-related anxiety returns home after a particularly stressful day at the office. At this point, cheerful or soothing music would be an annoyance, serving to mock rather than comfort him. He needs to reach an internal state of calm, and no superficial solution will aid him in achieving this goal. So, he finds a recording of music that joins his current mood. Its tense lyrics and aggressive tones show that the performers understand what he is going through — they have been there before. He finds this validating and reassuring, and vents his frustrations through the music. As the evening moves along, he slowly transitions to lighter selections, and emerges from despair.

If non-specialists use this process to treat themselves, how much more expert would David have been in applying it to Saul? David may have used his lyre to first produce harsh and dissonant tones, and then shift to more pleasant music, eventually bringing out the instrument's joyous qualities. Such a session would have left Saul more profoundly moved than if he had only heard uplifting sounds; gradual exposure to musical changes would have carried him through slight adjustments in mood without much resistance. The end result would have been what the Bible describes: a sense that the evil spirit had released its grip.

Summary

Though the musical healing described in 1 Samuel 16:14–23 is unique in biblical literature, there are at least five reasons to assume that music therapy was widespread in ancient Israel. First, healing is among the first and most pervasive uses of music, and virtually all societies, to a greater or lesser extent, utilize musical tones for therapeutic aims. Second, music is a traditional remedy in cultures like ancient Israel, where mental and physical ailments are attributed to divine punishment and demon possession. Third, the courtiers did not hesitate to recommend a musical treatment for the king, implying that music was a conventional and trusted remedy. Fourth, the men specifically sought someone who could play the *kinnor*, suggesting that the instrument was recognized as a healing device. Fifth, because the musical encounter between David and Saul was an effective and believable way of furthering the story of David's rise to power, healing music was probably widely known and accepted in biblical life.

More importantly, this passage indicates the high status given to

3. Therapeutic Functions of David's Lyre

music in ancient Israel. Israel substantially defined its national identity through David's kingship and the prominence of music in his biography served as an example for the population as a whole. Musical expertise was among the qualities that made David fit to be king, and was a means by which he connected with and drew energy from the divine. It was through music that David fostered an intimate relationship with Saul, and his skillful playing and poetry captured the people's hearts and minds. It is not incidental that David is held up as Israel's greatest and most musical king. Music accompanied him in battle, voiced his deepest sentiments, attracted and charmed the populace and became an official part of Israel's religious life under his rule. Music was a constant presence during David's career, and the many uses he had for it, including therapeutic, served as a model for how others could use musical tones to enrich and benefit their own lives and the lives of others. In this sense, David's lyre playing not only demonstrated the efficacy of healing music, but also encouraged and lent credibility to the wider employment of music therapy in that society.

Given the musically rich environment of ancient Israel, the incorporation of music as a healing art seems inevitable. The mood altering effects of music made it an indispensable part of both public gatherings and the private, intimate setting of therapy. Healing holds a prominent place among the assortment of functional music mentioned in the Hebrew Bible. And as we learn from the story of David's lyre — and can be assumed from the likely innumerable instances of musical healing not recorded in the Bible — the music of therapy, like that of worship and other religious settings, had an added quality of divinity.

These observations further suggest that therapy was only one of the private ways Israelites applied the emotional-psychological potency of sound. Taking the above descriptive analysis one logical step forward, it can be presumed that other types of calming music were also known and widely employed. From a categorical standpoint, all music with a soothing or restorative purpose can be seen as allied—whether or not they are medicinal—and the mention of one suggests that others were in place as well. Specifically, these would include genres designed to promote relaxation, such as lullabies and music that accompanies meditation. Like much of the expressly therapeutic music used today, this music probably would have lacked rhythmic and harmonic tension, thus conveying a fluid, almost timeless quality suited for inducing or sustaining a sense of tranquility. As we have seen with David's lyre playing, such experiences point to the potentially intense influence of musical sounds on the inner, spiritual realm. This compelling mixture of music, emotions and spirituality will be explored in the next chapter, which looks at the intersection of music and prophecy in the Bible.

Chapter 4

Sing unto God: Music in Prophetic Literature

A basic premise of biblical thought is that God does not abandon humans to their own devices, but provides them with guidance and intervention. The prophet occupies an essential place in this worldview, which saw politics, economics, social life, health, and virtually everything else as dependent upon and influenced by God. Biblical prophets served as intermediaries between humanity and the divine. They were charismatic individuals endowed with the ability to receive and impart divine messages, revealing to the people God's active engagement in the world and what their proper response should be. In addition to being divinely centered, the cultural milieu in which the prophets operated was also highly musical. It is therefore not surprising to discover that prophetic utterances, like many aspects of ancient Israel, were frequently aided by music. For this musical people, singing and instrumental accompaniment proved a natural and effective way to hear God's word.

The institution of prophecy in the Hebrew Bible has its beginnings in Joshua, Judges, First and Second Samuel, and First and Second Kings. The early forms of prophecy typically involved the discovery of the divine will in specific circumstances and for specific individuals. The prophets whose words and deeds are described in the Former Prophets possessed psychic gifts of seeing the future and divination. Some were members of organized prophetic bands that favored rapturous and miraculous behavior over formal, verbal pronouncements. Others were employed by kings or houses of worship, ready to offer a prediction or vision when needed. The Latter Prophets, who occupy the books of Isaiah, Jeremiah, Ezekiel and the Twelve, employed elegant poetry to sound warnings, stipulate moral and ethical principles, voice social criticism and address issues of cultural and political concern. In contrast to the mostly localized and interpersonal role of their prophetic forerunners, the Latter Prophets spoke to the nation in elegant and symbolic language, and saw their primary task as challenging the false values of society and exhorting the people to turn from their depraved ways and rediscover righteousness.[1]

A religious outlook dominates the books of both the Former and Latter Prophets, though it is expressed in differing ways. The historical element of the earlier prophets, like the Bible as a whole, is bound up with a spiritual message.[2] Accounts of prophetic activities comprise a historical narrative filtered through a prophetic lens. From these selective reports—with prophets as the central players and God's will as the principle concern—a general outline can be constructed of Israel's history from the settlement of Canaan to the Exile (roughly 1250 to 586 B.C.E.). A similarly spiritual tone resounds in the books of the Latter Prophets, but it comes through in the preaching element of prophecy rather than in a clear sequence of events. While historical figures and events are alluded to, placing the documents in the closing centuries of the two kingdoms and later years of Judah, it is the prophetic message that takes center stage.

Despite differences in style, the primarily action-oriented books of the Former Prophets and oration-oriented Latter Prophets shared similar agendas and utilized similar modes of stimulation and presentation. Both sets of prophets were concerned for the underprivileged, dedicated to the covenant of God and Israel, had an ardent sense of justice and morality, and occupied a position from which to criticize leaders and the general populace.[3] In addition, both groups used music to prompt and express prophecy.

The Bible records a few instances of earlier prophets transmitting their visions through song and dance and employing music to help achieve a prophetic state. For example, 1 Samuel 10:5 describes a group of young prophets coming down a hill playing instruments and prophesying, while 2 Kings 3:15 shows the prophet Elisha requesting a musician to help transport him to a frame of mind suitable for prophecy. Though examples of this sort are not abundant, they suggest a broader, institutional practice of music-assisted prophecy, and speak to music's perceived role as both a channel linking God and humanity and a force for propelling one to a realm of awareness that transcends the limits of ordinary language and experience.

The later prophetic books display poetic form, meter, accentuation and other musical-linguistic characteristics that indicate their messages were delivered in song or song-like speech.[4] N. Kershaw Chadwick considers the intersection of prophecy, poetry and music to be universal: "Always this [prophetic] knowledge is uttered in poetry which is accompanied by music, whether of song or instrument. Music is everywhere the medium of communication with spirits."[5] Historical and contemporary examples lend support to this claim of a widespread phenomenon. Ancient Assyrian sources, for instance, espouse the compatibility of genuine prophecy and psalmody.[6] Socrates identified music as a divine gift on the level of prophecy.[7] The preferred medium of pre–Islamic Arabic seers and soothsayers was melodic poetry.[8] There is a belief among Rwala Bedouins that music and dancing can help one retrieve divine messages sent during a dream state.[9] And a recent study on spirituality in the music of India highlights the direct correlation between music and divine inspiration in that culture.[10]

However, though these cross-historical and cross-cultural illustrations point to an apparently intuitive union of prophecy and music, they are not meant to imply that each tradition has a common view of or use for prophetic experiences. While Chadwick's observations are helpful in drawing attention to the general phenomenon of musical prophecy, they may, in their generalness, blur distinctions between prophetic practices. Since the focus here is on biblical material, it is worth noting the unique characteristics of the biblical prophets. In his seminal book *The Prophets*, Abraham Joshua Heschel explains that Israel's prophets were set apart from the rest of humanity—and from the prophets of other civilizations—not only because they had intimate contact with the one true God, but also for the exceedingly high standards to which they held individual and communal behavior, usually to the point of having no patience for human weaknesses or shortcomings. "The world is a proud place, full of beauty," Heschel writes, "but the prophets are scandalized, and rave as if the whole world were a slum."[11] They placed strict ethical demands on kings, priests, false prophets and average folk alike. Heschel elaborates: "To us a slight act of injustice—cheating in business, exploitation of the poor — is slight; to the prophets, a disaster. To us injustice is injurious to the welfare of the people; to the prophets it is a deathblow to existence: to us, an episode, to them, a catastrophe, a threat to the world itself."[12]

As this quote suggests, biblical prophets felt everything fiercely. While the average person might have been forgiving about lapses in actions or belief, the prophet was quick to condemn them in the harshest terms. From the prophetic viewpoint, even the minutest dealings of daily life matter to God. As Amos said: "The Lord swears by the pride of Jacob: 'I will never forget any of their doings.' Shall not the earth shake for this and all that dwell on it mourn?" (8:7–8). Through such proclamations, the invisible God became audible; His presence was felt through impassioned words received as blasts from heaven.[13] And, significantly, it was the emotional and otherworldly nature of these episodes that translated so naturally into the expressive, mystical language of musical tones.

This chapter examines the intersection of music and prophecy in the Hebrew Bible. It begins with a brief overview of the characteristics and functions of prophecy and the place of music within it. This is followed by an application of Rudolf Otto's theory of the numinous experience to sacred music in general and musical prophecy in particular. These discussions set the stage for an investigation into how music figured in the careers of three representative prophets: Elisha (2 Kgs. 3:15), Jeremiah (Jer. 20:7–13) and Habakkuk (Hab. 3). Through all of this, it will be argued that ancient Israel, a society that depended on divine words and regularly received these messages in the form of musical prophecy, came to know who they were largely through song.

Musical Prophets

In all ages there have been individuals concerned with charting the direction of society and the actions, thoughts and attitudes of the people who live within it. While this task is taken up by a variety of people in the contemporary West — religious and political leaders, artists, authors, journalists, attorneys, etc.— the primary moral and social critics in biblical times were prophets. However, unlike these contemporary examples, prophets were not the ultimate source of their messages, but

4. Sing unto God

"middlemen" of the divine word. Prophecy was a recognized profession throughout the ancient Near East, and held sway over the intellectual, spiritual and political life of Egypt, Canaan, Aram, Mesopotamia, Israel and Judah.[14] In each of these cultures, prophetic men and women used divination, omen and dream interpretation, miraculous feats and other techniques to address local and socio-political issues.

In the biblical conception, a prophet is neither a philosopher nor theologian, but a mediator who delivers God's message to the people in order to reform the present and shape the future.[15] The prophets of the Bible typically came into the profession against their will and were compelled to proclaim the holy word, whether or not the people wished to hear it (e.g., Ezek. 3:11). In this sense, the prophets of Israel can be classified as shamans—an anthropological term for those exhibiting spontaneous, charismatic religious behavior along with inborn talent for connecting with the spirit world.[16] Yet, at the same time, most prophets of the ancient world appear to have been well-trained professionals who specialized in a certain modality, had mastery of a set of skills, and were sometimes linked to an established institution, such as a palace or shrine.[17] Thus, following their seemingly random calling, it can be inferred that the prophets worked to refine their methods.

The element of cultivation should not be alarming, as the prophets' primary objective was to translate revelatory experiences into the language of the people—a purpose that would have required diligent practice, if not formal training. Their success, after all, was dependent on the extent to which the people could understand and relate to their messages.[18] Even though the prophets were known to engage in physical demonstrations, such as symbolic acts (e.g., 1 Kgs. 11:29) and wonder-working (e.g., 1 Kgs. 17:8), they functioned mainly as social commentators and prognosticators.

Prophets carefully packaged their messages for their audiences, and no two prophets operated in the same exact style. Their personalities came through in the prophetic modes they preferred, whether prayers, miracles, oracles, hymns, letters, parables, indictments, sermons, legal pronouncements, dirges or drinking songs. The sheer variety of methods points to the individuality of each prophet, as well as to the extent to which the divine word was refracted through a human prism.[19] Prophetic liturgies, for example, appeared in a variety of genres, such as entrance liturgies (e.g., Isa. 33), theophanies (e.g., Hab. 3), Zion songs (e.g., Mic. 4:1–4) and doxologies (e.g., Amos 5:8–9). The originality of these and other prophetic forms and the importance of carefully crafted words suggest that instead of being possessed by the spirit of God and suffering effacement of personality, the prophets were "word possessed"—that is, consumed by and commanded to impart the divine message, however they chose to deliver it. Though God's spirit initiated prophecy, the word was the revelation itself. As scholars have observed, "What makes [someone] a prophet is not the spirit which envelops or moves him—for this spirit also motivated elders, judges, Nazirites, and kings—but the word that he has heard and which he transmits to others."[20]

The prophets also served a variety of roles. Some were active in communal affairs and were consulted for advice or asked to deliver oracles. To cite a few examples, Jeroboam's wife called upon Ahijah (1 Kgs. 14:5), Jehoshaphat and Ahab turned to Micaiah (1 Kgs. 22:8) and Josiah sought Huldah (2 Kgs. 22:13). Like everyone else, the prophets needed to make a living. The Bible records instances of prophets receiving remuneration for their services in money (e.g., 1 Sam. 9:8), food (1 Kgs. 14:3) and treasures (2 Kgs. 8:9). Elsewhere, we find prophets influencing the political destiny of their people. Samuel, for example, chose Saul (1 Sam. 9) and David (1 Sam. 16) to be kings over Israel, Ahijah announced the selection and later the rejection of King Jeroboam (1 Kgs. 11:29–39; 14:1–18; 15:29), and both Amos (Amos 7:9, 11) and Hosea (Hos. 1:4–5) condemned Jehu's dynasty and predicted its collapse. Other prophets had a designated place within the royal court, including Nathan (2 Sam. 7) and Gad (e.g., 1 Sam. 22:5), who both served under King David. Since all of the prophets addressed current situations, their messages inevitably made reference to political strategies, corruption, injustices and other pressing matters.

Even as the prophets had unique styles, points of interest and stations in society, they were unified in their "covenant advocacy," demanding that God's call for a just government, humane social order and an upright populace be realized.[21] No matter how severely the people went astray or even worked at cross-purposes with God's plan for Israel and the world, the prophets remained a righteous remnant, faithful to God and ever ready to remind the people of His role in history and unfolding events.[22] In most cases, they concerned themselves with the future, warning of dire consequences if the people continued to abuse the covenant. Yet, while their predictions tended to be harsh, they were usually conditional, allowing the possibility that impending doom or defeat could be curtailed if the people turned from their transgressions and followed the way of the Torah. They can be regarded as contingent even when not explicitly stated as such, as in the story of Jonah. Although the language the prophets chose and the circumstances under which they prophesied were sometimes quite difficult — especially in the case of Ezekiel[23] — their goal was straightforward: establishing a holy society in which the leadership and broader population would be ethical, virtuous and religiously faithful.

One of the musically profound aspects of biblical prophecy is its poetic design. Most of the prayers and speeches of the later prophets—Isaiah, Jeremiah, Ezekiel, and the Twelve—can be classified as poems.[24] Scholars such as Robert Alter and Walter Brueggemann assert that this poetic form is a main reason prophetic materials continue to capture the imagination of contemporary readers.[25] Particularly instructive are these words from Alter: "poetry is our best human model of intricately rich communication, not only solemn, weighty, and forceful but also densely woven with complex internal connections, meanings, and implications, [and so] it makes sense that divine speech should be represented as poetry."[26] The import and severity of the prophets' proclamations demanded the potent language of poetry. But these elevated outpourings were not just for the benefit of the prophets themselves; they also helped catch the ear of the audience. Because human beings are profoundly attracted to and moved by art, it made perfect sense for divine messages to be expressed through aesthetic means. Beauty functions as a primary way of attracting and opening the heart to truth and goodness. In this sense, the aesthetic appeal of prophetic poetry aided the people in grasping divine truths and warnings that might have otherwise been difficult to fathom.[27]

Poetry is first and foremost an auditory medium. Repetition, rhyme, rhythm and other poetic features have their full impact only when they are heard. There is a linguistic musicality in the pitches, stresses and dynamics of prophetic declamations, and the use of theme and variation, consonant clusters, counterpoints and so on are likewise homologous to musical forms.[28] These are just a few of the ways in which poems of all types are related to music. This connection was especially explicit in the biblical world. Most poems were sung, or voiced with rhythmic accentuation and with a heightened speech that at times approached real singing.[29] This speech-melody marked poetry as distinct from prose, and cut through the monotony of ordinary verbal expression. The melodic quality imbued the words with their intended attention-grabbing effect, and in the case of religious poetry emphasized that the content of the verses was utterly separate from profane matters. This sense of being set apart lies at the heart of what constitutes the sacred, and aided the prophets in conveying that their words stemmed from a divine source.

The musical nature of the Bible's prophetic verses is sometimes illustrated using the example of Isaiah.[30] In addition to being a mostly poetic work, the Book of Isaiah makes several references to songs and singing. Chapter 12, for instance, presents a song of thanksgiving to be recited in an ideal age, and includes the lines "the Lord is my strength and song" (v. 2) and "Hymn to the Lord, for He has done gloriously" (v. 5). Chapter 25, a song of gratitude describing God's victory over sorrow, contains the verse "This is the Lord, in whom we trusted; let us sing and exult in His deliverance" (v. 9); while chapter 49, a song of comfort assuring the people that Zion's restoration is close at hand, includes the words "Shout, O heavens, and rejoice, O earth! Break forth into song, O hills!" (v. 13). These are but a sampling of the overt link between prophecy and song found in Isaiah and other prophetic books. Conrad Orelli explains the purpose of this musical presentation in his exposition on Isaiah's "Song of the Vineyard" (5:1–7), a parable in which God is portrayed as a farmer and Israel as a vineyard: "The prophet appears here as singer and musician, skilful in drawing forth the lovely tones of the lyre, but hiding behind his charming song a terrible truth, in order to bring it home to man with more brilliant and conclusive effect."[31]

Music also aided the prophets in preparing themselves for their task, and proved an effective way of establishing the lines of communication with God (e.g., 1 Sam. 10:5; 2 Kgs. 3:15; 1 Chr. 25:1). This owes mainly to the perception that music — perhaps more than any other mode of art or expression — hints at the presence of the transcendent. Sound is non-material, possessing a quality of limitlessness far beyond that which is visible or tactile. The impact of sound — and especially musical sound — is immediate, evoking emotional and kinesthetic responses without prior mental preparation. This led to Nietzsche's description of the musician as a "mouthpiece of the perseity of things," "telephone of the beyond" and "ventriloquist of God."[32] These metaphors encapsulate the essence of musical prophecy, pointing to a mystical experience in which the divine voice is channeled and expressed through a potent mixture of language and musical tones.

Rudolf Otto

Further insights into the role of music in facilitating and intensifying prophetic states can be gleaned from the work of German theologian Rudolf Otto (1869–1937). Unlike other leading scholars of his time, such as Durkheim, Freud and Marx, Otto does not believe the sacred to be a human construction, but a genuine presence "whose special character we can feel without being able to give it clear conceptual expression."[33] All religions, Otto maintains, have their basis in an experience of the holy or numinous — an unmistakable yet ineffable feeling of communion and transcendence consisting simultaneously of fear and trembling (*mysterium tremendum*) and utter fascination (*mysterium fascinans*). These mysterious and non-rational (or supra-rational) components of the religious experience are the subject of *The Idea of the Holy* (1917), Otto's argument for the objective reality of the "wholly other."

At the core of his thesis is the assertion that the numinous experience, which signals the presence of the sacred, is more fundamental than and exists prior to and independent of any belief or conceptual understanding of the experience. In Otto's words, it is "perfectly *sui generis* and irreducible to any other; and therefore, like every absolutely primary and elementary datum, while it admits of being discussed, it cannot be strictly defined."[34] Still, he acknowledges the necessity of rational reflection in interpreting such experiences to the degree that language allows. Because the holy encounter is known by the senses, it does have an intelligible component. But Otto feels that to frame the experience solely in what can be ascertained by sensory faculties would constitute a rejection of the wholly other that exists beyond it. In such experiences, Otto posits, "to know and to understand are two different things," and can even be "mutually exclusive and contested."[35] This view paints a distinction between the encounter itself (knowing) and later interpretations (understanding). It is through the gradual process of "rationalization and moralization" that numinous experiences gain "progressively rational, moral, and cultural significance," and are sometimes developed into religious systems.[36]

Despite the essentially inexpressible nature of the numinous encounter, Otto does attempt to describe its characteristics, though he admits in inadequate terms. He explains that it begins with a feeling of "personal nothingness" and submergence before the "awe-inspiring object directly experienced."[37] Elsewhere, he describes this feeling as "stupor," which "signifies blank wonder, an astonishment that strikes us dumb, amazement absolute."[38] Almost immediately, this awed state gives way to "shuddering," an overwhelming feeling consisting of dread and unease.

This mixture of fear and awe in the presence of the holy has parallel in the philosophical writings of Maimonides, who believes these emotions to be intrinsically linked or "mirror image" responses that naturally arise when one tries to grasp the vastness of the universe:

> When a man contemplates [God's] great and wondrous deeds and creations, and sees in them His unequaled and infinite wisdom, he immediately loves and praises and exults Him, and is overcome by a great desire to know His great Name.... And when he considers these very matters, immediately he withdraws and is frightened and knows that he is but a small, lowly, dark creature who, with his inferior and puny mind, stands before Him who is perfect in His knowledge.[39]

It is unclear whether Otto was influenced directly by Maimonides, but, like Maimonides, Otto finds sufficient basis for the numinous experience in the Hebrew Bible. In Genesis 28:17, for example, Jacob, who ascends to heaven, remarks, "How awesome is this place! This is none other than the house of God, and that is the gateway to heaven." According to Otto, Jacob's proclamation expresses a mixed sensation of elation and trembling in response to the overwhelming presence of this sacred place. It contains a combination of "primal numinous awe," "aweful veneration," and "immediacy."[40] Yet, while it is tempting to explain this reaction — and all sacred encounters — in terms of emotions, Otto is careful to distinguish this phenomenon from the realm of ordinary emotions, believing it to be a unique response, analogous to being afraid, yet ultimately distinct. More specifically, Otto sees the sacred experience as an indescribable combination of fear and awe, or *mysterium tremendum*.[41]

Significantly, Otto compares the sacred experience to "the beauty of a musical composition which no less eludes complete conceptual analysis."[42] Like a symphony, the enormity of the divine encounter occurs instantaneously, allowing little time for one to examine its complexities or decipher particular elements. This observation is echoed by Gerardus van der Leeuw: "If we ask whence it comes that the massive, the sublime, often moves us religiously, indeed seems to be an expression of the holy, we find that this lies in its overpowering character. We cannot express it; we find ourselves in the presence of the wholly other."[43] As an example of this all-consuming experience, van der Leeuw cites a psychological experiment in which the subject recounts how he is "swept away" by a piece of music: "We are on a ship. The waves are smashing violently against the sides of the ship. We feel different."[44] An interviewee in William James's *Varieties of Religious Experience* uses a similar analogy when comparing a mystical experience to "the effect of some great orchestra, when all the separate notes have melted into the swelling harmony."[45]

Before delving further into the correlation between music and the sacred experience, it bears mentioning that Otto is not without his critics. Most problematic is his assertion that, regardless of how the numinous experience is later interpreted, the event itself occurs prior to and independent of belief. In this way, he understands the sacred as a reality existing apart from a conceptual, religious framework. In contrast, Wayne Proudfoot and others have noted that in order to identify an experience as sacred, one must have prior reference to what constitutes the religious—that is, a theory or belief.[46] Such critiques have importance in the academic study of religion, but do not necessarily hinder application of Otto's theory to musically induced spiritual states, as in the examples of biblical prophecy. Rather, Otto's description is ideally suited for an analysis of these experiences, since the music is used to arouse or intensify a highly emotional, non-rational and fundamentally ineffable connection with the divine. It should, however, be reiterated that the divine message, not the altered state, was the central component of biblical prophecy. As such, it is inaccurate to portray prophecy as a phenomenon devoid of rational thought or prior belief. What is important in light of Otto is music's role in stimulating receptiveness to such messages.[47]

This stimulation is evident, though perhaps to a lesser degree, in churches and synagogues, where sacred music has long been employed to induce congregants to feelings approximating those that accompany holy encounters. In the Western Church, for instance, transcendence is sometimes conveyed in soft passages representing the silent awe felt in the presence of the divine.[48] The modal patterns of the Ashkenazi synagogue are likewise designed to move worshipers to specific moods linked to liturgical occasions and themes.[49] In fact, the words mode and mood seem to share a common linguistic root, and modal music of all types is usually tied to elementary emotions or affects.[50] Thus, for Otto's understanding of the numinous experience to find resonance in music, the music itself must possess a certain, though perhaps inexplicable, quality of sacredness.

Despite the problems inherent in labeling which musical styles or techniques are most appropriate for religious services—especially as sacred music is a culturally diverse form of religious expression—it is clear that for music to be considered sacred, it must convey certain "holy" qualities: peace, contentment, joy, unity, harmony, awe, majesty, etc. As Richard Viladesau, a Catholic priest and scholar, has written:

> Otto's theory throws a great deal of light on the relation of music and spirituality. It accounts for the difference between what is called serious and what is called light music, and shows why there is some sense to the idea of a sacred "style": those forms of music that have emotional and intellectual associations of sufficient "depth" to be appropriate carriers of sacred words or themes (while light or frivolous forms of music, although perhaps pleasant in themselves, may betray a sacred message by inappropriate associations that trivialize it). It also explains why music can be seen in religion as the height of spiritual expression or, alternatively, as the epitome of sensual depravity.[51]

In the worship setting, music that succeeds in capturing an intended religious atmosphere can inspire devotion and spiritual contemplation. Even if one fails to resonate with the message of a prayer, or is distracted from deep worship by worldly concerns, sacred music can stimulate an appropriate emotional state, disarming the rational mind, and inviting

4. Sing unto God

an embrace of the sacred moment. In a similar though more intensified way, several biblical prophets used music either as an aid for channeling the divine, or as a means of delivering prophetic messages. Thus, worshipers and prophets share a common acknowledgement of the power of musical tones, especially when set to religious language, to bring humanity closer to God. For Otto, this is mainly possible because music, like the sacred experience, can stir one to simultaneous feelings of fear and awe. Since biblical times, the elevated language of tones has been viewed as a signal of transcendence, able to conjure a sense of the divine presence, and as a medium apt for speaking to God.[52]

The intimate association of music and divinity is further suggested in the connection between *hozeh*, a biblical term for prophet meaning "seer," and *hazzan*, a later rabbinic term for the individual who sings the liturgy in Jewish prayer services. A number of prophets are identified by some version of the term *hozeh*, including Amos (Amos 7:12), Nahum (Nah. 1:1) and Ezekiel (Ezek. 7:13). The term is also applied to the Levitical singers Heman (1 Chr. 25:5), Asaph (2 Chr. 29:30) and Jeduthun (2 Chr. 35:15). Although *hozeh* is generally translated to imply "vision," it also refers to hearing the word of God. As such, a better translation might be "perception" and, in the case of the Temple singers and several of the prophets, "perception through song." It is this meaning that is preserved in the title of *hazzan*.

The *hazzan* functions as the "messenger of the congregation," sending the community's prayers toward the divine on the wings of song. In this capacity, he or she serves as an intermediary between the people and their God, facilitating a liturgical conversation through a blend of musical tones and religious language. Of course, this is not exactly the same as the biblical prophets, who were "messengers of God" rather than spokesmen of the people; but, like a prophet, the *hazzan* communicates directly with God through song and transmits an awareness of the divine presence to the listeners. One man remarked after hearing the singing of famed *hazzan* Leib Glantz: "I felt that this man was actually talking to God with great passion! His voice commands its way to the heavens—to be heard and to be answered."[53] This reaction gives support to the claim that music is "as nearly allied to prophecy as to poetry,"[54] and is what Yiddish novelist Joseph Opatoshu had in mind when he wrote, "Through true song one may rise to the power of prophecy."[55]

In their influential study, "The Philosophy and Theory of Music in Judeo-Arabic Literature," Eric Werner and Isaiah Sonne delineate two specific ways in which music functions in the prophetic experience: allopathic and homeopathic.[56] Allopathic music minimizes thoughts and feelings that make a prophetic state difficult to achieve. Without giving it a name, Hugo Gressman writes of this phenomenon in a statement based on Aristotle: "While enthusiasm manifests itself with the true prophets seemingly out of nowhere — without being sought — it has to be coaxed out of others with artificial means. This is done, aside from feasts, dances, honey and intoxicating beverages through music — in itself a child born out of enthusiasm."[57] Homeopathic music, on the other hand, amplifies the emotions already present in the prophet, thus heightening, clarifying and expanding the prophetic manifestations.

In both cases, musical sounds direct the prophets' attention and energies toward God, and foster or intensify the sensation of being filled with the spirit of God. Examples of these musical functions are seen in prophetic episodes involving Elisha (2 Kgs. 3), Jeremiah (Jer. 20:7–13) and Habakkuk (Hab. 3:1–19). Elisha utilizes music's allopathic properties when he calls upon a musician to stir him into a prophetic state. Jeremiah demonstrates the homeopathic role of music when he expresses his highly emotional prophecy in song. Habakkuk intensifies his prophecies by singing them in psalm form. Because these three examples offer such clear depictions of music's place in biblical prophecy, it behooves us to examine them in detail.

Elisha

Elisha's entrance into prophecy begins in 1 Kings 19:16, when God commands Elijah to anoint him as his successor. This is the Bible's sole example of a prophet selecting his own replacement, and its only reference to an anointing component of prophetic investiture.[58] Upon receiving this command, Elijah emerges from a cave on Mount Horeb, where he has been hiding from the vengeful Queen Jezebel after ordering the death of her priests (1 Kgs. 19:2). He finds Elisha plowing in his father's field and throws his mantle over him (1 Kgs. 19:19). The mere touch of Elijah's cloak signals that Elisha will have to leave home; and he soon becomes Elijah's devoted servant and outstanding disciple. Although Elijah is generally portrayed as a hermit-like prophet performing his deeds alone, this account suggests that he was at least minimally attached to a system in which student prophets served under a master, and was perhaps connected to the larger institution of prophetic bands and brotherhoods. This is further illustrated when Elijah ascends to heaven on a whirlwind, leaving Elisha with a double-portion of Elijah's prophetic spirit (2 Kgs. 2:9)—an allusion to the property inheritance custom in which the oldest son receives twice as much of his father's inheritance. With this, Elisha is signified as the rightful heir to Elijah's position, and the other disciples bow down before him (2 Kgs. 2:15).

Elisha prophesied in the Northern Kingdom of Israel for a sixty-year period spanning the reigns of Jehoram, Jehu, Jehoahaz and Joash (892–832 B.C.E.). Like Elijah, he was an oracular diviner and a wonder-worker. Miraculous actions are described throughout his prophetic career. For example, when a creditor threatens to seize a widow's two children as slaves, Elisha multiplies a jug of oil in her possession so that she can sell it to pay her debts and use the rest to help feed her family (2 Kgs. 4:1–7). In another instance, he rewards a wealthy woman for her hospitality by making her able to bear a son, and later heals the child from an ailment (2 Kings 4:8–37). During a time of famine, Elisha turns a pot of poisonous gourds into edible sustenance for the disciples of the prophets (2 Kgs. 4:38–41). He also multiplies twenty loaves of barley to feed a hundred men (2 Kgs. 4:42–44), cures leprosy (2 Kgs. 5:1–27) and makes an ax head float (2 Kgs. 6:1–7). These brief and isolated stories are linked by the common theme of Elisha's supernatural powers, and are presented as a cycle covering 2 Kings 4–6. They are atypical of simple miracle accounts in that they include details about surrounding circumstances and why his help was needed.[59] Most of these stories lack references to prayer or the divine presence, thereby focusing attention on Elisha as the source of wonderment.

2 Kings 3 shows an additional aspect of Elisha's prophecy: the use of music to initiate contact with God. The kings of Israel, Judah and Edom have joined forces to do battle with the Moabites, but realize that they have run out of water for their armies and animals (v. 9). Jehoshaphat, king of Judah, recalls hearing of Elisha the wonder-working prophet and suggests that the monarchs seek his assistance (v. 11). At first, Elisha is

reluctant to satisfy the request, since Jehoram was the son of the despised King Ahab and Jezebel and "did what was displeasing to the Lord" (v. 2). The indignant prophet tells Jehoram, "Go to your father's prophets or to your mother's prophets," but in the end agrees to help out of respect for Jehoshaphat (vv. 13–14). Elisha does not, however, transition immediately into a prophetic mode. Instead, he calls for a musician (v. 15).

Elisha needed the aid of music to get him past his initial resistance and to prepare him for divine contact. As Friedrich Wilhelm Krummacher puts it: "His mind, thrown out of its wonted composure, and disturbed in its depths by its indignant feelings towards the miserable monarch, required soothing and recollection."[60] Another nineteenth-century source notes: "To acquire that self-collection, that self-possession, which is the very essence of devotion, the prophet has recourse to the powers of music ... a state of solemn sedateness of mind was solicited by the prophet, as a preliminary to the advent of the prophetic spirit."[61] In a manner echoing that of King Saul, the prophet turned to the mood altering capacity of music to quiet his anger and cleanse his mind of distracting thoughts. Though we do not know what instrument was played for Elisha, it is entirely possible that is was a *kinnor*.[62] Just as David's use of the instrument brought Saul to a calm state of mind, its melody could have had a refining and/or uplifting impact on the prophet.

But tranquility of spirit was not Elisha's only desire, nor was it the music's exclusive effect. It is evident from the narrative that the musical tones induced the prophet to a state of receptivity and inspired him to prophesy. "As the musician played," the Bible reports, "the hand of the Lord came upon him" (2 Kgs. 3:15). The prophecy that results advises the kings regarding the water situation and assures them that they will be victorious: "Thus said the Lord: the wadi shall see no wind, you shall see no rain, and yet the wadi shall be filled with water ... [and the Lord] will also deliver Moab into your hands" (vv. 17–19). The musician's ability to facilitate a prophetic experience is rooted in many traditions of the ancient world.[63] The Assyrians recognized a strong compatibility between prophecy and psalmody, and the ancient Greeks viewed music as a divine gift intertwined with prophecy.[64] Israel's perception of the link between music and divine communication is repeated in a rabbinic story of Jonah ben Abitai, a musician who lives in such joy and piety that God prompts him to prophesy.[65]

4. Sing unto God

This ecstasy-inducing music is most closely associated with the *kinnor*, an instrument regularly identified as a tool of divine inspiration.[66] 1 Chronicles 25:1–3 gives an account of the use of various instruments, including the *kinnor*, in the prophetic activities of the Levitical musicians: "the sons of Asaph, of Heman, and of Jeduthun, who prophesied to the accompaniment of lyres, harps and cymbals ..." The *kinnor* likewise appears in 1 Samuel 10:5, which shows a band of prophets "coming down from the shrine, preceded by lyres, timbrels, flutes, and harps, and they will be speaking in ecstasy." Both of these passages relate music's stimulation of prophetic states and its role in supporting ecstatic words.

An interesting—though not exact—comparison can be drawn between prophetic music in the Bible and the role of music in Santería, a syncretic religion of West African and Caribbean origin. Though they are two distinct religious systems existing in widely separated geographical and historical milieus, the musical aspect of human-divine contact in both traditions speaks to the larger, perhaps universal, link between musical and sacred experiences. Religious music is often part of a trance experience, in which music combines with other sensual cues—like incense and bright ornate colors—to bring individuals into a sense of euphoria and perceived connection to the sacred realm.[67] In Santería, songs with repetitive and extended rhythmic patterns are played to call upon specific deities, known as *orishas*. As the music and dancing intensifies, participants are lifted into spiritual ecstasy. A typical ceremonial ritual might involve the following:

> It starts with *oro seco*, dry drumming without singing, performed in the *igbodú* [sacred grove of the festival] during which time no dancing or procession takes place. As in any ceremony, the Elegúa [god of the crossroads, messenger between gods and humans] must be saluted first. This is followed by the *oro del eyá* performed in the area of the house-temple where the uninitiated are permitted to enter. Here the *oro cantado* or sung prayer calls to the *orishas* in precise rhythms with specific meanings. Singing and dance are now incorporated in the ritual, and the increase in energy summons different *orishas* who respond to their specific musical themes and possess or "mount" their "horses."[68]

Rhythmic and chant sequences entice *orishas* to greet their "children"—the practitioners of Santería. Their energy builds as the ceremony progresses, and the musicians and dancers—driven by polyrhythmic textures and repetitive melodies—are prompted to perform for many hours. The end goal is spirit possession, in which *orishas* are believed to work within the possessed and deliver messages, advice and healing. The parallel with Elisha's prophetic episode is striking as he, too, was only able to connect with the deity after first becoming caught up in the music. And although Elisha is not shown dancing into a heightened state, an additional similarity can be drawn between the Santería ritual and the enraptured dances of Miriam and the women at the Red Sea (Exod. 15:20) and David and the Israelites before the Ark (2 Sam. 6: 5). Additionally, 1 Kings 18:26 mentions dance as a component of Canaanite prophecy, suggesting that the practice may have been regional.

Elisha's reliance on music also offers insights into the role of prophetic brotherhoods. Elisha does not appear to have been a musician himself but rather, like Saul, called upon music's transformative power. By requesting a musician, the prophet not only confirmed the suitability of music for inspiring divine contact, but also drew upon his association with musicians of the prophetic guild. Scholars have long maintained that Elisha used a musician from the disciples of the prophets.[69] Josephus concludes that these men were students of the great prophets[70]; and 2 Kings 2:15 shows them giving deference to Elisha following Elijah's ascent to heaven. Musical instruction seems to have been a major focus of these schools, and helps to explain how an individual might be trained to become a prophet—a vocation that in its purest form is initiated by divine calling. As Sendrey notes, "The sole prerequisite for admission was the wish and the aptitude for learning, the voluntary submission to the common discipline, and devotion to the religious and national ideals of Israel."[71] Along with methods of wonderworking, students were trained to perform music for the purpose of fostering human-divine communication. As such, these schools were a precursor to the Levitical guild of Temple musicians, who learned, performed and passed on traditions of devotional music.

The musical component of the prophetic brotherhood is evident from its first mention. It occurs in 1 Samuel 10:5, the aforementioned scene in which a band of prophets is shown "speaking in ecstasy" to the sound of musical instruments. Some have speculated that Samuel himself formed this band after his retirement from public affairs.[72] According to this theory, though he no longer served in an official capacity, Samuel remained the nation's spiritual leader and assembled groups of enthusiastic men to be taught in the prophetic arts. This program is, perhaps, alluded to in Samuel's address to Israel announcing his retirement: "I will continue to instruct you in the practice of what is good and right" (1 Sam. 12:23). Comparable prophetic schools existed in antiquity, reaching as far back as Sumeria, and almost without exception their course of study included musical training.[73]

1 Samuel 10:5 also alludes to the use of music at shrines and temples, especially those positioned on high places. These temples—the most prominent of which were found at Bethel, Shiloh, Shechem, Gilgal, Mizpah, Gibeah, Hebron and Beersheva—were the site of daily cultic activities, holiday rituals, family celebrations and private devotion. Such high places, according to Mircea Eliade, are more innately sacred than other places because of their closer proximity to the sky. "[B]eholding the sky," writes Eliade, "[man] simultaneously discovers the divine incommensurability and his own situation in the cosmos. For the sky, by its own mode of being, reveals transcendence, force, eternity."[74] As we see in the verse from Samuel, bands of ecstatics and musicians congregated at these elevated locales, where they were inspired to establish contact with God.[75]

Still, it should be stressed that 2 Kings 3 is the only place we see Elisha utilizing music to reach a prophetic state. In fact, this passage stands out as the Bible's singular episode in which a major prophet—that is, a prophet mentioned by name—requires external inducement to prophesy.[76] As the star pupil and successor of Elijah, Elisha was gifted with inborn talents and refined skills; and in numerous other verses he performs miracles and divination without the need for external aid. However, given his hatred for King Jehoram and his initial resistance to prophesying on his behalf, he called upon ecstatic music to propel him past his sour mood and prepare him for prophecy. Elisha put his trust in a musician to assist him in reaching the necessary receptive state.

Jeremiah

There is a wealth of biographical information contained in the Book of Jeremiah. From its superscription, the longest in the Bible, we learn that Jeremiah came from Anathoth, a town three miles north of

Jerusalem in the territory of Benjamin, and that he was a descendant of the Elide priest Abiathar, who was expelled from the Temple when Solomon appointed Zadok as the sole high priest (1 Kgs. 2:26–27). His prophetic career is placed between the thirteenth year of Josiah's reign (627 B.C.E.) and the eleventh year of King Zedekiah (586 B.C.E.), when the Temple was destroyed. These four decades spanned Judah's most calamitous period, in which the nationalism, reform, expansion and prosperity experienced under Josiah gave way to a series of disasters.[77] Jeremiah entered this volatile climate as an "outsider" priest (1:1), reluctant prophet (1:4–10), condemner of "false prophets" (e.g., 23:9–40; 33:9–40), supporter of Babylonia when most others favored Egypt (e.g., 25:1–29:32), and disputatious witness to the fall of Judah and the exile that followed — all of which made him profoundly unpopular, bitter and resentful. Yet despite his perpetual cynicism and the many plots fashioned against him, he could not keep from proclaiming the word of God.

The emotional content of Jeremiah's turbulent biography is expressed most vividly in his "confessions": first-person complaints addressed to God (11:18–23; 12:1–6; 15:10–12; 17:14–18; 18:18–23; 20:7–13; 20:14–18). These passages combine to paint an intimate portrait of Jeremiah's personality and inner struggles. Through them, we gain an understanding of how the prophet, whose message and character are constantly derided, comes to "incarnate in personal burden the perversity of a world in the wrong."[78] In both language and content, the confessions resemble the personal laments of the Psalter, which voice complaints of physical or mental anguish, protestations of innocence, and pleas for divine help.[79]

Because of their close similarity to these psalms, some scholars view Jeremiah's confessions as anonymous additions to the book.[80] But it is understandable that he would choose to express himself in this traditional form. The lament psalm is the quintessential vehicle in the Bible for personal emotional expression, and it is fitting that Jeremiah's deepest sentiments and concerns are conveyed through this poetic form. From a biographical standpoint, Jeremiah was a priest residing in Jerusalem and, if not a member of the Temple choir, certainly had intimate knowledge of the psalms.[81] This not only explains how he could have authored the confessions, but also suggests that he was a skilled musician. Just as scholars contend that the Bible's psalms and psalm-like passages were originally intended for musical presentation, there is a long-held contention that Jeremiah sang his confessions.[82]

Importantly, musicologists have emphasized the role of Levites and other secondary priests as liturgical musicians, citing their indispensable role as leaders of responsorial and corporate song.[83] Sendrey points to the unparalleled ability of Temple singers to express "joy, grief, love, triumph, and the inexhaustible gamut of human emotions ..."[84] When Jeremiah was compelled to pour forth his innermost feelings, he set his words to music, the "tonal analogue of emotive life."[85]

The confession found in Jeremiah 20:7–13 is comprised of two parts: Jeremiah's resentment of the isolation and mockery he endures (vv. 7–10), and his confident proclamation of thanksgiving (vv. 11–13). This combination of lament and exultation follows the structure of several lament psalms, where words of anguish are resolved in a concluding statement of assurance and praise (e.g., Pss. 6; 13; 30; 31; 35). These so-called "dynamic psalms" are characterized by a marked shift from doubt to hope or petition to praise, regardless of whether or not this change reflects a renewed state coming later.[86] Jeremiah 20:7–13 fits neatly into this genre and should therefore be read as a singular composition.

However, because 20:7–13 is the only one of Jeremiah's confessions to end with confident assurance, Robert Lundbom suggests that the discontinuity between the two parts "precludes there being a single composition, however dynamic."[87] Yet, whether or not this confession reflects an editorial conflation, its rhetorical movement is natural to biblical literature, and illustrates a major theme of the book: Jeremiah bemoans being chosen as a prophet and the suffering it entails, though he maintains a definite, if understated, joy in the word of God.

20:7 begins with Jeremiah calling out accusatorially: "You enticed me, God, and I was enticed; You overpowered me and You prevailed." This piercing statement hearkens back to Jeremiah's commission, when he protests his appointment as a prophet (1:6). Like Moses in Exodus 3:11–12, Jeremiah contends that he is unfit for prophecy; and as with Moses, God assures him that He will be with him (1:8). Importantly, this verse gives Jeremiah's call the added dimension of seduction and physical conquest. According to Marvin A. Sweeney, this formulation suggests rape and metaphorically captures how God's word causes pain and humiliation for Jeremiah.[88] Jewish commentators tend to overlook this sexual connotation, finding that it was the persuasiveness of God's argument — not its coercive force — that overpowered Jeremiah's objections.[89]

In either case, it is clear that Jeremiah's prophetic career brought him much distress. As he continues in 20:7: "I have become a laughingstock all the day, everyone mocks me." This complaint ties in with the beginning of the chapter where Passhur, a priest charged with keeping order at the Temple Mount, has Jeremiah imprisoned and flogged for a day (20:1–2).[90] Presumably, both during and after his imprisonment, Jeremiah is mocked for prophesying doom. This would suggest that the confession took place during the reign of Jehoiakim between 609 and 605 B.C.E., as conditions in Jerusalem were favorable enough for the masses to scoff at Jeremiah's forecast of a Babylonian invasion, which did not begin until 604.[91] Walter Baumgartner has drawn a connection between the mockery Jeremiah describes in this verse and several references to mockery in the psalms of lament (e.g., Pss. 22:8–9; 35:15–16; 40:16; 44:12–17; 69:11–13; 79:4).[92] The clearest example is found in Psalm 22:8: "All who see me mock me; they curl their lips, they shake their heads."

Psalm-like language also appears in Jeremiah 20:8, which begins: "For whenever I speak, I cry out; I cry out 'lawlessness and destruction!'" Baumgartner envisions Jeremiah declaiming these words as a cry for help, echoing the psalmist (e.g., Pss. 34:18; 77:2; 88:2).[93] Moreover, the phrase "lawlessness and destruction" has parallels in several psalm passages condemning rampant violence and injustice (Pss. 7:17; 11:5; 18:49; 25:19; 27:12; 35:11), and as an idiom appears in Jeremiah 6:7, Amos 3:10 and Habakkuk 1:3. This verse concludes with the wrenching statement, "For the word of the Lord is disgrace and scorn for me all day long," suggesting that Jeremiah is mocked each day he prophesies. The words used to convey mockery—"disgrace" and "scorn"—appear either individually or as a pair in Psalms 22:7; 31:12; 39:9; 44:14; 69:11; 79:4; and 89:42.

Jeremiah next describes his inability to keep his prophecy silent. "I said to myself: 'I will not mention Him, and I will no longer speak His name.' But there is a raging fire in my heart, confined in my bones; I wearied to contain it, but I could not" (20:9). This language is mirrored in Jeremiah 23:9, when the prophet cries out that God's word is crushing his heart and making his bones tremble. All of the prophet's attempts to conceal his message cause him mental and physical pain. He must continue to prophesy, even as it makes him a laughingstock. This is also evident in 4:19: "My heart moans within me, I cannot keep silent"; and in 6:11, the prophet says the same thing about God's wrath: "I am filled with the wrath of the Lord, I cannot hold it in." Thus, from the moment Jeremiah is called as a prophet, God's word wields tremendous power over him.[94]

Jeremiah 20:10 begins with a verbatim quote from Psalm 31:14: "For I hear whispering in the crowd: 'Terror-all-around!'" Earlier in chapter 20, Jeremiah renames Passhur "Terror-all-around," indicating that Judah's enemies will destroy him (20:3–4).[95] Here, Jeremiah's detractors use this phrase as a taunt against him, poking fun at his gloomy demeanor and predictions. This is followed by additional details of the crowd's activities: "'Inform! And let us inform about him!' And all my trusted friends watch for my fall." The people's anticipation of Jeremiah's demise bears a similarity to Psalm 56:7, where the psalmist protests, "They plot, they lie in ambush; they watch my every move, hoping for my death"; and Psalm 35:15 describes the enemies' glee as they watch a righteous man fall. By stating that even his close friends desire his undoing, Jeremiah brings to mind Micah 7:6: "a man's enemies are the men of his house." This is especially striking as Jeremiah gives his friends the intentionally ironic label "my friends of peace," suggesting that not only have his friends become his enemies, but also people of peace plotting violence.[96]

Jeremiah 20:10 concludes with the crowd saying, "Perhaps he can be enticed, and we will prevail over him, and take our revenge on him." Jeremiah uses two verbs employed in the seduction imagery of 20:7, "entice" and "prevail," though few commentators interpret these verbs the same in both verses.[97] Here, they imply deception instead of a physical act, referring to the crowd's scheming to discredit Jeremiah and his message.

At this point, the confession shifts abruptly in tone from sorrow to praise. Read in the context of Jeremiah's release from Passhur's prison, this movement indicates an emotional change within the prophet: he is temporarily alleviated of the burden of persecution and humiliation. "But the Lord is with me like a mighty warrior; thus my pursuers will stumble and will not succeed. They are very ashamed because they did not succeed, with eternal reproach they will not be forgotten" (20:11). This expectation of deliverance from "my pursuers" echoes the pleas voiced in Psalms 7:2 and 31:16, and the everlasting shame the prophet wishes upon them reflects his unwavering faith in divine justice. Even as Jeremiah's friends and enemies join together in craving his downfall, the prophet remains confident that God is with him. So, while Jeremiah's confession insinuates that God has abandoned him, this verse functions both as a reaffirmation of divine power, and a reminder to God that He is to serve as the prophet's protector.

He continues: "Lord of Hosts, who tests the righteous and sees the kidneys and the heart, let me see your vengeance upon them, for to You I have confided my case" (20:12). The prophet clearly sees himself as a righteous man constantly tested by his detractors. This, he insists, is readily apparent to God, who understands his emotions (kidneys), will (heart) and the "inner fire" that consumes him. Jeremiah's plea that God take vengeance upon his enemies alludes to Psalm 37, which counsels the righteous to wait for God to exact justice on their behalf.

Jeremiah 20:13 brings the prophet's confession to a climax: "Sing unto the Lord, praise the Lord, because he rescued the life of the needy from the hand of evildoers." With these words, Jeremiah again recalls the Psalter, where the injunction to sing to God is formulaic (e.g., Pss. 33:3; 68:5; 98:1; 113:1; 135:1; 117:1; 148:1; 150:1). Like the psalms Jeremiah may have sung in the Temple, this verse employs the plural command forms of the verbs "sing" and "praise." As such, the prophet appears to be assuming a sort of liturgical role, inviting the faithful among the crowd to join him in worshiping God. It is also apparent that Jeremiah views himself as the needy man in this verse, who has received divine deliverance from his enemies. Again, this draws on a recurring theme of the lament psalms, as seen in Psalm 40:18: "But I am poor and needy; may the Lord devise for me. You are my help and my rescuer; my God, do not delay" (cf. Pss. 9:19; 12:6; 35:10; 72:4, 13; 107:41; 132:15).

As this analysis shows, Jeremiah 20:7–13 closely resembles the biblical psalms of lament. It documents a profound shift from sorrow to praise, and portrays in strong language "a struggle, a movement, an active process occurring within a person."[98] But this inner transformation was probably not expressed through words alone. Both the lament psalms and Jeremiah's confessions were most likely sung rather than spoken. For the psalmist and Jeremiah, who composed his own psalms and was likely a priestly singer, the "whole worship, including the musical accompaniment of the praise or prayer, is conceived as an offering to God."[99]

The likelihood that Jeremiah sang his laments is supported by the long history of singing in the face of adversity. Communal and personal experiences of persecution, discrimination, conflict and disaster have given rise to countless songs of witness and hope.[100] While the musical tones of ancient Israel are not known, it is safe to assume that they were capable of stirring basic human emotions. Music's emotive potential is rooted largely in its ability to symbolically communicate the movement from tension to release[101] — the same process that characterizes Jeremiah's confession. So, in order to further dramatize his already intense words — and to express sentiments that lie beyond the limits of language to convey — Jeremiah turned to the "heightened speech" of music.

As already noted, Werner and Sonne identify the allopathic and homeopathic uses of music in prophecy.[102] While the allopathic function of music minimizes psychological and emotional states that make prophecy difficult to achieve (as in the Elisha example from 2 Kings 3), the homeopathic use amplifies the emotions already present in the prophet. Jeremiah 20:7–13 seems to exhibit this latter function. The humiliation, plots and inner torment he endures are the impetus for the confession, and its words unequivocally convey both the tragedy and hope the prophet feels in his darkest hour. By singing these words, Jeremiah allowed them to reach their highest emotive potential, and intensified his dialogue with God.

Habakkuk

In contrast to the detailed information found in the introduction to Jeremiah, the two superscriptions in the Book of Habakkuk (1:1 and 3:1) merely ascribe each section to the Judean prophet. Still, the book's historical context can be ascertained from its portrayal of the rise of the Chaldeans (1:6), the Neo-Babylonian Dynasty founded in 625 B.C.E., as well as the indication that Jerusalem had not yet fallen (e.g., 2:20). When the Chaldeans defeated Egypt and took control of Judah in 605 B.C.E., many in Judah viewed them as foreign oppressors. Habakkuk is representative of this camp. Like his contemporary, Jeremiah, he asks God why He would bring an oppressor against Judah: "You whose eyes are too pure to look upon evil, Who cannot countenance wrongdoing, why do You countenance treachery, and stand by idle while the one in the wrong devours the one in the right?" (1:13). Elsewhere, Habakkuk characterizes the Chaldean king Nebuchadnezzar as a wicked tyrant who will be destroyed by God (2:5–20).[103] All of this points to the likelihood that the prophecies were given between 605 and 600 B.C.E.[104]

The Book of Habakkuk does not provide explicit biographical details about the prophet, but the structure of the chapters and various linguistic indicators imply that he was at least familiar with the Temple's cultic and liturgical traditions,[105] if not a prophet-priest like Jeremiah.[106] Given the liturgical tone, language and formulae employed in the book, most scholars view Habakkuk as a Temple prophet who delivered his prophecies in that setting.[107] It is also intriguing that Bel and the Dragon, a late second-century apocryphal extension to the Book of Daniel, identifies Habakkuk as a Levite (Bel. 1:1). Although the prophet's appearance in that text is chronologically inaccurate, his link to the Levitical order, real or imagined, is instructive. The Levites were charged with guarding the Temple service and overseeing its musical activities. Such a role would account for Habakkuk's familiarity with the liturgical structure evident in his prophecies. But, no matter his relation to the Temple, it is clear that his favored prophetic mode was poetry, which would have been sung. For this reason, Habakkuk — like Jeremiah — can be described as a singing prophet.

Habakkuk is comprised of several oracles, or divine communications presented through an intermediary. The oracle was one of the basic methods employed by the biblical prophets and it took many forms (e.g., Josh. 7:6–15; 2 Sam. 5:23–24; Isa. 14:4–23; Ezek. 11:7–13; Nah. 2:14).[108] However, Habakkuk's oracles are unique in that they are arranged as a coherent, sequentially developed argument, instead of disjointed utterances offered at different times and places. This organization gives shape to the book and an impression of dramatic development. The oracles are primarily concerned with theodicy: justifying God's righteousness in threatening circumstances and in the face of great evil. Habakkuk's prophecy begins with a series of God-directed questions concerning injustices committed against Judah. These resolve in a vision of God as the conqueror of chaos, who instills in the prophet hope for future deliverance and courage to endure the gloomy present.[109]

Habakkuk is comprised of two distinct sections: a dialogue between the prophet and God (chs. 1–2) and a psalm (ch. 3). The dialogue can be divided into four parts.[110] The first is Habakkuk's complaint that God remains silent as injustices are perpetrated against Judah (1:2–4). The prophet gives a series of pointed, rhetorical questions, such as "How long, O Lord, shall I cry out and You not listen? Shall I shout to You, 'Violence!' and You not save?" (1:2). The second part consists of God's response to the prophet's complaint (1:5–11). Rather than providing consolation or reassurance, He states that the Chaldeans are His agents sent to eradicate injustice, and describes them as an almost unstoppable force "like vultures rushing toward food" and with horses "fleeter than wolves on the steppe" (1:8). Not surprisingly, Habakkuk is dissatisfied with this reply, especially as the rise of the Chaldeans does not seem like a "solution" but an exacerbation of the problem. He launches into the third section, in which he complains that the Chaldeans have overstepped their bounds, and reiterates his point that the wicked are oppressing the righteous (1:12–17). The fourth section is God's response to this complaint, in which He assures Habakkuk that despite the severity of the situation, the wicked will eventually be overthrown (2:1–20). The central message is this: the righteous must sometimes wait for redemption while those who do not deserve worldly power wield it over them.[111] From a musical and liturgical perspective, it is notable that this section closely resembles the content and structure of a lament prayer that would have been sung on a day of penitence.[112]

The musical aspect of Habakkuk is especially marked in chapter 3. The entire chapter reads like a self-contained psalm, complete with a superscription (v. 1), a petition to God to manifest His power (v. 2), a vision of God's power in the world (vv. 3–15) and a concluding expression of confidence in God (v. 19). Its content is derived from a theophany, or a "self-disclosure of God in specific places and particular forms in nature and in human society."[113] It employs standard theophanic imagery to underscore the awesomeness of God, such as His descent from a mountain in verse 3 (cf. Gen 12:8; Exod. 1:9; Ps. 48) and His role as a cosmic warrior in verses 7 to 15 (cf. Exod. 15:3; Deut. 33:2–3; Ps. 89).

The third chapter of Habakkuk is a "genuine psalm" with influences from the prophetic mindset, and may have been written or modified to its current shape for use in the cult.[114]

In addition to its psalmic structure, the chapter displays musical and liturgical instructions. These elements give the distinct impression that Habakkuk's psalm was recorded to be performed as a prophetic communication and as a musical composition. In the words of one scholar, it was "written in the form of a psalm and was probably designed to be sung by the Levites in the Temple services."[115] Most telling in this regard is its incorporation of three obscure musical cues original to the Book of Psalms: *shigionoth*, *selah* and *la-menazze'ah*.

Shigionoth is a term of uncertain meaning found only in the heading of Psalm 7 (in the singular form)—"A *Shiggaion* of David, which he sang to the Lord"—and the introduction to Habakkuk 3—"A prayer of the prophet Habakkuk. In the mode of a *Shigionoth*." It may derive from an Akkadian word for "lamentation," and possibly denotes a hymn, a song of distress or psalm accompanied with musical instruments.[116] It may also be an indication of how to interpret the text in performance, such as "a passionate psalm with strong emotion"[117] or a "wild, exuberant praise."[118] All of these options point to the term's musical function, and support the proposition that Habakkuk sang the verses. Indeed, *shigionoth* may have been added to the text when it was transcribed in order to capture the essence of Habakkuk's vocal performance, and ensure that the same feelings were imparted when the psalm was sung liturgically.

Another psalm term found in Habakkuk is *selah*. There is no agreement among scholars as to the precise meaning of the term, but many modern scholars ascribe to the word a musical meaning.[119] *Selah* occurs seventy-one times in thirty-nine Psalms, either at the end of a stanza (e.g., Pss. 32; 66; 89; 140) or, on four occasions, at the very end of a psalm (Pss. 3; 9; 24; 36). The only place *selah* appears outside of the Psalter is Habakkuk 3:3, 9, and 13, where it divides sections of the text. Like *shigionoth*, the use of *selah* in Habakkuk is strong evidence that it was a sung prophecy with liturgical overtones.

Numerous proposals have been offered as to the function of *selah*, both linguistic and musical. Medieval Jewish commentator Abraham Ibn Ezra (1089–1164) read it as a statement of emphasis, like "so it is," "thus" or "the matter is true and right."[120] Understood in this way, *selah* would have functioned similarly to *amen* ("so be it"). The Talmud likewise translates *selah* as a non-musical term meaning "forevermore."[121] But it is possible that this understanding is a carry-over from Temple worship, where *selah* may have functioned as a *fermata* signaling that the final note of a stanza be held for a long duration, thus conveying a sense of "foreverness."[122] The term is also interpreted as a dynamic marking, either derived from *salah* ("to lay low"), indicating a decrease in volume, or from *salal* ("to raise"), marking an increase.[123] Another intriguing theory comes from J. Steinberg, who suggests that *selah* was a cue to beat on a basket-shaped drum that marked a change in the music or the end of a psalm.[124] He sees a connection between *selah* and *sal*, a Hebrew word for basket, and points to the existence of similar drums in China and India. Jacob Beimel writes in support of Steinberg's theory: "In all probability ... the signals [of the drum] were designated for the musicians who accompanied the singers on musical instruments. Like the accompanying musicians of our time, who in most cases do not know the texts of the songs which they accompany, so the Levitic players also may not have known the words of the Psalms which the Levitic singers sang."[125]

The musical function of *selah* is supported as well by its frequent appearance with *la-menazze'ah*, a cue commonly translated as "for the choirmaster."[126] The term has also been viewed as a direction "to the chief musician"[127] and as a general indication that the psalm is to be performed.[128] Whatever its exact meaning, it is almost certain that *la-menazze'ah* is an instruction regarding the musical presentation of a prayer-song. It occurs in the title of thirty-one psalms in which *selah* is also found. Outside of the Psalter the term appears only in Habakkuk 3:19, following the three instances of *selah* (vv. 3, 9, 13). This employment of psalmic terminology is further evidence of Habakkuk's familiarity with and connection to Temple worship.

A final note on the musical nature of Habakkuk's prophecy also bears mention. Habakkuk is identified as *nabi* (1:1), the principle term the Bible uses for prophet. The term is probably related to the Akkadian root *nabu*, meaning roughly "one who has been called."[129] Though it can refer simply to the announcement of the divine word (e.g., 1 Kgs. 18:29; Ezek. 37:10), it is often found in the context of ecstatic prophetic experiences with song and instrumental accompaniment (e.g., Num. 11:25;

1 Sam. 10:11; 1 Kgs. 18:29). In addition, various forms of *nabi* appear in connection with prophets who are, at one point or another, depicted as singers. These include Moses (Deut. 33:1), Miriam (Exod. 15:20), Deborah (Judg. 4:4) and Jeremiah (Jer. 1:5). 1 Chronicles 25:1 uses the term in describing the Levitical singers: "David and the officers of the army set apart for service the sons of Asaph, of Heman, and of Jeduthun, who prophesied (*hanib'im*) to the accompaniment of lyres, harps, and cymbals," while 1 Samuel 10:5–6 tells of "a band of prophets (*n'vi'im*) coming down from the shrine, preceded by lyres, timbrels, flutes, and harps, and they will be prophesying (*mitnab'im*) in ecstasy." Viewed as a whole, these passages show that music helped prophets (and priests) enter into mystical states, where they were more receptive to divine messages. This further explains why Habakkuk, who was familiar with music's role in generating a sense of the divine presence during worship, chose song as a medium for connecting with God and relaying His word.

Summary

The use of music to induce and express communion with the divine is evident across cultures and throughout history. In biblical society, music played a significant role in prophecy—the primary medium through which God's concern for and involvement in human life was revealed. The prophets occupied the hallowed space between humanity and the divine. They used musical tones to become more receptive to God's word and transmitted these messages to the people in poetic song. Music helped clarify and amplify the emotional content of divine encounters, and enabled the content to better resonate among a populace well acquainted with music's vital place in devotion and everyday life. In this important way, ancient Israel—a society that relied on words given by God and received these messages through the music-infused medium of prophecy—substantially defined its collective identity through song.

As is apparent from this chapter's general discussion of the methods of biblical prophecy and deeper exploration of three representative prophets—Elisha, Jeremiah, and Habakkuk—prophetic episodes often included a musical component. Several of the prophets described in the

4. Sing unto God

books of the Former Prophets used song and dance to transmit divine messages and utilized music to reach a prophetic state. The poetic form, meter, accentuation and other musical-linguistic aspects of the Latter Prophets show a similar reliance on music to deliver God's word. Viewed more broadly, the intersection of music and prophecy can be grouped with many examples of music's prominence in biblical life. The prophets recognized the ability of musical sounds to establish divine contact, intensify holy words and attract the populace to urgent proclamations. In a less dramatic way, music continues to figure prominently in devotional settings, where the ultimate goal is to become enraptured in the language, themes and sentiments of the sacred moment.

The incorporation of music in prophecy and divine worship is reflective of an intuitive musical response that existed prior to and continued well beyond the development of these religious offices. In these related contexts, music's power lies in the mysterious yet effortless way it makes intimate a sense of something greater than oneself. On a fundamental level, music is transcendent: it rises above the monotony of speech and the noises of everyday living. Universally, the human ear distinguishes between musical and unmusical sounds, and even in clamorous environments like city streets and shopping malls we tend to gravitate, consciously or unconsciously, toward these organized sounds. The division between music and everyday noise is, then, analogous to the distinction between sacred and profane; and in a society as God-oriented as ancient Israel, it is fitting that holy words were musically offered and received.

Chapter 5
Music and Public Worship: Singing in the Book of Psalms

In his classic study, "Religion and Music" (1893), Waldo S. Pratt observes that religion operates on two levels: personal and communal. Calling religion "essentially a spiritual affair" between one's soul and the divine, he writes that the necessary outward manifestations of religion, such as ethics and institutions, make it a social affair as well.[1] Bonds between co-religionists, moral and spiritual instruction, a sense of God's presence and other elements central to religious life are strengthened when people engage in rituals and ceremonies together. As Pratt concludes, the "practical necessities of religion, the necessity of concrete manifestation and the twin necessity of the social value in such manifestation, have their fullest expression in the institution, historic everywhere, of public worship."[2]

Crucially, it is the public expression of religion that calls for and benefits from music. Pratt puts it thus:

> Music naturally belongs with the social side of religion rather than with its private side. The secret intercourse between the soul and God has no absolute need of music or any other sensuous formulation. Only so far as this inmost intercourse expands into a social institution, where outward expression is a necessity, is there a special demand for such a voice as that of music. The solitary worshiper may set his prayer and praise in forms of song as a fuller mode of utterance than cold words; but he is not likely to do this unless he has first learned the value of song as an implement of social intercourse.[3]

The Hebrew Bible provides examples of both hushed personal prayer and musical corporate prayer. The former is typified in 1 Samuel.

5. Music and Public Worship

The book begins with the story of Hannah, the beloved wife of Elkanah. Unlike Elkanah's other wife, Peninah, Hannah was unable to bear children. Peninah taunted Hannah, claiming that God had closed her womb. "This happened year after year" the Bible tells us. "Every time she went up to the House of the Lord, the other would taunt her, so that she wept and would not eat" (1 Sam. 1:7). During an annual pilgrimage to Shiloh, where the Holy Ark was stored, Hannah vowed that if she were able to have a son, she would dedicate him to divine service. Her prayer was answered and she bore Samuel, judge and prophet of Israel.

Hannah's prayer was personal, spontaneous and quiet. As the story relates, she "[prayed] in her heart; only her lips moved, but her voice could not be heard" (1 Sam. 1:12). Because this prayer involved only two parties—Hannah and God—there was no need to unite a community in shared consciousness or intent, and thus no need for musical rendering. Even so, the rabbis derived from this verse the general principle that true prayer, whether of a personal or collective kind, requires sincerity and concentration. They maintained that the worshiper should strive to be like Hannah, who made her heart attentive to God.[4] This became known as *kavvanah*: the intention necessary for the performance of religious duties. *Kavvanah* is the ideal devotional state, in which the individual is entirely focused on the words, activity and object of prayer. As Maimonides explains, "*Kavvanah* means that a man should empty his mind of all other thoughts and regard himself as if he were standing before the Divine Presence."[5]

Deep devotion and unhindered concentration was natural for Hannah, as she uttered her prayer in response to the painful realities of life. Unlike liturgical formulae, which are prescribed and usually communal in design, Hannah's petition was impromptu and private; it was an extemporaneous outpouring triggered by her spiritual and emotional state. This signifies a stark contrast between private and public worship. Whereas Hannah's prayer grew organically from her state of being, ceremonial ritual necessitates a common literature to guide participants through the themes and sentiments of worship. This typically involves collective language (we, us, our, etc.), general themes that speak to many circumstances, and a range of possible feelings congregants may be having (gratitude, elation, despair, etc.). Yet, while the highly structured service is critical for bringing people together and for assuring that individuals touch on the many moods of religious life, its static nature can make *kavvanah* difficult to achieve. Liturgy, by definition, is a prayer routine, and so it is not always engaged in with the same level of intensity as spontaneous devotion. This is an important reason why public worship is virtually everywhere linked with music.[6]

A prayer that is sung can affect one more intensely and immediately than when it is read or spoken. If one does not approach a given prayer with complete concentration, the musical setting can bring him or her into heightened awareness. Moreover, as a collective experience, worship music replenishes a sense of shared purpose and identity, and reminds participants of the beliefs, convictions and expectations that form the very basis of community.[7] Put simply, musical prayer plays a vitalizing role in congregational life.

This does not mean that song is completely absent in private devotion. It is common for individuals to reach out to God with singing in times of joy, anxiety, anguish and contemplation. In private settings removed from the communal environment of church or synagogue, strains of melody can be used to forge a connecting line between the human and the divine, and serve as an outlet for grief, gratitude, praise, frustrations and other religious and existential concerns. In these unrehearsed moments, when one need not worry about the quality of performance or the formalities of congregational participation, song takes on its purist form of "breathing out of the soul to God."[8] But even here, the social aspect of worship plays a crucial role. To restate Pratt's astute observation, though the solitary worshiper may sing prayers "as a fuller mode of utterance than cold words," this is unlikely to occur "unless he has first learned the value of song as an implement of social intercourse."[9] This is confirmed by the fact that many who sing private prayers turn to hymns and liturgical settings that they have become familiar with through repeated usage in a house of worship.[10]

Music's key place in public worship is attested in the Book of Psalms, "the prayer book of the Old Testament and the prayer book of Israel."[11] The psalms were canonized during the Second Temple period, perhaps in the fifth or fourth century B.C.E. Although the precise editors are unknown, the Psalter was likely a project of priestly circles in Jerusalem, who had an interest in making the psalms authoritatively available for use in worship.[12] Its place as the hymnbook of the Second Temple is widely asserted,[13] though it also contains psalms that originated in other locations, like the First Temple and early synagogues.[14] While questions regarding origins and authorship arise from the book's composite nature, two things are clear: the psalms were a part of public worship and are thoroughly musical in character.

This chapter details the connection between music and public prayer in ancient Israel, with special attention on music in the psalms. It begins with an examination of music's role as an aid to sacrifice and continues with a description of the centrality of Levitical musicians in Temple ritual. This sets the stage for an analysis of musical references and implications in the Book of Psalms, a look at Psalm 150 as a case study in musical praise, and an application of Levitin's concept of six world-shaping songs to the Psalter. These discussions combine to paint an extensive picture of musical worship in the Hebrew Bible, and show how ancient Israel's view of itself was informed through the musically rich institution of public worship.

Sacrifice

Helmer Ringgren writes, "All over the world, and throughout history, wherever mankind has worshiped divine beings, we encounter the practice of sacrifice."[15] Ancient Israel was no exception. Like the neighboring civilizations of Babylonia and Egypt, Israel had a highly developed, complex system of sacrifice. However, in contrast to the sacrifices of other peoples in the ancient world, Israel never considered the ritual to be a magical act that causes God to respond a certain way, but a sign of devotion, adoration and obedience.[16] To be sure, the sacrificial preparation incorporated aspects ostensibly symbolic of a meal, with the selection of choice pieces, the salting and cooking of meat, the inclusion of bread and wine, and use of the altar as a kind of "table"; but, unlike some other groups, Israel did not believe its deity to be dependent on food, drink or any form of worldly nourishment. These elements were probably a conservation of an older, more primitive ritual, and were emptied of their meaning in Israel's hands. Yehezkel Kaufmann makes this point: "Such terms and rites mean only that at one time sacrifice was considered food for the god."[17] That the God of Israel does not need sacrifice for sustenance is a theme emphasized in Psalm 50:10–13: "For mine is every animal of the forest, the beasts on a thousand mountains. I know every bird of the mountains, the creatures of the field are subject to Me. Were I hungry, I would not tell you, for mine is the world and all it holds. Do I eat the flesh of bulls, or drink the blood of goats?"

A few references to sacrifice are found in stories from the patriarchal age. Cain and Abel each presented "gifts" to God — Cain from his field and Abel from his flock (Gen. 4:3–4); and following the flood, Noah made a burnt offering (Gen. 8:20). As an implied or explicit practice, sacrifice also appears in the narratives of Abraham (Gen. 12:8; 21:3), Isaac (Gen. 26:25) and Jacob (Gen. 33:20; 35:7). The Bible records a covenant sacrifice involving Moses, during which Israel's relationship with God is sealed through burnt and peace offerings and the sprinkling of the animals' blood, half upon the altar and half upon the people (Exod. 24:3–8). In Canaan, the Israelites made sacrifices at various locales, including Bochim (Judg. 2:1-5) and Ophrah (Judg. 6:24–26). 1 Samuel cites the main center for ritual sacrifice as Shiloh (1 Sam. 1:3), though it mentions additional authorized sites, such as Beth-Shemesh (1 Sam. 6:14–15), Mizpah (1 Sam. 7:9), Ramah (1 Sam. 7:17) and Gilgal (1 Sam. 10:8). Under Saul, the primary place for sacrifice shifted to Nob (1 Sam. 21:1). With the dedication of Solomon's Temple, Jerusalem became the focal point of the ritual (1 Kgs. 8:5; 2 Chr. 5:6), although worshipers continued to frequent local high places (1 Kgs. 13:2; 2 Kgs. 14:4).

During the Second Temple period, Jerusalem was the sole official location of the sacrificial rite.[18] The importance of this centralized ritual is evidenced by its multiplicity of forms and functions: there were propitiatory (sin and guilt), dedicatory, burnt, meal, fellowship, libation, peace, thanksgiving, ordination and other types of sacrifices. Although libations of wine and meal offerings were an important feature of the ritual, the essential sacrifices were those of animals. The surrender of a living thing was in Israel's thinking a way of rendering the gift of life back to God. Such slaughter was crucial because it took the animal out of its everyday service, and sprinkled its life-carrying blood against the sanctified altar.[19] The extraction of blood was a powerful demonstration that life was being forfeited to God. The offering itself had to be the property of the one presenting it, and only domesticated animals raised to be eaten were deemed acceptable (Lev. 1:2). Such an animal was to be without blemish (Lev. 22:17–25) and could not be killed before it was eight days old (Lev. 22:26–30).

According to Eric Werner, all Temple music, regardless of the period, "was nothing more than an accessory to its sacrificial rite."[20] This view is supported in rabbinic literature, which links the Temple's musical activities with specific sacrifices.[21] However, Werner calls the relationship of music and sacrifice an "unsolved puzzle," and gives no expanded account of the connection between the two activities. The closest he comes is in comparing the fanfare associated with the ritual to a "banquet for honored guests, whereby quantities of burned meat, incense, and music were offered, to a sacred meal for a still anthropomorphically conceived deity, whose prestige demanded sacrifice, incense, praise, as well as musical entertainment."[22]

Though this is speculation on Werner's part, not the fruit of extensive investigation, his proposition does overlook the fact that Israel's sacrificial rite was, at its core, a way of focusing the worshipers' minds and hearts on God. Like the corpus of prayers that would later replace it, sacrifice was an external, routinized expression of what was ideally an inner and intensely felt attitude of dedication and gratitude to the divine source of life. It was an elaborate symbol of self-surrender and loyalty to the Almighty, which included a daily offering (*tamid*) representing a pledge of unbroken service to God, and the fragrant smoke of incense that served as a metaphor for prayers ascending heavenward.[23] Furthermore, as stated previously, the apparent anthropomorphic overtones of the sacrificial "banquet" were most likely a carry-over from earlier times, and were not foremost or even meaningful factors in Israel's consciousness.

Even so, Werner is right to point out that the Bible is silent on the issue of why music was sounded during sacrifice. Such silence, though, does not necessarily preclude any attempt at an explanation. There are at least two probable reasons for this musical accompaniment: one social and one theological. The social argument rests on the simple fact that Temple sacrifice was a communal affair. This was true of the two daily ceremonial offerings, which began and concluded each day's sacrifices, and was especially the case during annual feast days when multitudes of worshipers filed into the Temple from surrounding areas.[24] Feasts were not complete without guests, and public gatherings, religious or secular, were not complete without a musical backdrop.[25]

This basic explanation does bear some resemblance to Werner's idea of "banquet for honored guests"; but while he envisioned God at the center of the musical celebration, the argument that music stemmed from the ritual's social character merely draws a link between the Temple and other public gatherings where music was a natural and expected ingredient. This underscores the practical purpose of worship music in ancient Israel: it was meant for the people rather than for God, and was intended to draw attention to and enhance the collective tone of the event, amplifying feelings of common faith, heritage and purpose among participants.

Viewed theologically, the intent behind sacrifice's musical score was to help inspire the attentiveness and sincerity required of the ritual act.[26] As a focusing agent, music can bring increased sensitivity and engagement to what might otherwise be vacant or emotionless exercises. This has particular relevance for sacrifice, as several biblical prophets stressed the supremacy of intention over empty offerings, and the primacy of obedience over blood. From their pronouncements emerges a theme with relevance for later traditions of Judaism and Christianity: the insufficiency of devotional acts without undistracted mindfulness on the divine. In modern worship, music works as a safeguard against the mechanical tendencies inherent in the ritual routine, and provides sacred texts with a vehicle for spiritual elevation. In the sacrificial system, music (instrumental and vocal) would have aided in establishing a prayerful atmosphere and a mood suited for spiritual elevation.

The prophets of the First Temple were especially hostile toward what they perceived to be insincere sacrificial ritual (Amos 5:21–27; Hos. 6:6; Micah 6:6–8; Isa. 1:11–17; Jer. 6:20, 7:21–22). Isaiah, for instance, confronts Israel regarding God's disapproval of sacrifice without internal commitment: "What need have I of all your sacrifices?" says the Lord. "I am sated with burnt offerings of rams.... Bringing oblations is futile, incense is offensive to me" (Isa. 1:11–13). In place of such ritual, God commands: "Cease to do evil; learn to do good. Devote yourselves to justice; aid the wronged. Uphold the rights of the orphan; defend the cause of the widow" (Isa. 1:17). Jeremiah concurs that sacrifice is essentially worthless if presented by individuals who are uninterested in doing

5. Music and Public Worship

justice or are attracted to other gods (Jer. 7:1–11). God reminds the people of Israel that He did not direct their ancestors who fled Egypt to prepare burnt offerings, but to "Do my bidding, that I may be your God and you may be My people; walk only in the way that I enjoin upon you, that it may go well with you" (Jer. 7:23). In a succinct verse from Hosea, the people are instructed to ask God: "Forgive all my guilt and accept what is good; Instead of bulls we will pay the offerings of our lips" (Hos. 14:3).

These and other citations show that inner attitude was considered a prerequisite to any valid ritual expression. It is largely for this reason that music has been employed as an aid to prayer, inspiring and reinforcing contemplation and devotion throughout the ages. When one fails to resonate with the aim and message of ritual worship — be it sacrificial or linguistic — music can aid one in fully embracing the sacred moment. But this does not mean that music is a guaranteed antidote to the complacency that often comes with ritual behaviors. Prophetic condemnation of empty sacrifice was, after all, leveled against people who participated in the musical service of the Temple. The biblical prophets railed against elegant worship that lacked correspondence in the believer's inner experience. They also recognized that though sacred art may bring one closer to sacred truths, these truths have weight only when incorporated into one's life. For this reason, music did not always alleviate the problems inherent in the sacrificial routine. Nonetheless, it was used to guide worshipers into a proper state of mind. In short, music was associated with sacrifice because it was a powerful — if imperfect — defense against the disengagement that could occur during the ritual.

This brings us to a more general point regarding the suitability of musical accompaniment for religious ritual. As stated in previous chapters, music is linked to specific emotional responses. In Antiquity, considerable spiritual value was ascribed to the emotions stirred by music. Augustine, for one, defines music as "the art of good movement," believing that musical sounds have the potential to direct the soul toward divine communion.[27] Changes in musical properties, such as pitch, tone, timbre and dynamics, inspire corresponding changes in mood, which reflect alterations that occur in a person's inner state, or soul. Thus, the "good movements" in Augustine's definition are those of consciousness that lead the soul eventually into the "everlasting light of the divine One."[28]

Carrying this idea into the twentieth century, Herbert Antcliffe deems music to be the most effective means of conjuring feelings of adoration for God. He finds the sense of religion and the sense of music to be "intimately related in the minds of most people," and observes that in societies far and wide the complete expression of religious emotions requires the help of music.[29] The unparalleled capacity of music to foster and intensify religious sentiments and convictions is central to Antcliffe's high appraisal of the value of sacred music, as he considers religion without emotion to be impossible.

The emotional impact of the musical experience does much to support both the social and theological arguments for music's involvement in the sacrificial rite. Few forces are more powerful than music for consolidating the thoughts and feelings of a community. In biblical times as today, the unifying effect of music was an asset essential to public worship. Groups that hear or sing musical settings of the liturgy merge into a unified whole "like several flashlight beams splaying at random around a ceiling until they eventually land together superimposed in one brilliant burst of light."[30] On an individual level, the emotional pull of music helps focus the worshiper's attention on the spirit and subject matter of the sacred occasion. Prayers and ceremonies set to musical tones have an immediate and visceral effect. In other words, worship music is theology felt.

Music's emotionalizing effect was evidently a central and carefully constructed aspect of sacrificial worship. Beginning in the days of King David (1 Chr. 6:31–48), the music that accompanied sacrifice and other formal religious gatherings was performed mostly by Levites: a sacred caste charged with guarding the divine service and providing its musical support. From that point until the fall of the Second Temple in 70 C.E., the Levites served as the official and highly trained singers and instrumentalists of Israel, and were no doubt expert in music's mood stimulating properties and aptness for bringing people to divine devotion. As Israel's premiere class of musicians, they were knowledgeable and able to exploit to good purpose the musical conventions and associations that pervaded their culture. They evoked within listeners feelings appropriate for the occasion. It is also important to bear in mind that the music they performed was not abstract, but set to and guided by liturgical selections—many of which are preserved in the Book of Psalms.

Levites

According to the biblical account, when the Israelites' conquered the land of Canaan, each tribe was given a geo-political territory of its own. The only exception was the priestly tribe of Levi, which traced its lineage to Jacob's third son by Leah (Gen. 29:24) and produced Moses and Aaron (Exod. 2:1; 6:16–20; Num. 26:59). With the development of the Temple system, the Levites were designated as overseers of the Israelite religion and accorded special privileges and responsibilities. Those who were direct descendants of Aaron were delegated as high priests, set apart to lead the sacrificial service. The rest were assigned to the administration of tasks necessary for maintaining the divine service and keeping the Holy Ark (Num. 18). Some were trained as Temple architects and masons, gardeners, accountants, scribes, educators and street sweepers, while a select group was given the higher role of performing and supervising the music of divine worship, both vocal and instrumental.[31] According to 1 Chronicles 23:30, this caste of musicians was required "to stand every morning to thank and praise the Lord, and likewise in the evening." Their vocation was considered so important that those Levites who served as musicians were exempt from all other duties (1 Chr. 6:16).

Various explanations have been proposed for the appointment of Levites as religious functionaries. The most obvious is the divine selection of Moses and Aaron, which conferred upon the tribe special honor that was recognized by the other tribes. The Levites also earned distinction for not having shared in the heresy of the golden calf (Exod. 32:39), and for the actions of Phinehas, one of their tribesmen whose piety stayed a plague that was on course to destroy the sinning Israelites (Num. 25:1–15). On a more practical level, the standardization of the service benefited from the selection of a single, closely knit clan or group as its overseeing body. The Levites acted on behalf of all Israelites, and so helped to unify beliefs and practices throughout the tribal territories.

Jewish literature provides further rationale, giving attention to Levi's position as the ancestor of Moses, Aaron and the priestly class. He is described as a visionary to whom the rituals of the priesthood were revealed,[32] an expert in the laws of God[33] and a prophet who knew the mysteries of God[34]—all of which accounts for his unique place in Israel's history. From a linguistic standpoint, the name Levi comes from *lavah*, meaning "to join," "be connected" or "cling to." Therefore, some see it as an omen that Levi's descendants were destined to cleave to the service of God.[35] The Zohar takes a different approach, stating that it was those who listened to Levitical music who became attached to God: "Why were the Levites selected to sing in the Temple? Because the name Levi means cleaving. The soul of him who heard their singing at once cleaved to God."[36]

Much of what can be discerned regarding the activities of the Levitical musicians is found in First and Second Chronicles. The anonymous author — who was apparently himself a Levite and possibly a member of the Temple choir or orchestra[37] — elaborated on music's inclusion in the ritual life of ancient Israel. For instance, 1 Chronicles 6 lists David's chief musicians as Heman, Asaph and Ethan, each of whom led groups of Levitical musicians when the Ark was brought to Jerusalem. 1 Chronicles 23:5 recounts how, for special ceremonial events, David would appoint 4,000 of the Levites to praise God with "instruments which I devised for singing praises." At the dedication of Solomon's Temple, the Chronicler reports that the "trumpeters and the singers joined in unison to praise and extol the Lord" (2 Chr. 5:13). On the occasion of the crowning of the boy-king Joash, "The singers also played on instruments of music and led the singing of praise" (2 Chr. 23:13); and when Hezekiah ascended the throne to restore the Temple service, he ordered the Levites to play cymbals, harps and lyres, and sing praises with joy (2 Chr. 29:25–30).

The liturgical function of the Levitical musicians reached full force in the Second Temple. One hundred twenty-eight Levite singers are said to have returned from the Babylonian exile (Ezra 12:41), and during the inauguration of the Second Temple, the priests played trumpets while the Levites played cymbals and sang praises to God (Ezra 3:10–13). Nehemiah 12:27–43 describes the dedication of Jerusalem's wall, including a processional of two groups of priestly musicians marching in opposite directions and singing, blowing trumpets, playing cymbals and plucking harps and lyres. Rabbinic literature, which contains later recollections of Second Temple worship, explains that "There were never fewer than twelve Levites standing on the platform [as a choir] but there was no limit on the maximum number of singers."[38] The Levite orchestra is described as having two to six harps, nine or more lyres, two to twelve pipes and one cymbal.[39] In addition, some of the Levites are credited with developing techniques of virtuoso singing. For example, when the singer Hugras sang his virtuoso passages, he reportedly inserted his thumb into his mouth and placed his index finger under his nose, thereby producing unusual tones that astonished the attending priests.[40]

During the greater part of the Second Temple period, the Levites appear to have functioned exclusively as singers and gatekeepers. Their division into these positions was determined by family, as stipulated in 1 Chronicles 9:17–44.[41] Whereas the high priests conducted sacrifices and blew trumpets at the altar, the Levite choirs and orchestras were stationed on an adjacent dais.[42] A training period of five years was required for all Levitical work, beginning at age twenty-five (Num. 8:24), and the singers were admitted into the choir when they were thirty years old (1 Chr. 23:30). The choristers were required to serve until they reached age fifty,[43] when the singer's voice generally begins to decline. The Talmud adds that members of the Levite choir could continue singing until their voices were judged inadequate for divine service.[44]

Given that music in those days was passed on orally and that large quantities of liturgical songs had to be memorized, the actual training (informal or otherwise) most likely began much earlier than the prescribed age of twenty-five. This is confirmed in a rabbinic account, which states that junior choristers of Levite stock were known to join in the Temple singing.[45] The practice of apprenticeship is reminiscent of the prophetic schools described in the previous chapter, and is further suggested by evidence that Levitical musicians were divided into guilds.[46] Though children were not as a rule permitted to take part in the Temple service, the participation of child singers-in-training was allowed:

> None that was not of age could enter the Temple Court to take part in the service save only when the Levites stood up to sing; and they [the children] did not join the singing with harp and lyre, but with the mouth alone to add spice to the music. R. Eliezer b. Jacob says: They did not help to make up the required number [twelve Levites], nor did they stand on the platform; but they used to stand on the ground so that their heads were between the feet of the Levites.[47]

It should be reiterated that Levitical music, first and foremost, was an accessory to the sacrificial rite. Their music accompanied the daily (*tamid*) offerings, additional (*musaf*) sacrifices, the offerings of the people and so forth.[48] This ritualized worship environment necessitated an equally standardized set of liturgical offerings. The Levites chanted passages from the Pentateuch and presented a variety of psalms that covered a range of religious emotions, themes and circumstances. Among the uses of the psalms was the singing of *Hallel* (Pss. 113–118) on the three festivals, the singing of Psalm 30 at the bringing of the first fruits, and the various "psalms of the day."[49]

Following the destruction of the Second Temple, the centralized sacrificial rite and its musical accompaniment fell into near oblivion. According to Idelsohn, roughly two generations later the Levites themselves lost technical knowledge of the music.[50] Without the need for their services, and with the incorporation of instruments in worship all but abandoned — partly out of mourning for the Temple[51] — Levites had neither the desire nor the discipline needed to retain their skills. Moreover, their position as directors of the service was taken over by worship leaders in local synagogues — an institution that had its start during the Second Temple and replaced it after the fall of Jerusalem. Despite all this, the vocal intonations of the Psalter and Pentateuch were transplanted into the synagogue, and retained the character — if not the actual tones — of Levitical singing. Over time, psalmody and scriptural cantillation combined with a growing body of statutory prayer-chants to form the musical repertoire of the early synagogue.[52]

It is impossible to know for sure how the Levites' psalmody actually sounded. With the Diaspora that followed the Temple's destruction, Jews were scattered to various parts of the globe. This migration brought with it the practical and inevitable development of regional traditions, which shared a common core — holy scriptures, sacred history, ritual calendar, etc. — but took on diverse modes of cultural expression, including varied musical styles. Indeed, scholars have long recognized that no single melody is common to all Jewish groups.[53] Like the Jewish people, Jewish music does not exist in a vacuum; and whatever musical unification may have existed in the Temple has long since been erased by generation after generation of Jews living throughout the world and adapting local sounds as their own. In the words of one researcher, "Basic to all Jewish musics are their close ties to the musical traditions of their non–Jewish neighbors."[54]

The Book of Psalms

The Book of Psalms is a collection (or, more accurately, a collection of collections) of poetic prayers. The composite nature of the book is seen in its inclusion of smaller liturgical units, like the Song of Ascents (Pss. 120–134), the so-called Elohist psalms, which refer to God as Elohim instead of Lord (YHVH), and prayer clusters that begin or end with "hallelujah"—which may have originally been independent sub-collections.[56] The Psalter was not arranged with an overriding principle in mind; and since prayers of similar form are found elsewhere in the Hebrew Bible (e.g., 2 Sam. 23:1–7; Jon. 3; Hab. 3), it would seem that the book, while certainly prominent, was not the sole definitive source of psalms in ancient Israel. What is almost certain, though, is that the various chapters of the Psalter were preserved through usage in the Second and, in some cases, First Temple liturgies.[57]

The dating of the psalms is notoriously difficult. This is partly because they contain few overt references to specific events or people, and partly because their language tends to be archaizing, drawing upon older-sounding words. Added to this, many of the psalms containing historical references actually come from entirely different contexts and were only later attached to the event described.[58] To take two examples, both Psalms 57 and 142 are placed in the context of 1 Samuel 24:3–4, when David hid in a cave from his pursuer, King Saul. Each psalm fervently pleads for God's protection from enemies, a theme appropriate for the fleeing David: "I seek refuge in the shadows of your wings, until danger passes" (Ps. 57:2), and "save me from my pursuers, for they are too strong for me" (Ps. 142:7). However, this setting appears to be the editor's interpretation, intended to set the atmosphere in which the psalms were to be read; and the "cave" in the heading of Psalm 142 is viewed by some modern commentators as a metaphor for prison.[59]

The dates ascribed to certain psalms have also been subject to change according to trends in biblical scholarship. Critical scholars in the nineteenth century generally regarded the psalms as the product of the Maccabean era.[60] In later years, several of the psalms were dated back to the pre-exilic period; and current thought places a number of them in the exilic and postexilic ages.[61] Many researchers also maintain that during the earlier part of the Second Temple period, several psalms were composed, organized into collections and brought together with older collections to form the bulk of the Psalter as we have it today.[62] Others are content with the broad view that the Psalter was gradually compiled over a period of nearly six centuries.[63] It is also probable that some psalms contain an ancient core that was revised and expanded upon prior to the sealing of the book.[64]

Opinions differ as well regarding the authorship of the psalms. A tradition going back to biblical times attributes the entire book to King David, the sweet singer of Israel (1 Sam. 16:17–23), archetypal musician (Amos 6:5) and founder of the Temple's musical system (2 Chr. 23:18). This tradition is reinforced by chapters that include the phrase "a psalm of David" in their superscriptions, and link the text to an event in his life (Pss. 3; 18; 34; 51; 56). David as psalmist is a theme found in later texts as well. For instance, 2 Maccabees 2:13 refers to the "writings of David," and several New Testament passages mention psalms spoken by David (e.g., Mk. 12:36; Lk. 20:42). A version of Psalms from the Dead Sea Scrolls goes so far as to attribute 3,600 psalms to David, along with 450 additional "songs."[65]

The Psalter itself is much more modest in designating Davidic authorship, giving this pedigree to 73 of its 150 psalms. While these poems display the deep faith and artistic flare one would expect from a person like David, linguistic and contextual clues suggest that these headings were not original to the psalms, but rather derived from the conventional portrayal of David as a pious and uniquely gifted poet and musician.[66] So, as with the ascription of Proverbs to Solomon, Lamentations to Jeremiah and so forth, the identification of David as author of the psalms was perhaps a way for the ancients to assert the authority and divine inspiration of the text.[67]

A somewhat similar, though not entirely parallel, motivation led to the identification of Solomon as the author of Ecclesiastes. Solomon's attributed authorship has been viewed variously as part of the wider custom of putting wisdom in the mouths of monarchs,[68] a reference to Solomon's legendary wisdom,[69] and a way of framing the book as the king's autobiography.[70] Another possibility is offered by Brevard S. Childs, who argues that the popular view of the book as the final reflections of the wise king was intended to give weight to its verses attacking wisdom (e.g., 1:8), as if Solomon realized in his later years that the truly

5. Music and Public Worship

wise know the limits of wisdom.[71] But whatever the motivation, the book's content and language place it in the post-exilic period, well after Solomon's time, and its ascription to the king most certainly aided its reception as a definitive, sacred text.[72]

Even so, some recent scholarship questions the conventional tendency to disregard the historical veracity of the authorship and settings found in the psalms' superscriptions. Bruce Waltke *et al.* have outlined seven arguments in defense of the originality of the superscriptions, and the unlikelihood of editorial manipulation.[73] It is important to note that while these arguments can be used to support the authenticity of psalmic introductions in general, they aim primarily is to vindicate the notion of David as author. First, they note that the superscriptions appear in the earliest versions of the Psalms; no documentary evidence exists to deny their originality. Second, rubrics similar to biblical superscriptions are found in ancient liturgical texts of neighboring peoples, including the Sumerians, Akkadians and Egyptians. Third, some of the psalms ascribed to David are clearly of ancient origin, such as Psalm 29, which depends on a Canaanite background. Fourth, the words, images and parallelism found in Davidic psalms are attested in Ugaritic texts of David's time. Fifth, every biblical hymn found outside the Book of Psalms is affixed with a superscription (e.g., Exod. 15:1; Judg. 5:1; 1 Sam. 2:1; 2 Sam. 23:1; Isa. 38:9; Hab. 3:1), implying that these opening words are original with the text. Sixth, technical terms in these headings were obscure to the rabbis of the Tannaitic period (c. 70–200 CE), pointing to a gap in time between the composition of the psalms and their later Aramaic (and Greek) translations. Seventh, there are marked differences between the linguistic, structural, thematic and theological elements of the psalms and those of later imitative psalms found at Qumran. According to Waltke *et al.*, all of this indicates that the superscriptions predate editorial tampering and therefore leave open the possibility that David, "Israel's poet laureate," was indeed a psalmist.

These arguments are not without controversy. Others have pointed to inconsistencies in the superscriptions of different versions of the Book of Psalms, such as the Syriac Peshitta[73] and Greek Septuagin,[74] showing that depending on the agenda or point of view of the translators/editors, superscriptions were added or taken away with relative ease — a process that may have also occurred before and/or during the canonization of the Hebrew text.[75] It also bears mention that the Hebrew preposition "*le*," most regularly translated "of"—e.g., "of David," "a psalm of David" and the like—is a fluid term, and could mean "to David," "for David," "by David," "pertaining to David," "in honor of David" or "written in the style of David."[76] Some posit that the preface *le-David* merely signifies that the psalm received David's approval, was part of a series of "David-authorized" psalms, or was scribed by a subsequent king of the Davidic dynasty.[77] However, while such perspectives should not be dismissed out of hand, ascriptions of this type commonly denote direct authorship in Semitic languages, and so "of David" stands as the most accurate translation.[78]

Even with the claim of Davidic composition—within and outside of the Psalter—less than half of the psalms are actually attributed to him, and several other psalmists are mentioned by name. Asaph, a choirmaster who played cymbals before the Holy Ark (1 Chr. 16:4–7), is credited with a dozen psalms. The Korahites, a Levitical group descendant from a man who rebelled against Moses (Num. 16:1–34), are attached to eleven psalms. Two psalms bear Solomon's name, while Heman, Ethan and Moses grace the titles of one psalm each. The remaining chapters are of anonymous authors.

From a purely devotional standpoint, it can be assumed that the precise dating and authorship of the individual psalms did not have a significant impact on their liturgical value. Just as these issues matter little to present-day worshipers, the people of ancient Israel were presumably more interested in the message than historical details. Rather than being tangled up in specific ancient contexts, the psalms address a remarkable array of emotions and situations that speak to the common experiences of people of faith. Despite their sundry original contexts, the psalms give the impression of being a comprehensive "worship book of Israel," and "microcosm of the Bible as a whole."[79]

Most psalms fall into three general categories: hymns of praise, complaints (or laments) and thanksgiving prayers. Smaller subcategories also exist, most notably royal hymns (e.g., Pss. 2; 36; 119), psalms of God's enthronement (e.g., Pss. 93; 97; 99) and wisdom psalms (e.g., Pss. 1; 90; 127). The texts may utilize first person singular (individual) or plural (collective) language, and some exhibit movement from an individual to collective voice. But, whether they appear as personal or group prayers, all psalms are the property of the community by virtue of their inclusion in the Psalter and public performance.[80] Each psalm conveys a desire to reach out to the divine, experience His presence and maintain the lines of communication between earth and heaven. With heavy use of metaphors, imagery and lush language, they address spiritual and existential needs, stipulate ethical and behavioral guidelines, delineate doctrine and theology, and establish the mood and intent of the worship setting. The Psalter's extensive treatment of these central areas of religious life has ensured its place as an indispensable source of inspiration, contemplation and comfort across the ages.

Several prominent figures have written of the Psalter's lasting relevance and appeal. John Calvin, for instance, comments:

> [The Book of Psalms is] an anatomy of all parts of the soul, for there is not an emotion of which any one can be conscious that is not here represented as in a mirror. Or rather, the Holy Spirit has there drawn to the life all the griefs, sorrows, fears, doubts, hopes, cares, perplexities, in short, all the distracting emotions with which the minds of men are wont to be agitated.[81]

In like fashion, Martin Luther asks:

> Where does one find finer words of joy than in the Psalm of praise and thanksgiving? There you look into the hearts of all saints ... yes, as into heaven itself.... On the other hand, where do you find deeper, more sorrowful, more pitiful words of sadness than in the Psalms of lamentation? There again you look into the hearts of all the saints, as into death, yes, as into hell itself.... And that they speak these words to God and with God, this, I repeat, is the best thing of all.[82]

While much of the psalms' religious value owes to their potent and wide-ranging content, their literary form has also contributed to their popularity in ancient times and subsequent eras. The psalms were composed in a rhythmic style, usually regarded as poetry.[83] This is musically relevant, since poetry is an auditory medium closely related to (and often identical with) music. In psalm poetry especially, there is a direct link between structure and mode of delivery — that is, singing.[84]

The most common poetic technique employed is parallelism, where the second line of a verse corresponds to the first. Typical of this form is synonymous parallelism, in which both parts of the verse state essentially the same thing.[85] For example, Psalm 6 contains the verse, "The

Lord will hear my pleading, the Lord will accept my prayer" (v. 9). A number of psalms are also written in acrostics, with the first letter of each verse flowing through an alphabetical sequence (e.g., Pss. 9; 25; 34; 112; 145). This device shows a concern for aesthetics, attention to pleasing the ear and a desire to effectively communicate a message.[86] Other poetic tools found in the Psalter include chiastic arrangement (ABBA or ABCBA), which arranges concepts or ideas in a symmetric pattern (e.g., the sequence of wicked-righteous-righteous-wicked in Ps. 1:5–7), and *inclusio*, where a specific word or line is found at the beginning and ending of a psalm. This is seen, for example, in the identical first and last verses of Psalm 136: "O give thanks to the Lord for He is good, His steadfast love endures forever."

Poetic ingredients such as these support the view of the Psalter as an anthology of song lyrics. Indeed, it is often stated that most (if not all) of the psalms were originally meant to be sung.[87] With the institution of the elaborate Temple service, the Psalter—even in its earliest and simplest form—became the liturgical hymnal of Israel.[88] While the selection of prayer-texts for inclusion in the Psalter certainly owed to factors of content—ritual function, historical significance, richness of language, etc.—it can be asserted that its editing was guided in part by musical considerations. Because music played a large role in the public worship of ancient Israel, the efficacy of sacred texts stemmed from both the power of the words and their adaptability to musical rendering.[89] Thus, the psalms included in the Bible are likely those that proved from experience to be the most "singable."

The importance of praising God with music is affirmed throughout the Book of Psalms. The term "psalm" derives from the Greek *psalmos*, an adaptation of the Hebrew *mizmor*, meaning "a song with string accompaniment." The Hebrew title for the book in rabbinic and subsequent Jewish literature is *Sefer Tehillim*, which roughly translates to "Book of Praises." The fundamental essence of the book is revealed when both names are combined: it is a collection of musical prayers that, whether voicing thanksgiving or lament, heap praise upon God. Significantly, too, early rabbinic writings propose that it was the very act of singing and playing that compelled the psalmists to compose their prayers, underlining the intuitive link between music and worship.[90]

Of the 150 biblical psalms, fifty-seven are designated *mizmor* and thirty are titled *shir* ("song"). Singing is referenced over sixty times, and musical instruments are named throughout the book, including various types of plucked strings, pipes, trumpets and hand percussion. These instruments—sometimes labeled "instruments of song"—were closely united with vocal music. They provided rhythmic support and accentuation, performed introductions, interludes and conclusions for the psalms, and perhaps played melodies in unison with the singers, as is still heard in some Eastern traditions.[91]

Moreover, it should not escape our notice that the majority of technical terms unique to the Psalter have musical connotations. Superscriptions contain instructions for performance, like *la-menazze'ah*, a cue for the musical director found in fifty-five psalms, and *maskil*, a sign calling for a specific skill to be used in the musical presentation of thirty-three psalms. Other headings are thought to specify familiar melodies to which the psalms were to be sung. These include *Al Shoshanim*, "On the Lillies" (Pss. 45; 69; 80), *Al Tashhet*, "Do Not Destroy" (Pss. 57–59), *Al Mahalat*, "For Sickness" (Pss. 53; 88), and *Al Ayyelet ha-Shahar*, "On the Hind of the Morning" (Ps. 22). Still others specify instruments to be played, such as *Al ha-Gittit*, "On the Gittith" (Pss. 8; 81; 84), *Al ha-Sheminit*, "On an Eight-Stringed Instrument" (Pss. 6; 12) and *Al Alamot*, on a type of flute or pipe (Ps. 46). Two musical terms are also found in the body of numerous chapters: *selah*, a term marking a change in performance found in thirty-nine psalms, and *higgayon*, a musical instruction signaling a glissando or flourish found in Psalms 9, 19 and 92.[92]

We cannot hear the ancient music of the psalms, and so any attempt at describing its various qualities is, in the end, hypothetical. Notwithstanding, the book itself does give sufficient evidence for the antiphonal singing of many of the psalms. This style of performance would have featured a musical back and forth between the choir and congregation, two semi-independent choirs, or soloist and choir.[93] Antiphonal singing is used to achieve a dual aim: stressing the central message of a verse through a reiterating exchange, and in the case of group responses, facilitating participation through the interplay of intricate passages sung by skilled singers and formulaic statements sung by the laity.[94]

In the Temple, this latter method was both a practical way to appease the worshipers' urge to add their voices to divine petition and praise, and to skirt potential problems rooted in the fact that the populace was not entirely familiar with the psalm texts or the manner of their performance. This was accomplished with the responses of "Blessed be the Lord," "Amen and Amen," "His faithfulness is forever" or some other brief refrain, and is alluded to in the proclamation in Psalm 89:16: "Happy are those who express these joyful shouts; O Lord, they walk in the light of your presence."

Hermann Gunkel finds evidence for antiphonal liturgical song in Nehemiah 12:27, where the Levites "wherever they lived, were sought out and brought to Jerusalem to celebrate a joyful dedication [of the wall] with thanksgiving, and with song, accompanied by cymbals, harps, and lyres."[95] According to Gunkel, these dedication songs were sung by twin choirs, who started at a common point and circled the walls in opposite directions, singing back and forth. Gunkel locates additional hints of this practice—which he describes as "one choir throw[ing] a ball to the other ... and the other catch[ing] it in order to return it to the first"—in Psalms 19:3, 42:8, and 65:9.[96]

The probability of antiphonal singing between soloist and choir is addressed, among other places, in rabbinic commentaries on Psalm 118.[97] This victory psalm was likely reformulated to celebrate the return from the exile and rebuilding of the Temple, and may have been sung liturgically as part of a ceremony upon entering the Temple. Its function as a processional is suggested in verses 18 and 19: "Open the gates of victory for me that I may enter them and praise the Lord. This is the gateway to the Lord—the victorious shall enter through it." Importantly, the text alternates between individual and collective praise, implying a prescribed exchange between leader and choir. This is evidenced in antiphonal snatches in the psalm's opening verses (1–4):

> *Leader:* Praise the Lord for He is good,
> His steadfast love is eternal. Let Israel declare,
> *Choir:* His steadfast love is eternal.
> *Leader:* Let the house of Aaron declare,
> *Choir:* His steadfast love is eternal.
> *Leader:* Let those who fear the Lord declare,
> *Choir:* His steadfast love is eternal.

The musical details in the Psalter are not matched by cultic descriptions. None of the psalms provide explicit information about the type of priestly ceremonies to which they were attached. Even the section called

5. Music and Public Worship

Shir ha-Ma'alot, "Song of Ascents" (Pss. 120–134), may or may not be, as the Mishnah posits, an allusion to the fifteen steps on which the Levitical musicians stood during the "drawing of water" ceremony of Sukkot.[98] Some scholars simply group *ma'alot* with the other musical terms in the book, signaling some sort of gradational style of musical execution.[99] Still, there is ample reason to support the relationship of cult and liturgy in ancient Israel. Arguing from a utilitarian standpoint, Nahum M. Sarna writes "without some association between the two it would be extremely difficult to account for the preservation and transmission of the individual compositions over long periods of time until they became gathered into collections and ultimately canonized as a corpus."[100]

The place of the psalms within the cult is treated extensively in the writings of Sigmund Mowinckel. Taking a "cult functional" approach, Mowinckel maintains that all of the psalms were connected to the cult in terms of origin and intention. As such, their content was not the result of private experiences, but the direct expression of the Temple singers who composed them for liturgical worship. In this view, psalm themes—even when they appear linked to an event or scribed in first person singular language—are in fact intended as universal, linking the individual to the community. Not unlike Durkheim, Mowinckel sees Israel's cultic rituals as a means of bringing people together in a sacred force, and argues that it was through these communal acts—not private devotion—that individuals received divine blessing.[101]

Placing this general claim in a specific setting, Mowinckel connects more than forty psalms to a hypothetical autumnal New Year festival.[102] His grounds for this celebration come from the Babylonian New Year feast, which celebrated the rule of the chief deity Marduk and the corresponding earthly reign of the king of Babylonia. The king played a major role in this dramatic celebration, and was a central figure in cultic activities more generally. Mowinckel proposes that this festival, which had pre–Davidic roots but apparently lingered in the Israelites' consciousness, was the basis for Israel's own autumn New Year commemoration linked with the seasonal harvest (Exod. 23:16; 34:24; Lev. 23:23–24). According to Mowinckel, the ceremonies culminated with the procession of the Ark to the Temple, representing God's enthronement, and the singing of "enthronement psalms" praising God as king (e.g., Pss. 47; 93; 95–99). Following Babylonian practice, this ritual coincided with the reaffirmation of the Israelite king, and was proclaimed in "royal psalms" that affirmed his status as the earthly embodiment of God's heavenly kingship (e.g., Pss. 2; 89; 110).

Though Mowinckel constructed this festival without direct biblical support, the Bible does contain a few indications of liturgical ritual. For example, there is the priestly benediction (Num. 6:22–26) with which Aaron and his sons blessed the Israelites, and the cultic liturgy of the first fruits (Deut. 26:1–11). Solomon's Temple included "prayer and supplication" (1 Kgs. 8:28), while prophetic books attest to a statutory Temple liturgy (e.g., Isa.1:15; Jer. 33:11; Amos 5:23). From the early stages of public worship to its highpoint in the Second Temple, set liturgies played a central part in the ceremonials of Jerusalem and local shrines. Whether the occasion was a national festival or regular offering, the singing of psalms would have been a regular component of public worship.

It can, then, be concluded that much of the Psalter was sung during the sacrificial ritual, especially in the highly developed system of the Second Temple. A tradition likely developed that paired psalm sets with certain sacrificial events so that, as Sendrey argues, "the daily burnt, expiatory, laudatory offerings and libations had all a different musical layout, which was strictly regulated like any other part of the ritual."[103] As mentioned, the Psalter itself lacks obvious clues as to which psalms were employed at which times; but rabbinic literature helps fill in the gaps, even as some of its comments reside in the realm of conjecture. The Mishnah lists psalms designated for each day of the week. It describes the Levites singing Psalm 24 on the first day, Psalm 42 on the second, Psalm 82 on the third, Psalm 94 on the fourth, Psalm 81 on the fifth, Psalm 93 on the sixth, and Psalm 92 on the Sabbath.[104] These psalms, it claims, were intoned when the High Priest initiated the daily libation offering.[105]

Though it is impossible to recapture the setting and sound of the psalms' original performance, the Psalter's unique beauty and religious value has ensured its continued popularity in Jewish and Christian worship. Just as the psalms' aptitude for expressing adoration, offering thanks, confessing sin, seeking forgiveness and voicing petition motivated Israel to retain them after the Temple was destroyed, these qualities account for the important place they still hold. Though they voice the concerns and worldview of a specific place, time and culture "wholly at variance with our own," the psalms are remarkably timeless.[106] They appear frequently in the liturgical traditions of both Judaism and Christianity, and have for centuries been a source for private reflection and devotion. Medieval Jewish literature notes the psalms' enduring applicability, writing "Whatever David says in his book pertains to himself, to all Israel, and to all times"[107]; and Christian worshipers have "not yet sung them dry."[108]

The infusion of psalms into modern worship represents a continuity of religious practice from ancient days, as well as a persistent awareness of the spiritual significance of prayerful words set to music. For example, *Kabbalat Shabbat*, the Jewish service that welcomes the Sabbath, begins with the singing of Psalms 95–99 and 26. These psalms not only express a common theme of God as master of the universe — a concept central to the weekly commemoration of Creation — but also contain language linking song and praise: "Come, let us sing joyfully to the Lord" (Ps. 95); "Sing a new song, sing to the Lord, all the earth" (Ps. 96); "Raise a shout to the Lord, all the earth, break into joyous songs of praise" (Ps. 98); and so on.

Psalms are likewise essential to Christian religious expression, holding "a place in the services of every church of Christendom where praise has been offered."[109] In the nineteenth century, Edward Irving observes that psalm singing helped forge common ground between theologically and ritually opposed Christian groups. Following St. Ambrose, who says that psalmody "unites those who disagree, makes friends of those at odds, brings together those who are out of charity with one another,"[110] Irving writes:

> From whatever point of view any Church hath contemplated the scheme of its doctrine, by whatever name they have thought good to designate themselves, and however bitterly opposed to each other in Church government or observance of rules, you will find them all, by harmonious consent, adopting the Psalms as the outward form by which they shall express the inward feelings of Christian life.[111]

Psalm 150

The Psalter's most striking musical depiction is found in Psalm 150. Walter Brueggemann describes the psalm as "nothing other than a glad offer of self in lyrical surrender to the God appropriately addressed in praise."[112] Another scholar characterizes it as "a powerful exhortation to the people of God to praise Him in whatever way possible."[113] While most psalms include reasons for praising God, Psalm 150 provides no specific motivation. It focuses instead on the appropriateness of worshiping God through music, listing a variety of instruments to be played in His service. In the framework of the Psalter, Psalm 150 functions as a return to a primal mode of communication with the sacred, in which the complexities of theology and existential questions are replaced by "a joyful noise."[114] It uses the command to praise—*hallelu*—in each of its six short verses, and the entire psalm reads as a directive to heap glory and honor upon the divine by way of musical sounds:

> Hallelujah.
> Praise God in His sanctuary;
> praise Him in the sky, His stronghold.
> Praise Him for His mighty acts;
> praise Him for His exceeding greatness.
> Praise Him with blasts of the horn;
> praise Him with harp and lyre.
> Praise Him with timbrel and dance;
> praise Him with lute and pipe.
> Praise Him with resounding cymbals;
> praise Him with loud-clashing cymbals.
> Let all that breathes praise the Lord.
> Hallelujah.

Psalm 150 is among the Bible's hymns of praise—a psalm-type that also includes Psalms 8, 19, 29, 33, 65, 67, 68, 96, 98, 100, 103–105, 111, 113, 114, 117, 135 and 145–149.[115] Of all the chapters in the Psalter, these hymns are perhaps the most readily adaptable to communal devotion. Each exudes a sense of urgency, as if the author could not help but sing praises to God and invite others to do the same. The impulse to sing joyous songs to deities is common to most ancient and modern faiths. Hymns are listed among the oldest and most universal religious acts; whether they are spontaneous outbursts or structured liturgical pieces, these songs are a natural and integral part of the human-divine relationship.[116] While joy and gratitude inspire words exalting God, the emotions accompanying such words find most suitable expression in music.

5. Music and Public Worship

Augustine derives a concise definition of hymns from his analysis of the Book of Psalms: "Hymns are praises of God with song; hymns are songs containing the praise of God. If there be praise, and it is not of God, it is not a hymn; if there be praise, and praise of God, and it is not sung, it is not a hymn. If it is to be a hymn, therefore, it must have three things: praise, and that of God, and song."[117] Augustine recognizes the essential partnership of text and music in praising the divine. Because God transcends human vocabulary, and because moments for extolling God tend to be highly emotional, we instinctively set praise to music, the language beyond words. As he explains, hymn singing is "the voice of a soul poured out in joy and expressing."[118]

The majority of hymn psalms were originally sung at the Jerusalem Temple and other holy places during festival celebrations.[120] For the most part, they consist of two main sections: a summons to praise and the reasons or motivation for praise, such as God's manifest goodness or might. A succinct example of this structure is Psalm 117:

> Praise the Lord, all the nations;
> extol Him, all you peoples,
> for great is His steadfast love toward us;
> the faithfulness of the Lord endures forever.
> Hallelujah.

Significantly, this rhetorical movement is absent from Psalm 150, the closing doxology of the Book of Psalms and "the most extreme and unqualified statement of praise in the Old Testament."[121] Unlike other hymns, which call attention to certain characteristics and/or feats of God, Psalm 150 is a statement of "pure praise," implying that God is praiseworthy simply because He is God. It is located literally and theologically at the end of the Psalter, after Israel's deepest thoughts and feelings have been fully conveyed. Brueggemann points out that when all the laments have been voiced and all the pleas have been uttered, what remains is this glad offering "without vested interest, calculation, desire or hidden agenda."[122] Psalm 150 is a triumphant "Hallelujah chorus," putting a seal of praise on what is the Bible's longest book and most profound articulation of the complex relationship of God and humanity.

The Psalter's 150 chapters are organized into five books. This structure is meant to draw a link between Psalms and the Torah, which is comprised of the five books of Genesis, Exodus, Leviticus, Numbers and Deuteronomy. The relationship of these two anthologies is emphasized in Psalm 1, a prayer selected to introduce the entire collection specifically because it stresses the importance of Torah study.[123] A tenth-century *midrash* on that psalm states, "Moses gave the five books of the Torah to Israel, and David gave the five books of the Psalms to Israel."[124] However, this arrangement came about relatively late and reflects the book's evolution from a liturgical collection, as used in the Second Temple, to a Torah-like book suitable for study.[125]

Each of the five divisions concludes with a doxological statement. The doxologies marking the end of the first four books are written as formulaic blessings. Book I, containing Psalms 1 to 41, concludes "Blessed is the Lord, God of Israel, from eternity to eternity. Amen and Amen" (41:14). Book II, comprised of Psalms 42 to 72, ends with the words, "Blessed is the Lord, God of Israel, Who alone does wondrous things; blessed be His glorious name for ever, and let His glory fill the whole world. Amen and Amen. End of the prayers of David son of Jesse" (72:18–20). Book III, spanning Psalms 73 to 89, finishes with the verse, "Blessed be the Lord to eternity. Amen and Amen" (89:53). Book IV, made up of Psalms 90 to 106, closes with "Blessed is the Lord, God of Israel, from eternity to eternity. And let all the people say Amen. Hallelujah" (106:48). Book V includes Psalms 107 to 150, and has as its closing doxology the entirety of Psalm 150. Rather than employing a simple formula like the other four books, the fifth uses the exuberant verses of the final psalm as its own conclusion and the culmination of the Psalter as a whole.

As mentioned, Psalm 150 lacks specifics regarding God's attributes and justification for giving Him praise. However, it does present explicit directions of *how* God should be worshiped. It decrees that Israel praise God with ram's horn, harp, lyre, timbrel, dance, lute, pipe, resounding cymbals and loud-clashing cymbals— a diverse array of instruments perhaps symbolic of the manifold attributes of God. Jewish thought maintains that the tones produced on these instruments were capable of arousing the full spectrum of human emotions[126]; and by devoting half of the six-verse psalm to naming wind, string and percussion instruments, the psalmist seems to imply that God should be praised in every way possible.[127] Additionally, it relates where God is to be praised: in

"His sanctuary"—the Temple where formal ritual takes place—as well as in the "sky, His stronghold"—a metaphor intimating that, since God occupies the vast expanses of the heavens, He can be approached anywhere in the world.[128]

The previous 149 psalms explore the wide scope of liturgical expression, crying out to God in anguish, expressing confidence in His mercy, promising to praise Him for anticipated deliverance, and celebrating His presence and deeds in the world. They stem from a steadfast belief in the efficacy of prayer: the ability of pleas and praises to demonstrate faithfulness to God.[129] Psalm 150, however, draws attention to the insufficiency of words—even when they are sung—to express divine praise. It functions simultaneously as the euphoric climax of the Psalter and a humble recognition that, while God is certainly deserving of glory, the diverse, heartfelt and often lengthy psalm texts cannot fully capture the vastness of His works or character. For instance, Psalm 68, an extended and detailed hymn of praise, expounds God's punishment of the wicked, uplifting of the downtrodden, manifestation in nature, and involvement in specific episodes in Israel's history. But its message remains confined within the limits of words. Heschel notes that such texts require music to "[reach] out toward a realm that lies beyond the reach of verbal propositions."[130] Psalm 150, then, seems to announce that the effectiveness of praise is dependent more on its musical presentation than its exalted words.

This is further seen in the psalm's final verse: "Let all that breathes praise the Lord." Judah Halevi, the twelfth-century Hebrew poet, interprets this phrase to mean "every breath," referring to the endless possibility of melodies that can be sung in praising God.[131] Importantly, this verse does not use the standard psalmic injunction to "sing" to God. Instead, it endorses the use of breath to create melody, drawing a distinction between song (words set to music) and the vocal instrument itself.

The human voice has been called "the fine instrument of God's making."[132] A nineteenth-century poem echoes this sentiment: "No melody is so charming as vocal music. How divine a thing is the human voice!—divine, indeed, literally, since God made it; whereas the sweetest instrument of music that ever soothed the heart of the sorrowful was, after all, but of man's creation."[133] All other species of musical instruments—aerophones, idiophones, membranophones, chordophones and electronic—are fashioned by human hands; but the voice, theologically understood, is an instrument God created specifically for the purpose of giving Him praise. This does not mean that every sentiment one utters must be explicitly directed toward the divine, but that the sounds that emanate from the mouth, whether of tones or language, are imbued with the potential to glorify God. This seems to underlie the rabbinic teaching that with every breath one takes (i.e., every vocalization) one must praise God.[134] Musically, this position alludes to the fact that words sung to a melody are limited in time and expressiveness: when the words end, so does the melody. However, a wordless tune can be repeated endlessly, allowing the singer to pour out the contents of his or her soul without the hindrance of specific concepts or images, or self-conscious awareness of musical form.

Interestingly, the merging of joy, devotion and wordless songs is treated in the writings of Augustine. He describes the effectiveness of wordless songs in communicating an all-consuming sense of divine joy. In his commentary on Psalm 33:3, Augustine asks: "What does singing in jubilation signify? It is to realize that words cannot communicate the song of the heart."[135] He argues that this inner-song is best expressed through what he called *jubilus*: a spontaneous, wordless musical outpouring of one's spirit before God. "In this way," he writes, "the heart rejoices without words and the boundless expanse of rapture is not circumscribed by syllables."[136]

Augustine's position is nearly identical to that of Hassidic leader Rabbi Shnuer Zalman of Liadi (1747–1813), who sums up the impetus behind wordless devotional tunes known as *niggunim*: "Melody is the speech of the soul, but words interrupt the stream of emotion."[137] Although these men lived in vastly different times and places, and espoused beliefs that were in many ways incompatible, they recognized the limitations of language and the power of wordless tunes to harness, convey and amplify the joy felt in God's presence. Underlying the *niggun* and *jubilus* is a common belief that when it comes to the emotional side of religious experience, music speaks louder than words.

In addition to its liturgical role, the Psalter is widely employed as a source of healing. The psalms most frequently used to this end are the laments, which describe a situation of distress and cry out to God for

5. Music and Public Worship

assistance. They are characterized by words of tension and hope for release, and have obvious resonance for those struggling with illness or other hardship. This lament formula is encapsulated in the opening words of Psalm 102: "A prayer of the lowly man when he is faint and pours forth his plea before the Lord." But there is also potential for healing within the psalms of praise, particularly as they fervently endorse the creation of music. Music responds to illness more naturally than speech. As a form of psychological and medical treatment, music is used to ease anxiety in surgical patients, aid in physical rehabilitation, treat the elderly, put cancer patients more at ease, and so forth.[138] The ability of musical tones to promote wellness, relaxation and healing inspired the development of the field of music therapy. In times of despair, when the restrictive precision of speech gives way to "a thousand moods and ten thousand shapes," music is an especially powerful vehicle of expression.[139]

Of particular interest is the healing power of the wordless melodies mentioned above. In Jewish practice, these continuous chants, consisting of "nonsense" syllables (like *Yai dai dai*), are used to bring stillness to the mind and restfulness to the spirit, subduing negative or distracting thoughts as they arise. The singing of these melodies is perhaps the most unfettered form of musical production, free of the intellectual demands of remembering words to be sung or notes to be played, and exhibiting a level of repetition and predictability that is far more soothing than the patterns of ordinary speech.[140] There are, in fact, many quantifiable health benefits associated with the sounding of the vocal instrument. For instance, a Swedish study of over twelve thousand people found that singing promotes longevity,[141] and the deep breathing required of singing has been shown to enhance the immune system.[142]

It is therefore appropriate that Rabbi Nachman of Breslov (1772–1810) included Psalm 150 in his list of ten "healing psalms." Nachman considered these psalms a general remedy (*tikkun hak'lali*), and recommended that they be recited when one feels diminished.[143] They vary in subject and mood, moving from joy (Ps. 10) to forgiveness (Ps. 32), suffering (Ps. 41), longing (Ps. 42), deliverance (Ps. 59), affliction (Ps. 77), human finitude (Ps. 90), thanksgiving (Ps. 105), restoration of Jerusalem (Ps. 137) and musical praise (Ps. 150). With their wide range of themes, concerns and contexts, these carefully chosen chapters are a representation in miniature of the entire Book of Psalms, in which Psalm 150 provides affirmation of music's healing qualities.

Six Songs in the Psalter

As Psalm 150 demonstrates, the performance of liturgical prayers in the Temple aroused and reinforced a profound awareness of God. Whether its theme is praise or petition, rejoicing or suffering, each psalm reinforces the belief that the entirety of human experience is influenced and judged by God.[144] This God-consciousness was a defining trait of ancient Israel, as Charles H. Spurgeon notes in his commentary on Psalm 29: "God is everywhere conspicuous, and all the earth is hushed by the majesty of his presence."[145] Traveling through a range of theological insights, historical reflections, ethical teachings and inspirational verses, the Psalter served as a guidebook for how to conceive of and address God, and how to form and live within a good society. As this chapter has shown, it was not the text alone but words wed to music that helped shape and bolster Israel's worldview.

To better understand the influence of psalm singing on biblical life, it is worthwhile to examine the work of neuroscientist and musician Daniel J. Levitin, who sees six types of songs—friendship, joy, comfort, knowledge, religion and love—as playing a necessary role in facilitating the development of human society. In Levitin's analysis, based on a combination of scientific research and anecdotal findings, these song-types comprise the "soundtrack of civilization." In every age, they have provided a medium for sharing information, strengthening bonds, asserting identities, imparting wisdom and facilitating a host of other actions and attitudes that define a people. It should, then, come as no surprise that the Book of Psalms—Israel's anthology of song lyrics[145] and the "mapping of Israel's life with YHWH"[146]—includes several chapters that fit into Levitin's six categories.

Of course, this does not imply that the rich content of the psalms lends itself to easy stereotyping or reduction to a single, basic concept—especially as many of them cross genres and address more than one theme. Still, it is notable that these songs, fundamental to the development and maintenance of a culture, are found throughout the Psalter.

5. Music and Public Worship

To illustrate this point, it will suffice to examine a few psalms rather than placing each of them into one of these six genres—an endeavor that, while possible, exceeds the limits of this study. Such an overview will contribute to an understanding of the Psalter as Israel's defining songbook, as well as give further credence to the view of Israel as a musical people.

Levitin observes that throughout human history friendship songs have encouraged and accentuated bonds between members of a group, and bolstered unity in activities ranging from warfare to worship.[147] According to Levitin, the combination of these songs' content — stressing common beliefs, sentiments and goals— and communal musical production — bringing people into synchronized feelings and movements— cultivates trust and solidarity among participants.[148] Whether they are sung in unison or performed by professionals in a public setting (as with the Levitical musicians), the emotions stirred by such songs lead people to specific collective actions: battle, ritual enactments, interpersonal dealings, etc.

Psalm 133 is the Psalter's clearest example of a friendship song. It begins with the verse, "How good and how pleasant it is that brothers dwell together" (v. 1), and continues with a blessing of Zion (vv. 2–3). Though difficult to interpret, these words most probably expressed hope for the reunification of the ancient kingdoms of Israel and Judah.[149] Viewed in light of Levitin, this recognition of common identity and longing for unity was not intended as an idle statement, but as a call to take some sort of action toward this goal, however futile it may have been. On a general level, the psalm reminded worshipers of the goodness of fellowship, and of their common membership in a sacred community. A similar theme is explored in Psalm 117, the shortest hymn in the Psalter. Rather than intra-group cohesion, it conveys the desire that all peoples of the earth recognize their unity under the one true God: "Praise the Lord, all you nations; extol Him, all you peoples, for great is His steadfast love toward us; the faithfulness of the Lord endures forever. Hallelujah." This is friendship in the grandest sense, and its impassioned singing caused worshipers to reflect on the thread of unity, drawn by the Creator, that binds humanity as a whole.

Another of the Psalter's recurring motifs is singing out for joy. The seemingly natural convergence of song and joy is made explicit in several psalms (e.g., Pss. 4; 9; 16; 32; 68; 100), and dozens more allude to the connection. According to Levitin, ebullient texts set to appropriately joyous melodies usually accompany a positive outlook.[150] They not only brighten the listeners' mood, lifting them from the doldrums or heightening positive emotions already felt, but also serve as mental inspiration, encouraging the listener to embrace the optimistic point of view of the song's creator.

The association of music and joy is made in psalms of praise. These prayer-songs are indicative of a phenomenon innate to the human experience: it is oftentimes not enough to simply speak or read words of elation and gratitude; these emphatic statements beg for musical accompaniment. The suitability of song in moments of great delight is described in Psalm 98: "Make a joyful noise to God, all the earth, break into joyous songs of praise" (v. 4.). Evidently composed following a military victory, the psalm extols God for displaying "His triumph in the sight of the nations" (v. 2). The author, consumed with jubilation, invites all of humanity to join him in singing divine praise. He even imagines things of nature — trees, hills, rivers, etc. — forming a chorus to glorify their maker: "Let the sea and all within it thunder, the world and its inhabitants; let the rivers clap hands, the mountains sing joyously together at the presence of God ..." (vv. 7–8). As such, Psalm 98 illustrates two natural impulses: translating joy into song and viewing the world as a reflection of our own emotional states. As Levitin would point out, the psalm verifies the positive outlook that comes with joyful singing, and depicts the psalmist inspiring others to sing along, thereby adopting his optimism.

Songs of comfort also have a beneficial impact. Most songs contain repetitive elements, such as rhythms and melodic motifs, which supply a degree of redundancy lacking in plain speech. Levitin finds in this predictability a uniquely soothing quality, especially when the content of the song relates to hardship and loss.[151] In ancient days as in the present, music was understood to unlock emotional dimensions of faith that would otherwise be out of reach.[152] This is apparent in lament psalms, the largest single category in the Psalter.[153] The music of these psalms likely provided comfort for performers and listeners. Through the act of singing to God for physical healing, security, refuge or victory over enemies,[154] worshipers presumably gained a sense of confidence or security, regardless of the ultimate outcome. Thus, lament psalms can be understood as an ancient form of community music therapy, in which the group attains a sense of comfort or catharsis through communal singing. By singing them on fast days and other times of communal mourning or uncertainty, the psalms were able to impart a pleasant feeling of social wellbeing.

Psalm 44 is illustrative of the intersection of music, text and comfort found in lament psalms. It is scribed in communal language, reflecting the need for the community to remain unified through difficult situations. The psalm's three sections — invocation, request and motivation — are written in first-person plural form. It begins with a hymn appealing to God's past deliverance: "our fathers have told us the deeds You performed in their time, in days of old" (vv. 2-9). This is followed by a three-part request, consisting of a complaint about the Israelites' current situation ("You do not go with our armies") (vv. 10-17), a protestation of innocence ("Our hearts have not gone astray") (vv. 18-23), and the petition itself ("Awaken, do not reject us forever") (vv. 24-26). The final verse offers a motivation: "redeem us, as befits Your faithfulness" (v. 27). Like other psalms of lament, Psalm 44 acknowledges that the realities of life often run counter to religious teachings, hard times are only temporary, and continued dedication to God and community will bring about positive change. It was in this way that Psalm 44 — and lament psalms in general — imbued worshipers with a sense of solace and wellbeing.

Psalm singing was also a mode of teaching theology and ethics. The poetic features of these prayer-songs — meter, assonance, alliteration, etc. — combined with presumably memorable melodies to help in the recall of information and ensure the lasting impact of the message. As Levitin notes, songs give form and structure that jointly fix, and limit possible alternatives, in word choices.[155] Through the mutually reinforcing constraints of text and melody, the message is seared into the memory, and can be recreated at virtually any time in near perfect performance.

Many psalm texts exhibit music's didactic role. Of course, without knowledge of the actual music or precise performance of the psalms, it is impossible to determine exactly how singing contributed to the transmission of the texts. But, by applying what is known today of the effective use of music in imparting ideas, it can be asserted that singing was essential to their transmission. To cite one example, Psalm 46 reminds worshipers to have confidence in God. The psalm is attributed to the Korahites, a branch of Temple singers. It begins with the words, "God is our refuge and stronghold a help in trouble, very near" (v. 2), and later states that God "puts a stop to wars throughout the earth, breaking the bow, snapping the spear, consigning wagons to flames" (v. 10). The psalm encourages hope and reinforces three central aspects of the Israelites' understanding of the divine: dependability, justness and might. With its depiction of God as guardian and protector, it persuades worshipers to adopt an attitude of collective confidence; they will be safe as long as the group stays together.

Psalm 73 likewise exemplifies the disciplinary function of liturgical song. It is the first in a collection of psalms ascribed to Asaph (Pss. 73–83), a prominent Levite who established a guild of Temple singers (1 Chr. 25). The psalm presents an unambiguous moral lesson, recounting the experience of a man who nearly rejects the notion that God rewards the upright and punishes the wicked. It begins, "God is truly good to Israel, to those whose heart is pure. As for me, my feet had almost strayed, my steps were nearly led off course, for I envied the wanton; I saw the wicked at ease" (vv. 1–3). After a series of verses questioning how the wicked can "scoff and plan evil" (v. 8), "set their mouths against heaven" (v. 9) and "pound His people again and again" (v. 10), yet remain "ever tranquil, [and] amass wealth" (v. 12), the psalmist answers with a message to all who are tempted to abandon moral scruples in their striving for success: "Those who keep far from You [eventually] perish; You annihilate all who are untrue to You. As for me, nearness to God is good; I have made the Lord my refuge, that I may recount all Your works" (vv. 27–28). This liturgical song confirms a system of reward and punishment for behavior, and in so doing reiterates social standards.

Levitin lists religion songs as another musical genre crucial to human life. The Psalter is, of course, a thoroughly religious book. But what Levitin means by religion is more precisely its ritual or ceremonial aspects. Music helps infuse these practices with meaning, and works to imprint sacred history, beliefs and moral guidelines into the memories of participants. The messages of these sacred songs tend to resonate long after the ceremony has ended, and their ritualized expression ties the

5. Music and Public Worship

community both to the event itself and to the flow of history in which similar events have already occurred and will occur again.[156] In short, religion songs play a major part in forming and articulating religious identity.

It is probable that most (if not all) of the psalms were assigned to a particular ritual.[157] However, the exact context of their performance is not always readily derived. There is much conjecture and debate regarding the original usage and liturgical placement of the majority of psalms.[158] Still, several psalms are generally understood to have accompanied specific ceremonial moments or events in the Jerusalem Temple. For instance, Psalm 24, with its requirements for participation in worship (vv. 3–6) and reference to the opening of gates (vv. 7, 9), is identified as part of the entrance liturgy. In contrast, Psalm 121 was probably a song of dismissal from the Temple, concluding with the message that "The Lord will guard your coming and going, now and forever" (v. 8). Psalm 81 was likely sung during a festival, as indicated in verse 4: "Blow the horn on the new moon, on the full moon of our feast day," while Psalm 107 seems to have been part of a thanksgiving ceremony.[159] These liturgical psalms point to the ritual function of the Psalter, and illustrate the various instances in which psalms would have helped infuse the community with beliefs, moral guidelines, communal-consciousness and a sense of identity.

Love is another theme explored in the Book of Psalms. Levitin recognizes love songs as vital to human life largely because they generate an awareness of something greater than ourselves: "Whether [a song expresses] love of another, of country, of God, of an idea, love is fundamentally an intense devotion to this notion that something is bigger than us."[160] They remind us that even when things are uncertain, there exists a powerful, steadfast force that can be drawn upon for consolation and uplift. This is certainly the case with songs of divine love, as presented in the Psalter. Love of God is a commandment found in Deuteronomy 6:5: "You shall love the Lord your God with all your heart, with all your soul, and all your might." This all-consuming love is not mere emotion; it requires appropriate response in thought and action. One shows love for God by reflecting on His word, apprehending Him, delighting in Him, following His will, worshiping Him and, ultimately, leading others to do likewise.[161]

Psalms of love sung during Temple worship would have made tangible the intimacy and affection that marked Israel's relationship with God. In a sense, all psalms — whether of petition, praise or thanksgiving — are imbued with this feeling of affection: they praise God's faithfulness, exude gratitude for His favor and express devotion to His ways. They are liturgical pronouncements of the powerful bond between the people and their deity. Psalm 19:15 succinctly communicates the love that comes with sincere devotion: "May the words of my mouth and the prayer of my heart be acceptable to You, O Lord, my rock and my redeemer." Psalm 103:1–5 gives a similar depiction of divine allegiance: "Bless the Lord, O my soul, all my being, His holy name. Bless the Lord, O my Soul and do not forget his bounties." This is followed by a list of ways God returns affection to His devotees, demonstrating the covenantal nature of the relationship: "He forgives all your sins, heals all your diseases. He redeems your life from the Pit, surrounds you with steadfast love and mercy. He satisfies you with good things in the prime of life, so that your youth is renewed like the eagle's."

Anthropologists have theorized that music originated as a means of achieving tribal unity.[162] Levitin concurs, adding that six kinds of songs — friendship, joy, comfort, knowledge, religion and love — paved the way for and have remained integral to large-scale cooperative undertakings, the transmission of information and other complex social behaviors.[163] As the above examples attest, these song-types are found throughout the Book of Psalms. This gives support to the notion that the six songs are universal, and indicates their important role in shaping and upholding a civilization immersed in a specific worldview, system of ethics and collective identity. In no small way, incorporating these prayer-songs into the Temple service helped to define and strengthen the beliefs, concepts and sentiments that characterized ancient Israel, and provided the people a common vocabulary — both linguistic and musical — through which to communicate their unity.

Summary

Music is a natural part of public worship. In contradistinction to spontaneous moments of personal devotion, which generally give rise

5. Music and Public Worship

to quiet words of the heart, communal worship entails a number of individuals joining together in thought, movement and emotion. This merging of many into one is usually accomplished through liturgy — which provides a common script addressing a range of spiritual, theological and existential concerns — and music — which brings participants together in shared feelings and kinesthetic responses, and focuses collective attention on the text, occasion and the group itself. The prayer text consolidates minds, while its musical accompaniment consolidates hearts. Considering the extent to which Israel's worldview and sense of unity were imparted and reinforced through the institution of public worship — and given the highly musical nature of that activity and the Levitical priests who conducted it — it is no exaggeration to claim that the people came to know themselves with the aid of musical tones.

The social and religious value of liturgical song was well known in biblical times. From the prayer-song of Moses, Miriam and the Israelites following the Red Sea crossing (Exod. 15:1–21) to the highpoint of liturgical music in the Second Temple, there appears an indelible link between community, worship and musical sounds. This chapter has explored several ways music aided both the spiritual and national life of ancient Israel. Music was a constant companion of the sacrificial rite, establishing the devotional mood needed for that regulated ritual routine. The designation of the Levites as Temple singers and players ensured the establishment and perpetuation of an elevated sacred sound to which corporate prayers would be set. Throughout the Psalter we encounter references to singing and instruments, stage directions and musical signals, and the recognition of music as an appropriate means of offering hymns, petitions and thanksgiving to God. The musical character of Israel's worship is perhaps best displayed in Psalm 150, with its list of musical instruments and call for vocal outpourings of praise. And by viewing the Book of Psalms through Levitin's theory of six world-shaping songs, we gain an appreciation of the important role the Psalter played in fostering, defining and asserting a cultural and religious worldview.

Aside from its immediate purpose of drawing attention to the divine presence in the world — creating the ambience of sacred times and exploring themes essential to a religious outlook — the Psalter was also integral to the social aims of facilitating interpersonal bonding and communication, imparting behavioral and doctrinal guidelines, and instilling a collective mission and consciousness. It is thus apt to view the psalms as part of the larger phenomenon of practical music in the Bible. Though its content was scribed and presented by professionals with specialized training and advanced skills, the musical rendering of the psalms shares the functional quality of other forms of music in ancient Israel, such as work songs, military marches, music therapy and sung prophecy. The glorious setting and aesthetic appeal of Levitical music surely conveyed an element of performance. Yet, like religious singing in our own day, its beauty was not intended to arouse mere pleasure or to entertain an appreciative audience, but to stir worshipers to desired thoughts and feelings. It was music with an expressed purpose, not for its own sake. The richness of imagery, diversity of subjects, and divine awareness housed in the psalms were enhanced by their musical presentation, and these constituent parts have made the Psalter a continuous source of spiritual and musical inspiration for Jews and Christians throughout the ages.

Moving from these descriptive insights to a more conceptual one, it is instructive to view the Psalter as a definitive songbook, not just for ancient Israel but also for humanity as a whole. As noted, it contains examples of all the major song types as identified by Levitin: friendship, joy, comfort, knowledge, religion and love. Though the Book of Psalms was compiled for and delivered in a worship environment — and continues to influence liturgical traditions — its individual chapters can be taken as archetypes of songs both sacred and secular, Semitic and non. By classifying the psalms according to their main themes and universalizing their intent, it becomes apparent that ancient Israel knew the range of music's potential functions and used songs to achieve similar aims and address similar concerns as we do today. As such, it is not difficult to envision the people singing secular versions of the types sung in the Temple: love songs, friendship songs, learning songs and so forth. It can be said that the inclusion of these genres in the Psalter is a reflection of their widespread usage in that culture — something we would expect from such a musical people.

Conclusion

In virtually all societies, music is used to teach, comfort, communicate, celebrate, strengthen bonds and announce allegiances. It figures in a host of settings and activities, and is a storehouse of cultural heritage and information. However, while every culture has music, not every culture is equally musical. The emphasis placed on musical expression varies from society to society, and certain populations are more inclined or encouraged to be music-makers than others. This was as true in the ancient world as it is today.

Relics and writings from the ancient Near East show a degree of overlap in the music-cultures of that region. Civilizations spanning from Egypt to Mesopotamia used similar instruments—flutes, lyres, trumpets, etc.—and had common occasions for musical performance—royal processionals, cultic rites, storytelling, etc. And since there was regular interaction between them, we can assume they shared some musical conventions and/or styles, though we have no record of the sounds they made. But even when we acknowledge that music pervaded all groups, there is reason to consider Israel an especially musical nation.

As this book highlights, Israel excelled in functional music. Again, the same might be said for other civilizations, but the frequency with which such music is integrated into the biblical text is so remarkable as to demand special notice. Generally speaking, functional music is music with a purpose. It has a much longer lineage than music composed or played for aesthetic effect, or "music for entertainment." Among ancient peoples, there was probably no such thing as music for its own sake; it was a utilitarian art pursued to enrich an extra-musical event or undertaking.

Functional music involves two main aspects, which exist either separately or in conjunction. First, it is designed to influence physical states, behaviors, moods and attitudes. It might be used to stir people to common purpose, induce a peak experience, stimulate relaxation, promote therapeutic ends and so on. What distinguishes this from music in general is intent: it is selected and/or created to achieve a specific goal. A second feature of functional music is its association with a task or activity. The music is defined by its use and setting, whether it be ritual, work or play. In ancient Israel, distinct music was found in nearly every social context, including military, religious, vocational and educational. In these instances, the music's identifying features are determined by function, not aesthetic gratification (although such enjoyment is possible and often desired).

When music appears in the Hebrew Bible, it is typically not the focus of a prose passage or poetic verse. Rather, it is included to further a plot, fill out a description or indicate the means of performing a text. Music most often comes as an incidental element in prayer-poems (like psalms and prophetic verses), communal settings (like family gatherings and royal processionals) and larger narratives (like the exodus and David's rise to power). Moreover, many of these citations relate music to theological and spiritual awareness. This is to be expected, as the Bible is a document concerned with elucidating God's existence, characteristics, relationship with Israel and involvement in worldly affairs. This accounts for the scarcity of references to secular music. But the link between music and religion is more than just a result of the authors' agenda. The resounding association of music with religious experience and expression—as in the cases of prophecy and psalmody—is a testament to music's cultural value. It is no small thing that in a world ever conscious of God, the divine presence was perceived musically. These functional and theological observations paint a compelling musical portrait of biblical life.

Throughout this book, I have aimed to develop the conception of music as more than a peripheral element of biblical society. It was not enough to simply acknowledge that Israel incorporated music into certain rituals and activities—a fact that is apparent upon first glance at a list of musical citations—nor was it deemed beneficial to take a limited or esoteric route, like hypothesizing about possible meanings of obscure musical terms or attempting the reconstruction of instruments. Those challenges have been met admirably elsewhere. The task instead was to portray ancient Israel as a musical people; to show how functional music was integrated into Israel's daily life; and to describe the multi-faceted nature of its music through an in-depth look into four main topics: the Song of the Sea, David's lyre, prophecy and the Book of Psalms. The result is a work that identifies reasons for — and not just the existence of — music in biblical life, and shows how these four areas helped shape the self-identity of ancient Israel. Put succinctly, Israel's birth as a free nation was marked by the Song of the Sea, its monarchic system was defined by the archetypical musician-king David, its divine correspondences were delivered in sung prophecy, and its appointed institution for mediating worship was designed and officiated by a class of priestly musicians.

Complications

It is worthwhile to revisit two problems in the study of music in the Bible: the mythological character of much of the text, and the absence of sonic records from biblical times. The first poses obvious problems for a study grounded in the written word. It is naive to contest the lack of archaeological evidence for the exodus and Davidic kingship; and stories of miracles, transcriptions of poetry and attribution of verses to specific individuals have long been suspect outside of devotional circles. These objections and debates are doubtless applicable to material explored in this book.

Even so, I have decided to examine the text as it is rather than determine its accuracy or inaccuracy. Admittedly, such a discussion will probably not satisfy those who desire a purely historical investigation of music in biblical times. I have made mention of archeology, iconography and textual criticism where relevant; but it was not my purpose to challenge a given passage or provide an alternate scenario. This has been meticulously explored elsewhere. Instead, I treated the text as a coherent story peppered with pertinent musical details— real or imagined. Such a study is reasonable when we consider the world of the biblical authors.

The overarching aim of this cultural-sociological study has been to glean broader implications from cherished texts. Even if the details of an episode discussed are embellished or are an invention of later times, what the Bible says about music is an accurate representation of how Israel appraised musical sounds. Thus, a story like David's lyre playing may not be historically precise, but it is culturally valid since it shows how music was understood, utilized and performed in biblical society.

The Hebrew Bible can therefore be read as a source that divulges musical information. This is sometimes done with depth and other times with subtle clues. These references are valuable cultural artifacts that offer glimpses into everyday life. The central claim is this: the way music is described in the Hebrew Bible and the settings in which it appears are indicative of a musically sophisticated society. Israel's familiarity with music is seen in references to singing and instrument playing in minor episodes and as a side feature in significant storylines. These occurrences are typically bereft of detail, suggesting that the people were familiar with musical practices and did not require long descriptions.

Our inability to hear music from biblical times is also a potential drawback. While the text has been carefully preserved, protected and passed on from one generation to the next, no such continuity exists for the music it describes. This is understandable, given that music—both instrumental and vocal—was an oral tradition that did not persist long enough to be notated. The tides of history have swept away any reliable trace of a musical heritage. This silence poses obvious obstacles for a study of music, an art form that exists in sound. Indeed, audible material is typically the starting part of a musical examination, be it theoretical, musicological, ethnographic or otherwise. But recreating the music of ancient Israel would be more imaginative than instructive.

From a purely musical standpoint, biblical passages might seem of little value. Standard questions remain unanswerable: Which musical conventions were experienced as joyful, melancholy, soothing or energizing? Did Israel develop systems of scales and modes? What was their concept of rhythm and harmony? What were their aesthetic preferences? Did musical choices divide one group from another? What were the signatures of a given genre? Were there regional variations and musical subcultures? Because such information is unobtainable, a complete study is helplessly out of reach. We are left to speculate about features such as tonal range, stylistic variants and performance techniques—elements that would ordinarily be of paramount interest.

But an appraisal of music's role in biblical life does not rely on how the music sounded. From the vantage point of music and culture, musical citations in the Hebrew Bible are remarkably instructive. The text paints a vivid (though composite) picture of a society in which music was regularly interwoven into non-musical activities. Because the music was functional, context and usage — not style and form — are of prime importance. We can assume that however it sounded, it was appropriate for its purpose: funeral music was suitably sorrowful, battle songs were appropriately aggressive, feast songs were fittingly festive, and so on. This position is especially justified when we consider that, outside of perhaps Temple worship, aesthetics were not a foremost concern. In this way, neither the mythic aspects of the text nor the absence of audible records prevent us from claiming that music was pervasive and influential in biblical life.

Observations

A brief review of the examples explored in the previous chapters gives sufficient proof of music's ubiquity in ancient Israel. First, the Song of the Sea (Exod. 15:1–21), which arose in response to the miraculous escape from the Egyptian forces, is a quintessential case of common people — newly freed slaves — uniting in voice and sentiment. It is a song of assertion, not only of God's victory, but also of collective gratitude, identity and solidarity. Its text is an expression of divine praise and nationalism, and its arrangement and textual clues suggest that it was responsorial, accompanied by dance and fueled by drums — all of which would have reinforced the participants' self-understanding as a cohesive and God-fearing people. Through a mixture of music, words and coordinated movements, the Israelites transcended (at least momentarily) any sense of individualism, and proclaimed their identity as a favored and triumphant people.

It is not accidental or insignificant that the Israelites chose song as their first collective act as a "reborn" nation. As slaves, they witnessed the use of music in Egyptian worship and likely incorporated work songs into their daily toils. They were intimately familiar with the power of singing to express shared emotions and bolster communal bonding, and

Conclusion

turned to music to mark the transition from slavery to freedom, voice divine praise and emphasize the shared nature of the experience. As a central moment in time and a model for later hymns, the Song had a lasting impact on biblical theology and practice. Its language, structure and setting influenced later praise songs, and its themes of God as warrior, protector and redeemer resonate throughout the literature. As a celebrated example of what appears to be an intuitive activity — in biblical times and since — singing at the Red Sea shows the ease with which ordinary people engaged in song and dance, and the unity of thought and spirit such activities fostered in settings big and small, extraordinary and everyday.

Second, David's playing of the lyre to calm the anguished King Saul (1 Sam. 16:14–23) indicates that musical healing was a known practice in ancient Israel, and that music in general had an exalted place in Israel's monarchy. David, Israel's greatest king, was distinguished for many things: his strategic mind, bravery in battle, divine appointment, piety, charisma and — not insignificantly — musical expertise. His skill at the lyre was among the qualities that made him fit to be king, and was a direct way in which he channeled the divine presence. It was through music that David entered into a relationship with Saul; and it was largely because of his playing, singing and poetry that he managed to capture the hearts and minds of the people.

David is held up as a model king and superb musician. In addition to his adeptness at music therapy, David used song to accompany himself in battle, voice feelings and concerns, attract and charm the populace and as a fundamental part of his vision of Israel's public religion. Music was, in short, integral to many aspects of David's career, and the various uses he had for it established a strong connection between music and kingship — a relationship that persisted in battle, liturgy and official ceremonies (e.g., Pss. 20; 21; 45; 2 Chr. 7:6; 20:21; 29:27).

Third, music was closely associated with the institution of prophecy. Prophets used music to become more receptive to God's word and to transmit these messages to the people. Several prophets sang their proclamations in poetic verses, drawing upon musical tones to clarify and amplify the emotional content of their divine encounters, and to help their words resonate among the people. The significance of music in prophecy should not be overlooked. Prophecy was the primary modality by which God's involvement in human life was revealed and prophets attracted special attention for their position as intermediaries between humanity and the divine. Moreover, the prophets' recognition of the capacity of musical sounds to foster human-divine contact, emotionalize holy words and call the people to urgent pronouncements was carried into worship settings, where the ultimate aim is to feel the divine presence — if with lesser intensity — and become wrapped up in the language, themes and sentiments of the sacred moment.

Fourth, the Book of Psalms displays the extent to which sound was a fundamental part of public worship. Communal worship involves a group of individuals joining together in thought, gesture and emotion. In the Jerusalem Temple (and particularly the Second Temple), this merging of many into one was accomplished through a combination of liturgy — a common script addressing a range of spiritual, theological and existential concerns — and music — an expressive medium that consolidates feelings, evokes shared kinesthetic responses and focuses collective attention on the text, occasion and the group itself.

It is also significant that the experts and main presenters of this devotional music were priests. The Levites were entrusted as Temple singers and players, and oversaw the establishment and perpetuation of the "Temple sound" to which corporate prayers were set. The Psalter contains ample references to stage directions and musical signs, singing and instrumental playing and a persistent message that song was the most appropriate means of offering communal hymns, petitions and thanksgiving. In addition to their immediate purpose of drawing attention to religious ideals and creating the ambience for a given sacred time, the Levites (through their music) accomplished the social aims of facilitating interpersonal bonding, imparting behavioral guidelines, teaching theology, instilling a collective consciousness, promoting a common purpose and so on. Their music was part of the wider goals of stirring people to desired thoughts and feelings, and building and preserving a good society.

These four examples illustrate the degree to which music helped inform the self-identity of Israel. At key junctures and in core institutions, musical tones were used to formulate and deliver messages, convey and heighten emotions, assert and strengthen communal bonds and establish human-divine contact. To be sure, some situations and settings relied more heavily on musical expression than others. For instance, music's role was more formally integrated into the Temple service than the individualized utterances of prophetic poetry; but in both cases, song proved an effective means of transmitting ideas and stirring souls. It should also not be overlooked that the crossing of the Red Sea — a pinnacle and transformative moment in Israel's history — and the kingship of David — the model monarch and national hero — were both filled with music. The Song of the Sea, monarchy, prophecy and priesthood thus demonstrate music's integration into the social structure of ancient Israel.

Implications

The musical content of these biblical examples can be taken a step further. Though most of the episodes and genres discussed in this book constitute exalted illustrations of Israel's music-making, their inclusion in the biblical account suggests musical usages outside of the narrative and ritualistic scope of the text. When we apply the twofold argument that music in the Bible is a selective record of a vast musical output and that the people did create secular music — even though songs of a religious nature are the Bible's predominant musical concern — the vision of Israel as a musical people comes into clearer focus. The topics addressed in this study contribute to this view of Israel's music-culture.

The Song of the Sea constitutes a mature musical form, involving solo singing, group singing, percussion instruments, dancing and the inclusion of men and women — all of which came together to provide an outlet for emotions wrapped up in the victorious crossing. The exalted language of the spontaneous poetic outburst could not be adequately expressed in plain speech. At that early stage in Israel's development, the populace already engaged in a complete musical experience, both in terms of the components employed — melody, words, dance, instruments, etc.— and its value as a bonding agent, didactic tool and so forth. Israel was a fully evolved musical people at the moment the Song was performed, and later passages show that a sophisticated music-culture was maintained throughout their history. Furthermore, if we consider that what is revealed in the Bible is only a religious snapshot of ancient

Israel, we can assume that day-to-day life in that society was enriched with all sorts of musical production, secular and sacred, public and private.

Indeed, evidence of music's general functions can be extracted from the episode of King Saul and David's lyre. Though this is the Bible's sole depiction of music therapy — and its only explicit reference to music's calming effect, medicinal or otherwise — the naturalness with which the courtiers sought a lyre player for the ailing king suggests an awareness and application of the emotional-psychological potency of sound in private settings. Because all types of music with a restorative function can be understood as allied, mention of one form suggests that others were employed as well, such as lullabies and music accompanying meditation. In this sense, David's lyre is symbolic of Israel's wider exploitation of the interaction of music and mood.

Similarly, the use of instruments and singing as an aid to prophecy was an outgrowth of an intuitive musical response. Music can and often does generate feelings of something greater than oneself; musical delivery and reception of divine messages helps impart the transcendence of the experience and the sacredness of the words. Music rises above the monotony of speech and the unorganized noises of everyday existence, creating a sonic division between the ordinary and holy. In a society as God-conscious as ancient Israel, it was only fitting that musicality and religiosity — two important components of its collective identity — came together in prophecy, the most direct and profound mode of connecting with the deity. Viewed theologically, it can be claimed that our innate capacity for and attraction to music-making — and singing in particular — was ordained by God for the purpose of perceiving Him.

A deeper, conceptual observation can also be made regarding the Psalter. The psalms exhibit all of the major song types, as derived by Levitin: friendship, joy, comfort, knowledge, religion and love. If we group the psalms according to their genres and universalize their intent, it is clear that ancient Israel was aware of the range of music's potential functions and used songs to achieve similar aims and address similar concerns as we do today. It is reasonable to presume that these functions were not limited to the sacred songs of Temple worship, but were also expressed in songs of a secular and/or less formal kind.

When coupled with the Bible's mention of music at family feasts, community festivals, national events, royal processionals, religious devotion and other occasions — however passing they may be — these insights reveal a general acknowledgement that vocal and instrumental music was effective in stimulating moods, expressing sentiments, imparting ideals, asserting convictions, encouraging cooperation and bolstering affiliations. Furthermore, while the bulk of biblical verses alluding to music are religious in nature — depicting worship or some other type of human-divine contact — we can conclude that the existence of religious music points to the musically rich environment of ancient Israel as a whole.

Further Suggestions

No study is without limitations, self-imposed or otherwise. This truism is magnified when the subject is the Bible, a book that has been analyzed for centuries and from seemingly all conceivable angles and perspectives. This book has strived to keep the discussions as succinct and focused as possible. As a result, some minor music-related verses and tangential details were purposely skipped over. It is also the position of this study that a full picture of Israel's music-culture emerges from the four topics chosen, and other passages not included or addressed in depth were either deemed redundant — as with the musical references in Isaiah — or too abstruse to be developed here — as with Job 38:7, which describes the morning stars singing together at the creation of the world. Additionally, because of the interdisciplinary range of this study, it was not possible to present a comprehensive set of arguments drawn from a particular specialization. Giving such consideration to a single field or line of investigation would have interrupted the flow of the analysis, and distracted attention from the larger purpose of creating a holistic view of music in biblical society.

It likewise goes without saying that this book is neither the first nor final word on the subject of music in the Bible — an area that has been a fruitful, if minor, subgenre of biblical studies for many decades. Since the subject has received relatively sparse consideration, there is still much to be learned about music's place in biblical life. Even the points made in these pages can be further developed and taken into different directions. Some possible avenues would be applying the musical "truths" found in the Bible to other contexts, expanding the examination to include the New Testament, exploring at greater length what the Bible has to say about music in modern worship, and assembling a verse-by-verse commentary that focuses on musical functions. More attention could also be given to exploring biblical musical examples using ethnomusicological theories and tools, and to expanding connections and/or citing differences between ancient Israel's music-culture and our own. These and other endeavors would shine additional light on music's role in biblical life, and help give music a more prominent voice in the field of biblical studies.

Chapter Notes

Preface

1. A. Sendrey, *Music in ancient Israel* (New York: Philosophical Library, 1969), 259.

Introduction

1. J. Stainer, *The music of the Bible: with some account of the development of modern musical instruments from ancient types* (London: Novello, 1914); C. Engel, *Music of the most ancient nations, particularly of the Assyrians, Egyptians, and Hebrews* (London: William Reeves, 1929); and A. Sendrey, *Music in ancient Israel* (New York: Philosophical Library, 1969).

2. E. Hutchinson, *Music of the Bible: or, explanatory notes upon those passages in the sacred scriptures which relate to music* (Boston: Guild and Lincoln, 1864); G. Larrick, *Musical references and song texts in the Bible* (Lewiston, NY: Edwin Mellen, 1990); D. Thiessen, *Selah: a guide to music in the Bible* (Chicago: Cornerstone, 2002); and H. Lockyer, Jr., *All the music in the Bible: an exploration of musical expression in scripture and church hymnody* (Peabody, MA: Hendrickson, 2004).

3. J. Braun, *Music in ancient Israel/Palestine: archaeological, written and comparative sources* (Grand Rapids: Wm. B. Eerdmans, 2002); J. Montagu, *Musical instruments in the Bible* (Lanham, MD: Scarecrow, 2002); and Y. Kolyada, *A compendium of musical instruments and instrumental terminology in the Bible* (London: Equinox, 2009).

4. O. Borowski, *Daily life in biblical times* (Atlanta: Society for Biblical Literature, 2003).

5. Braun, *Music in ancient Israel/Palestine*, 1.

6. S. T. Wine, *A provocative people: a secular history of the Jews* (Farmington Hills, MI: IISHJ and Milan, 2012), 45–46.

7. J. A. Smith, "Musical aspects of Old Testament canticles in their biblical setting," *Early music history* 17 (1998): 228.

8. Smith, "Musical aspects of Old Testament canticles in their biblical setting," 228.

9. BT *Rosh Hashanah* 31b.

10. Wine, *A provocative people*, 197.

11. Wine, *A provocative people*, 197.

12. See I. Finkelstein and N. A. Silberman, *The Bible unearthed: archaeology's new vision of ancient Israel and the origin of its sacred texts* (New York: Touchstone, 2001), 141–145.

13. A. Ha'am, *Selected essays* (Philadelphia: Jewish Publication Society, 1912), 308–309.

14. M. Slobin, "Learning the lessons of studying Jewish music," *Judaism* 44:2 (1995): 223.

Chapter 1

1. L. Ryken, J. Wilhoit, and T. Longman, *Dictionary of biblical imagery* (Downers Grove, IL: InterVarsity Press, 1998), 589; E. F. Davis, "Reading the song iconographically," in P. S. Hawkins and L. C. Stahlberg, ed., *Scrolls of love: Ruth and the Song of Songs* (New York: Fordham University Press, 2006), 176.
2. P. J. King and L. E. Stager, *Life in biblical Israel* (Louisville, KY: Westminster John Knox, 2001), xix; and O. Borowski, *Daily life in biblical times* (Atlanta: Society for Biblical Literature, 2003), 13.
3. King and Stager, *Life in biblical Israel*, 1.
4. W. E. Mills and R. A. Bullard, ed., *Mercer dictionary of the Bible* (Macon, GA: Mercer University Press, 1990), 590; King and Stager, *Life in biblical Israel*, 285; M. Wade-Matthews, *Music: an illustrated history* (London: Hermes House, 2002),17; and T. W. Burgh, *Listening to the artifacts: music in ancient Palestine* (New York: Continuum, 2006), 106.
5. Burgh, *Listening to the artifacts*, 106.
6. T. Frymer-Kensky, *Studies in Bible and feminist criticism* (Philadelphia: Jewish Publication Society, 2006), 162.
7. I. Reznikoff, "Intonation and modality in the music of oral tradition and antiquity," in T. A. Sebeok and J. Umiker-Sebeok, ed., *The semiotic web 1986: a yearbook of semiotics* (New York: Walter de Gruyter, 1987), 542.
8. D. Kunej and I. Turk, "New perspectives on the beginnings of music: archaeological and musicological analysis of a middle Paleolithic bone 'flute,'" in N. L. Wallin, B. Merker and S. Brown, ed., *The origins of music* (Cambridge: MIT Press, 2001), 235; and C. P. Kottak, *Cultural anthropology* (New York: McGraw-Hill, 2004), 383.
9. S. Mithen, *The singing Neanderthals: the origins of music, language, mind and body* (London: Weidenfeld and Nicolson, 2005), 267.
10. E. Dissanayake, "A review of the singing Neanderthals," *Evolutionary psychology* 3 (2005): 375.
11. B. Nettl, *The study of ethnomusicology: thirty-one issues and concepts* (Urbana: University of Illinois Press, 2005), 47.
12. *The Christian Examiner* 25 (1839): 31.
13. B. Seemann, "Proceedings of the society," *Journal of anthropology* 1 (1870): clv–clvi.
14. G. Herzog, "Music's dialects: a non-universal language," *Independent journal of Columbia University* 6:10 (1939): 1–2.
15. R. B. Whyte, "Religion and music," *Music educators journal*, 32:6 (1946): 18; L. Rowell, *Thinking about music: an introduction to the philosophy of music* (Amherst, MA: University of Massachusetts Press, 1984), 1; P. J. B. Slater, "Birdsong repertoires: their origins and use," in N. L. Wallin, B. Merker and S. Brown, ed., *The origins of music* (Cambridge: MIT Press, 2001), 49; and W. A. Haviland, E. L. Prins, and B. McBride, *Cultural anthropology: the human challenge*, 11th ed. (Belmont, CA: Thomson Wadsworth, 2005), 383.
16. J. T. Titon, L. Fujie, D. Locke, T. Cooley, D. P. McCallester, A. K. Rasmussen, and D. B. B. Peck, *Worlds of music: an introduction to the music of the world's people* (Belmont, CA: Wadsworth, 2005), 18.
17. Dissanayake, "A review of the singing Neanderthals," 375.
18. A. P. Merriam, *The anthropology of music* (Evanston, IL: Northwestern University Press, 1964), 219–226.
19. B. Nettl, *The study of ethnomusicology: thirty-one issues and concepts* (Urbana: University of Illinois Press, 2005), 46–47.
20. H. W. Longfellow, *The prose works of Henry Wadsworth Longfellow* (London: David Bogue, 1851), 4.
21. T. Gioia, *Work songs* (Durham: Duke University Press, 2006), 12.
22. Titon *et al.*, *Worlds of music*, 386–388.
23. R. H. Lavenda and E. A. Schultz, *Core concepts in cultural anthropology*, 2d ed. (New York: McGraw-Hill, 2003), 69–70.

Notes. Chapter 2

24. M. Stokes, *Ethnicity, identity, and music: the musical construction of place* (New York: Berg, 1997), 5.
25. A. D. W. Malefijt, *Religion and culture: an introduction to anthropology of religion* (Prospect Heights, IL: Waveland, 1968), 197.
26. P. M. Zeltner, *John Dewey's aesthetic philosophy* (Amsterdam, PA: John Benjamins, 1975), 94.
27. B. Nettl, *The study of ethnomusicology*, 47.
28. C. Pegg, H. Myers, P.V. Bohlman, and & M. Stokes, "Ethnomusicology," in S. Sadie, ed., *The new grove dictionary of music and musicians*, 2d ed., vol. 8 (New York: Grove's Dictionaries, 2001), 367.
29. See, for example, F. Jacox, *Bible music: being variations, in many keys, on musical themes from scripture* (London: Hodder and Stoughton, 1871); and S. Bacchiocchi, "Biblical principles of church music," *Endtime issues* 3:4 (2000): 1–32.
30. See, for example, I. Heskes, *Passport to Jewish music: its history, traditions, and culture* (New York: Tara, 1994), 66; and J. L. Friedmann, comp., *The value of sacred music: an anthology of essential writings, 1801–1918* (Jefferson, NC: McFarland, 2009), 6.
31. J. Beimel, "Divinity and music: a Jewish conception," *Jewish music* 1:1 (1934): 114.
32. Beimel, "Divinity and music: a Jewish conception," 114.
33. Beimel, "Divinity and music," 114.
34. Beimel, "Divinity and music," 114.
35. Beimel, "Divinity and music," 115.
36. Beimel, "Divinity and music," 115.
37. W. F. Crafts, *Trophies of song: Articles and incidents on the power of sacred music* (Boston: D. Lothrop, 1874), 47.
38. See, for example, J. L. Chapman, *Singing and teaching singing: a holistic approach to classical voice* (San Diego: Plural, 2006), 2; and A. Karpf, *The human voice: how this extraordinary instrument reveals essential clues about who we are* (New York: Bloomsbury, 2006), 303.
39. Crafts, *Trophies of song*, 5.
40. Crafts, *Trophies of song*, 57.
41. G. L. Beck, "Introduction," in G.L. Beck, ed., *Sacred sound: experiencing music in world religions* (Waterloo, ON: Wilfrid Laurier University Press, 2006), 3–4.
42. E. Fubini, *The history of music aesthetics* (London: Macmillan, 1990), 261–308.

Chapter 2

1. J. J. McDermott *Reading the Pentateuch: a historical introduction* (New York: Paulist, 2002), 118; and J. J. Collins, *A short introduction to the Hebrew Bible* (Minneapolis: Fortress, 2007), 61.
2. C. Stern, *Gates of prayer: the new union of prayer* (New York: Central Conference of American Rabbis, 1975), 167.
3. B. Lemmelijn, "'Genesis' creation narrative: the literary model for the so-called plague tradition?" in A. Wénin, ed., *Studies in the book of Genesis: literature, redaction and history* (Leuven: Peeters, 2001), 407–420; and J. J. Collins, *Introduction to the Hebrew Bible* (Minneapolis: Fortress, 2004), 118.
4. S. K. Langer, *Feeling and form: a theory of art developed from philosophy in a new key* (New York: Charles Scribner's Sons, 1953), 27.
5. L. Ginzberg, *The legends of the Jews*, vol. 3 (Philadelphia: Jewish Publication Society, 1920), 34.
6. Haviland *et al.*, *Cultural anthropology*, 385.
7. E. Werner, *From generation to generation: studies on Jewish musical tradition* (New York: American Conference of Cantors, 1967), 2–3.

Notes. Chapter 2

8. S. Hofman, *Miqra'ey musica: a collection of biblical references to music in Hebrew, English, French and Spanish* (Tel Aviv: Israel Music Institute, 1999).

9. R. Lachmann, *Jewish cantillation and song in the isle of Djerba* (Jerusalem: Hebrew University, 1940); and S. Manasseh, "A song to heal your wounds: traditional lullabies in the repertoire of the Jews of Iraq," *Musica Judaica* 7 (1991–92): 1–29.

10. Werner, *From generation to generation*, 16.

11. Sendrey, *Music in Ancient Israel*, 60.

12. Sendrey, *Music in Ancient Israel*, 60; and Shiloah, *Jewish musical traditions* (Detroit: Wayne State University Press, 1995), 39.

13. Sendrey, *Music in Ancient Israel*, 60.

14. N. Sarna, *Songs of the heart: an introduction to the book of Psalms* (New York: Schocken, 1993), 8–9.

15. N. P. Lemche, *The Old Testament between theology and history: a critical survey* (Louisville, KY: Westminster John Knox, 2008), 117.

16. P. D. Wegner, *Journey from texts to translations: the origin and development of the Bible* (Grand Rapids: Baker Academic, 2004), 55.

17. J. J. Nattiez, *Music and discourse: toward a semiology of music* (Princeton, CT: Princeton University Press, 1990), 60.

18. G. Hartman, "Imagination," in A. A. Cohen and P. Mendes-Flohr, ed., *Contemporary Jewish religious thought: original essays on critical concepts, movements, and beliefs* (New York: Free Press, 1988), 451–472; and F. L. Cohen, "Jewish music," in J. L. Friedmann, comp., *Music in Jewish thought: Selected writings, 1890–1920* (Jefferson, NC: McFarland, 2009), 52–58.

19. L. Salzman, "To figure or not to figure: the iconoclastic proscription and its theoretical legacy," in C. M. Soussloft, ed., *Jewish identity and modern art history* (Berkeley: University of California Press, 1999), 67–86.

20. P. T. Forsyth, *Christ on Parnassus: lectures on art, ethic, and theology* (London: Independent, 1911), 43.

21. T. E. Miller and A. C. Shahriari, *World music: a global journey* (New York: Routledge, 2008), 42.

22. Lavenda and Schultz, *Core concepts in cultural anthropology*, 72–73.

23. D. J. Levitin, *The world in six songs: how the musical brain created human nature* (New York: Dutton, 2008), 191.

24. Werner, *From generation to generation*, 6–7.

25. M. B. Edelman, *Discovering Jewish music* (Philadelphia: Jewish Publication Society, 2003), 12–15.

26. E. E. Gendler, "Community," in A. A. Cohen and P. Mendes-Flohr, ed., *Contemporary Jewish religious thought: original essays on critical concepts, movements, and beliefs* (New York: Free Press, 1987), 81–83; and J. Neusner and W. S. Green, *Dictionary of Judaism in the biblical period*, vols. 1 and 2 (New York: Macmillan, 1996), 128–129).

27. Gendler, "Community," 82.

28. E. Dickinson, "Oratorio performance in Europe and America," in W. L. Hubbard, ed., *The American history and encyclopedia of music* (New York: Irving Squire, 1909), 1; and C. Morey, *MacMillan on music: essays on music by Sir Ernest MacMillan* (Toronto: Dundurn, 1997), 157.

29. See, for example, H. Myers, *Ethnomusicology: historical and regional studies* (New York: W. W. Norton, 1993), 453; and S. Brown, "'How does music work?' toward a pragmatics of musical communication," in S. Brown and U. Volgsten. U., ed., *Music and manipulation: on the social uses and social control of music* (New York: Berghahn, 2006), 3.

30. P. V. Bohlman, *"The land where two streams flow": music in the German-Jewish community of Israel* (Urbana: University of Illinois Press, 1989), 110.

31. Stokes, *Ethnicity, identity, and music*, 5.

32. J. J. Collins, *Introduction to the Hebrew Bible*, 466.

33. M. Marttila, *Collective reinterpretation in the Psalms: a study of the redaction history of the Psalter* (Tübingen: Mohr Siebeck, 2006), 23–24.

Notes. Chapter 2

34. Marttila, *Collective reinterpretation in the Psalms*, 23–24.
35. H. M. Schueller, *The idea of music: an introduction to musical aesthetics in antiquity and the middle ages* (Kalamazoo: Medieval Institute, Western Michigan University, 1988), 233.
36. A. G. Johnson, *The Blackwell dictionary of sociology: a user's guide to sociological language* (Malden, MA: Blackwell, 2000), 46.
37. L. May, *The socially responsive self: social theory and professional ethics* (Chicago: University of Chicago Press, 1996), 29; and Johnson, *The Blackwell dictionary of sociology*, 46.
38. May, *The socially responsive self*, 29; and S. A. Grunlan and M. K. Mayers, *Cultural anthropology: a Christian perspective* (Grand Rapids: Zondervan, 1988), 214.
39. E. Durkheim, *Emile Durkheim on morality and society*, ed. Robert Bellah (Chicago: University of Chicago Press, 1973), 110.
40. Durkheim, *Emile Durkheim on morality and society*, 63.
41. E. Durkheim, *The elementary forms of religious life* (New York: Oxford University Press, 2001), 31.
42. M. L. Anderson and H. F. Taylor, *Sociology: the essentials* (Belmont, CA: Wadsworth, 2010), 105.
43. Durkheim, *Emile Durkheim on morality and society*, 69.
44. E. Tiryakian, "Durkheim, solidarity, and September 11," in J. C. Alexander and P. D. Smith, ed., *The Cambridge companion to Durkheim* (New York: Cambridge University Press, 2005), 308.
45. L. A. Tole, "Durkheim on religion and moral community in modernity," *Sociological inquiry* 63:1 (1993): 3.
46. A. E. Komter, *Social solidarity and the gift* (New York: Cambridge University Press, 2005), 104.
47. R. A. Rappaport, *Ritual and religion in the making of humanity* (New York: Cambridge University Press, 1999), xv.
48. Durkheim, *The elementary forms of religious life*, 46.
49. Durkheim, *The elementary forms of religious life*, 43.
50. See, for example, A. Radcliffe-Brown, *Structure and function in primitive society: essays and addresses* (New York: Free Press, 1952); and M. Douglas, *Purity and danger: an analysis of concepts of pollution and taboo* (New York: Routledge and Kegan Paul, 1966).
51. J. S. Fish, *Defending the Durkheimian tradition: religion, emotion and morality* (Burlington, VT: Ashgate, 2005), 103.
52. Durkheim, *The elementary forms of religious life*, 317.
53. K. Schrock, "Why music moves us," *Scientific American mind* 20 (2009): 32–37.
54. R. Robinson and A. Winold, *The choral experience: literature, materials, and methods* (New York: Harper's College, 1976), 4.
55. A. B. Ehrenreich, *Dancing in the streets: a history of collective Joy* (New York: Macmillan, 2007), 2; and J. L. Friedmann, *Music and Jewish religious experience: social and theological essays* (Saarbrücken: VDM Verlag, 2010), 82–90.
56. A. P. Merriam, *The anthropology of music* (Evanston, IL: Northwestern University Press, 1964), 226.
57. J. L. Kugel, *The idea of biblical poetry: parallelism and its history* (New Haven: Yale University Press, 1981), 116–118.
58. C. Houtman, *Exodus* (Leuven: Peeters, 1996), 242.
59. W. T. Miller, *The book of Exodus: question by question* (New York: Paulist, 2009), 81.
60. A. Brenner and F. van Dijk-Hemmes, *On gendering texts: female and male voices in the Hebrew Bible* (Boston: Brill, 1996), 40; and E. Frankel, *The five books of Miriam: a woman's commentary on the Torah* (New York: HarperCollins, 1997), 110.
61. Thiessen, *Selah*, 3; and Lockyer, Jr., *All the music in the Bible*, 16.
62. P. A. Mellor, "Sacred contagion and social vitality: collective effervescence in *Les formes élémentaires de la vie religieuse*," in W. S. F. Pickering, ed., *Émile Durkheim: critical assessments of leading sociologists*, vol. 2. (New York: Routledge, 2001), 175.

63. Durkheim, *The elementary forms of religious life*, 228.
64. X. Hang, *Encyclopedia of national anthems* (Lanham, MD: Scarecrow, 2003).
65. R. Sosis and C. Alcorta, "Signaling, solidarity, and the sacred: the evolution of religious behavior," *Evolutionary anthropology* 12:6 (2003): 266.
66. H. R. Haweis, "Music, emotions, and morals," in J. L. Friedmann, ed., *The value of sacred music: an anthology of essential writings, 1801–1918* (Jefferson, NC: McFarland, 2009), 100.
67. Haweis, "Music, emotions, and morals," 100.
68. Haweis, "Music, emotions, and morals," 100.
69. Z. Mach, "National anthems: the case of Chopin as a national composer," in M. Stokes, ed., *Ethnicity, identity, and music: the musical construction of place* (New York: Berg, 1997), 61.
70. H. Befu, "Symbols of nationalism and nihonjinron," in R. Goodman and K. Refsing, ed., *Ideology and practice in modern Japan* (New York: Routledge, 1992), 26.
71. Mach, "National anthems," 62.
72. F. M. Cross, Jr., and D. N. Freedman, "The song of Miriam," *Journal of Near Eastern studies*, 14:4 (1955): 237.
73. B. Kadden and B. B. Kadden, *Teaching tefillah: insights and activities on prayer* (West Orange, NJ: Behrman House, 1990), 49.
74. D.E. Hast, J. R. Codery and S. A. Scott, *Exploring the world of music: an introduction to music from a world music perspective* (Dubuque: Kendall/Hunt, 1999), 39; and L. A. Hoffman, *The art of public prayer: not for clergy only* (Woodstock, VT: SkyLight Paths, 1999), 176.
75. E. Feldman, "Shirat hayam: a triumphant song of Jewish history," *Hayenu* 45:8 (2000): 5.
76. A. W. Binder, *Biblical chant* (New York: Philosophical Library, 1959), 16; and M. Nulman, "The shirah melody in the Ashkenazi and Sephardic traditions," *Journal of Jewish music and liturgy* 7 (1984): 12.
77. Thiessen, *Selah*, 3–4.
78. J. Neusner, *Judaism: the basics* (New York: Routledge, 2006), 41.
79. Sendrey, *Music in Ancient Israel*, 167.
80. See, for example, BT Sot. 30b; H. Avenary, "Formal structure of psalms and canticles in early Jewish and Christian chant," *Musica disciplina* 7 (1953): 3; and B. D. Russell, *The song of the sea: the date of composition and influence of Exodus 15:1–21* (New York: Peter Lang, 2007), 37.
81. Sendrey, *Music in Ancient Israel*, 164; S. Weitzman, *Song and story in biblical narrative: the history of a literary convention in Ancient Israel* (Bloomington: Indiana University Press, 1997), 28; and Russell, *The song of the sea*, 32.
82. Thiessen, *Selah*, 3.
83. J. A. Smith, "Musical aspects of Old Testament canticles in their biblical setting," in I. Fenlow, ed., *Early music history*, vol. 17 (New York: University of Cambridge Press, 1998), 232–234.
84. BT Sot. 30b.
85. W. C. Stafford, *A history of music* (London: Constable, 1830), 77.
86. Lockyer, Jr., *All the music in the Bible*, 16–18.
87. *Exodus Rabbah* 1:23; and *Numbers Rabbah* 13:19.
88. J. H. Tigay, "Exodus: introduction and annotations," in A. Berlin and M. Z. Brettler, ed., *The Jewish study Bible* (New York: Oxford University Press, 2004), 129.
89. Idelsohn, *Jewish Music*, 3–4; Trigger *et al.*, *Ancient Egypt: a social history* (New York: Cambridge University Press, 1983), 91–92; and Kamil, *The ancient Egyptians: life in the old kingdom* (Cairo: American University in Cairo Press, 1996), 176.
90. D. M. Randel, *The Harvard dictionary of music* (New York: W.W. Norton, 2003), 282.
91. M. Slobin, "Learning the lessons of studying Jewish music," *Judaism: a quarterly journal of Jewish life and thought* 4:2 (1995): 223.

92. Edelman, *Discovering Jewish Music*, 9.
93. L. Ramey, *Slave songs and the birth of African American poetry* (New York: Macmillan, 2008), 53.
94. R. M. Radano, *Lying up a nation: race and black music* (Chicago: Chicago University Press, 2003), 162.
95. Sendrey, *Music in Ancient Israel*, 164.
96. A. Wilson-Dickson, *The story of Christian music: from Gregorian chant to black gospel* (Minneapolis: Fortress, 1992), 17.
97. F. Muchimba, *Liberating the African soul: comparing African and western Christian music and worship styles* (Colorado Springs: Biblica, 2008), 7.
98. Shiloah, *Jewish musical traditions*, 8.
99. Lachmann, *Jewish cantillation and song in the isle of Djerba*; Werner, *From generation to generation*, 4; and Shiloah, *Jewish musical traditions*, 8.
100. A. G. Zornberg, *The particulars of rapture: reflections on Exodus* (New York: Doubleday, 2001), 229–231; F. S. Spencer, *Dancing girls, loose ladies, and women of the cloth: the women in Jesus' life* (New York: Continuum, 2004), 49; A. B. Ehrenreich, *Dancing in the streets: a history of collective joy* (New York: Macmillan, 2007), 31.
101. J. L. Hanna, *To dance is human: a theory of nonverbal communication* (Chicago: University of Chicago Press, 1997), 99.
102. W. H. McNeill, *Keeping together in time: dance and drill in human history* (Cambridge: Harvard University Press, 1995), 2.
103. K. K. Shelemay, *Soundscapes: exploring music in a changing world* (New York: W.W. Norton, 2001), 183.
104. H. F. van der Leeuw, *Sacred and profane beauty: the holy in art* (New York: Oxford University Press, 2006), 73.
105. R. S. Schmidt, *Exploring religion*, 2d ed. (Belmont, CA: Wadsworth, 1988), 395.
106. Spencer, *Dancing girls, loose ladies, and women of the cloth*, 17.
107. G. P. H. Pasture, *Powwow* (Cody, WY: Buffalo Bill Historical Center, 1989), 38.
108. Lachmann, *Jewish cantillation and song in the isle of Djerba*, 115; Shiloah, *Jewish musical traditions*, 211; and Braun, *Music in ancient Israel/Palestine*, 29.
109. J. M. Edwards, "Women in music to ca. 1450," in K. Pendle, ed., *Women and music: a history* (Bloomington: Indiana University Press, 2001), 40.
110. C. Sachs, *The history of musical instruments* (New York: W.W. Norton, 1940), 108; M. Nulman, *Concise encyclopedia of Jewish music* (New York: McGraw-Hill, 1975), 251; and Braun, *Music in ancient Israel/Palestine*, 30.
111. Braun, *Music in ancient Israel/Palestine*, 29.
112. T. G. Foltz, "Drumming and re-enchantment: creating spiritual community," in L. Hume and K. McPhillips., ed., *Popular spirituality: the politics of contemporary enchantment* (Burlington, VT: Ashgate, 2006), 136.
113. Wilson-Dickson, *The story of Christian music*, 23.
114. Wilson-Dickson, *The story of Christian music*, 23.
115. Tam. 7:3.
116. Edwards, *Women in music to ca. 1450*, 40.
117. See S. Rothchild and S. Sheridan, *Taking up the timbrel: the challenge of creating ritual for Jewish women today* (London: SCM, 2000); and M. Osherow, *Biblical women's voices in early modern England* (Burlington, VT: Ashgate, 2009), 15.
118. See S. Barzilai, *Chassidic ecstasy in music* (Frankfurt am Main: Peter Lang, 2009).
119. Wilson-Dickson, *The story of Christian music*, 19.

Chapter 3

1. See, for example, R. Wolfe, *The twelve religions of the Bible* (Lewiston, NY: Edwin Mellen, 1982), 145; J. Kirsch, *King David: the real life of the man who ruled Israel* (New York:

Notes. Chapter 3

Ballantine, 2000), 48; and Bilu, "The taming of the deviants and beyond: an analysis of dybbuk possession and exorcism in Judaism," in M. Goldish, ed., *Spirit possession in Judaism: cases and contexts from the middle ages to the present* (Detroit: Wayne State University Press, 2003), 77.

2. See, for example, K. A. Bock, "Harp music eases pain from lupus," *The harp therapy journal* 4:1 (1999): 4; S. Williams, "Patients with Parkinson's disease find relief with harp music," *The harp therapy journal* 6:1 (2001): 6–7; and L. Freeman *et al.*, "Music thanatology: prescriptive harp music as palliative care for the dying patient," *American journal of hospital palliative care* 23:2 (2006): 100–104.

3. W. Latham and C. Eagle, "Music for the severely disabled child," *Music education journal* 38:49 (1982): 30.

4. See, for example, Bunt, *Music therapy: an art beyond words* (Hove, UK: Psychology Press, 1994), 185–188; Wigram *et al.*, *A comprehensive guide to music therapy: theory, clinical practice, research, and training*, vol. 1 (Philadelphia: Jessica Kingsley, 2002), 150; and J. During, "Therapeutic dimensions of music in Islamic culture," in D. Koen, ed., *The Oxford handbook of medical ethnomusicology* (New York: Oxford University Press, 2008), 362–365.

5. A. Kovach, "Shamanism and guided imagery and music: a comparison," *Journal of music therapy* 22:3 (1985): 154–165; J. J. Moreno, "The music therapist: creative arts therapist and contemporary shaman," in D. Campbell, ed., *Music: physician for times to come* (Wheaton, IL: Quest, 1991), 167–186; Gioia, *Healing songs*, 49–68; and D. A. Olsen, "Shamanism, music, and healing in two contrasting South American cultural areas," in D. Koen, ed., *The Oxford handbook of medical ethnomusicology* (New York: Oxford University Press, 2008), 331–360.

6. Gioia, *Healing songs*, 69–88.

7. B.J. Crowe, *Music and soulmaking: toward a new theory of music therapy* (Lanham, MD: Scarecrow, 2004), 8.

8. R. Sankaran, "Homeopathic healing in music," in D. Koen, ed., *The Oxford handbook of medical ethnomusicology* (New York: Oxford University Press, 2008), 393–409.

9. Gioia, *Healing songs*, 133–134.

10. L. M. Zimmerman *et al.*, "Effect of music and patient anxiety in coronary care units," *Heart lung* 17:5 (1988): 560–566; and P. Updike, "Music therapy results for ICU patients," *Dimensions of critical care nursing* 9:1 (1990): 39–45.

11. S. B. Hanser, "Music therapy and stress reduction research," *Journal of music therapy* 12:4 (1984): 193–206; A. Oldfield and M. Adams, "The effects of music therapy on a group of profoundly mentally handicapped adults," *Journal of mental deficiency research* 28 (1990): 37–40; and C. Davis, "The effects of music and basic relaxation instruction on pain and anxiety of women undergoing in-office gynecological procedures," *Journal of music therapy* 24:4 (1992): 202–216.

12. D. M. Prinsley, "Music therapy in geriatric care," *Australian nurses journal*, 15:9 (1986): 48–49.

13. Gioia, *Healing songs*, 36.

14. B. J. Crowe, *Music and soulmaking: toward a new theory of music therapy* (Lanham, MD: Scarecrow, 2004), 8.

15. S. Munro and B. Mount, "Music therapy in palliative care," *Canadian medical association journal* 199:9 (1978): 1029–1032.

16. C. Sachs, *World history of the dance* (New York: Seven Arts, 1952), 201–202.

17. D. A. Matthews and C. Clark, *The faith factor: proof of the healing power of prayer* (New York: Viking, 1998), 45–46.

18. S.M. Clift and G. Hancox, "The perceived benefits of singing," *Perspectives in public health* 121:4 (2001): 248–256.

19. Matthews and Clark, *The faith factor*, 45.

20. F. Rosner, "Moses Maimonides on music therapy and his responsum on music," in M. Nulman, ed., *Essays of Jewish music and prayer* (New York: Yeshiva University Press, 2005), 130.

21. F. Rosner, *Moses Maimonides' three treatises on health* (Haifa: Maimonides Research Institute, 1990), 35.
22. J. L. Gorfinkle, *The eight chapters of Maimonides on ethics* (New York: Columbia University Press, 1912), 69–70.
23. Rosner, *Moses Maimonides' three treatises on health*, 147.
24. Rosner, "Moses Maimonides on music therapy and his responsum on music," 121.
25. Rowell, *Thinking about music*, 70.
26. Rosner, *Moses Maimonides' three treatises on health*, 147.
27. Kirsch, *King David*, 48.
28. Collins, *Introduction to the Hebrew Bible*, 226.
29. P. D. Miscall, *The workings of Old Testament narrative* (Minneapolis: Fortress, 1983), 83.
30. N. P. Lemche, "David's rise," *Journal for the study of the Old Testament* 4:10 (1979): 18.
31. Thiessen, *Selah*, 21.
32. Thiessen, *Selah*, 22.
33. Sendrey, *Music in ancient Israel*, 530.
34. G. von Rad, *Old Testament theology: the theology of Israel's historical traditions* (Louisville, KY: Westminster John Knox, 2001), 309.
35. J. M. Miller and J. H. Hayes, *A history of ancient Israel and Judah* (Louisville, KY: Westminster John Knox, 1986), 153.
36. See F. A. Spina, "1 Samuel 17," in R. Van Harn, ed., *The lectionary commentary: the Old Testament and Acts* (Grand Rapids: William B. Eerdmans, 2001), 185–188.
37. J. G. Frazer, *The golden bough: a study in magic and religion* (London: Macmillan, 1919), 54.
38. S. Bar-Efrat, "First Samuel," in A. Berlin and M. Z. Brettler, ed., *The Jewish study Bible* (New York: Oxford University Press, 2004), 593.
39. L. O. Richards, *Bible reader's companion* (Colorado Springs: David C. Cook, 2002), 178.
40. Thiessen, *Selah*, 21.
41. Sendrey, *Music in ancient Israel*, 76.
42. BT B.B. 14b.
43. BT Pes. 117a.
44. J. A. Sanders, *The Dead Sea Psalms scroll* (Ithaca: Cornell University Press, 1967), 91–93.
45. B. Bayer and A. Shiloah, "David, music," in *Encyclopedia Judaica* 5 (2007): 457.
46. N.H. Imber, "Music of the Psalms," *Music: a monthly magazine* 6 (1894): 586–588.
47. Braun, *Music in ancient Israel/Palestine*, 2.
48. Braun, *Music in ancient Israel/Palestine*, 2.
49. Sendrey, *Music in ancient Israel*, 263.
50. J. H. Eaten, *The Psalms: a historical and spiritual commentary with an introduction and new translation* (New York: Continuum, 2006), 10.
51. Sendrey, *Music in ancient Israel*, 267–268.
52. Sendrey, *Music in ancient Israel*, 269.
53. Braun, *Music in ancient Israel/Palestine*, 17.
54. Stainer, *The music of the Bible*, 25.
55. H. Gressman, *Musik und musikinstrumente im Alten Testament* (Giessen: J. Rickler, 1903), 24.
56. Sendrey, *Music in ancient Israel*, 226.
57. Sachs, *The history of musical instruments*, 106.
58. Nulman, *Concise encyclopedia of Jewish music*, 133.
59. Nulman, *Concise encyclopedia of Jewish music*, 134.
60. BT Ar. 13b.

61. *Ant.* vii. 12.3.
62. *Shilte ha-Gibborim*, ch. 9.
63. Braun, *Music in ancient Israel/Palestine*, 18.
64. Braun, *Music in ancient Israel/Palestine*, 18.
65. C. H. Cornill, *The culture of ancient Israel* (Chicago: Open Court, 1914), 113; and Nulman, *Concise encyclopedia of Jewish music*, 134.
66. *Ant.* vii. 12.3.
67. Cornill, *The culture of ancient Israel*, 113.
68. Sachs, *The history of musical instruments*, 108.
69. A. Sendrey and M. Norton, *David's harp: the story of music in biblical times* (New York: New American Library, 1963), 113.
70. Braun, *Music in ancient Israel/Palestine*, 18.
71. Werner, *From generation to generation*, 63; Sendrey, *Music in ancient Israel*, 266; and Nulman, *Concise encyclopedia of Jewish music*, 134.
72. BT Ar. 13a.
73. Sendrey, *Music in ancient Israel*, 276.
74. J. W. N. Sullivan, "Beethoven: his spiritual development," in R. Katz and C. Dahlhaus, ed., *Contemplating music: source readings in the aesthetics of music* (Hillsdale, NY: Pendragon, 1993), 60.
75. See, for example, M. Budd, *Music and emotions: the philosophical theories* (New York: Routledge and Kegan Paul, 1985), 121–177; and P. Kivy, *Music alone: philosophical reflections on the purely musical experience* (Ithaca: Cornell University Press, 1990), 146–172.
76. D. M. Edwards, "Joy," in J. Orr, ed., *The international standard Bible dictionary*, vol. 3 (Chicago: Howard-Severance, 1915), 1755.
77. Crowe, *Music and soulmaking*, 330.
78. Gioia, *Healing songs*, 114.
79. Kirsch, *King David*, 325.
80. R. H. Pfeiffer, *Introduction to the Old Testament* (New York: Harper, 1941), 347.
81. R. Lack, *Twenty four frames under: a buried history of film music* (London: Quartet, 1997), 284.
82. M. Cobussen, *Thresholds: rethinking spirituality through music* (Burlington, VT: Ashgate, 2008), 16.
83. S. B. Finesinger, "The shofar," *Hebrew union college annual* (1931–32): 203.
84. Gressman, *Musik und musikinstrumente im Alten Testament*, 9.
85. Sendrey, *Music in ancient Israel*, 497.
86. BT M.K. 26a.
87. Wigram *et al.*, *Music therapy training*, 289.
88. C. O. Aluede and D. B. Ekewenu, "Healing through music and dance in the Bible: its scope, competence and implication for the Nigerian music healers," *Studies on ethnomedicine* 3:2 (2009): 160.
89. S. Bar-Efrat, "First Samuel," in A. Berlin and M. Z. Brettler, ed., *The Jewish study Bible* (New York: Oxford University Press, 2004), 588.
90. A. E. Meremi, "Traditional African concept of sound/motion: its implication for and application in music therapy," *British journal of music therapy* 11:10 (1997): 66–72.
91. J. Seidel, "Possession and exorcism in the magical texts of the Cairo Geniza," in M. Goldish, ed., *Spirit possession in Judaism: cases and contexts from the middle ages to the present* (Detroit: Wayne State University Press, 2003), 77.
92. Neusner and Green, *Dictionary of Judaism in the biblical period*, 400.
93. V. Erlmann, "Trance and music in the Hausa Bòorii spirit possession cult in Niger," *Ethnomusicology*, 26:1 (1982): 49–58; P. Berliner, *The soul of mbira: music and traditions of the Shona people of Zimbabwe* (Chicago: University of Chicago Press 1993), 186–206; and R. C. Jankowsky, "Music, spirit possession and the in-between: ethnomusicological inquiry and the challenge of trance," *Ethnomusicology forum* 16:2 (2007): 185–208.
94. Sachs, *The history of musical instruments*, 150.

95. D. C. Benjamin, *The Old Testament story: an introduction* (Minneapolis: Fortress, 2003), 193.
96. G. Rouget, *Music and trance: a theory of the relations between music and possession* (Chicago: University of Chicago Press, 1985), 154–158.
97. See, for example, H. G. Farmer, "The influence of music from Arabic countries: a lecture delivered before the musical association," lecture delivered before The Musical Association on 27 April 1926, London, 12; and Merriam, *The anthropology of music*, 11.
98. J. S. Peters, *Music therapy: an introduction* (Springfield, IL: C.C. Thomas, 2000), 3.
99. J. M. Honeycutt and M. E. Eidenmuller, "Communication and attribution: an exploration of the effects of music and mood on intimate couples' verbal and non-verbal conflict resolution behaviors," in V. L. Manusov and J. H. Harvey, J.H., ed., *Attribution, communication behavior, and close relationships* (New York: Cambridge University Press, 2001), 28.
100. See, for example, D. Campbell, *The Mozart effect: tapping the power of music to heal the body, strengthen the mind, and unlock the creative spirit* (New York: HarperCollins, 2001), 25; and Honeycutt and Eidenmuller, "Communication and attribution," 28.
101. E. L. Gatewood, "The psychology of music in relation to anesthesia," *American journal of surgery, anesthesia supplement* 35 (1921): 47–50.
102. F. Stein and S. K. Cutler, *Psychosocial occupational therapy: a holistic approach* (Florence, KY: Cengage Learning, 2002), 551.
103. T. West and G. Ironson, "Effects of music on human health and wellness: psychological measurements and research design," in B. Koen, ed. *The Oxford handbook of medical ethnomusicology* (New York: Oxford University Press, 2008), 423.
104. C. Brewer, "Orchestrating learning skills," *Open ear* 1 (1996): 14–15.
105. T. V. Sairam, "Therapeutic usefulness of music," *Music therapy today* 7:1 (2006): 115.
106. J. Jaaniste, "Cultural meaning and the art therapies in recovery," *Synergy* 2:1 (2006): 5.

Chapter 4

1. L. Boadt, *Reading the Old Testament: an introduction* (New York: Paulist, 1984), 307.
2. W. S. Lasor et al., *Old Testament survey: the message, form, and background of the Old Testament* (Grand Rapids: Wm. B. Eerdmans, 1996), 133.
3. A. J. Heschel, *The prophets: an introduction* (New York: Harper, 1962), 3–5; Boadt, *Reading the Old Testament*, 307; and Lasor et al., *Old Testament survey*, 133.
4. E. Rubin and J. H. Baron, *Music in Jewish history and culture* (Detroit: Harmonie Park, 2006), 5–6.
5. N. K. Chadwick, *Poetry and prophecy* (New York: Cambridge University Press, 1942), 14.
6. J. W. Hilber, *Cultic prophecy in the Psalms* (Berlin: Walter de Gruyter, 2005), 226.
7. *Ion*, 524.
8. M. Zwettler, *The oral tradition of classical Arabic poetry: its character and implications* (Columbus: Ohio University Press, 1978), 101.
9. A. Mursil, *The manners and customs of the Rwala Bedouins* (New York: American Geographical Society, 1928), 411.
10. S. Thielemann, *The spirituality of music* (New Delhi: APH Publishing, 2001), 134.
11. Heschel, *The prophets*, 5–6.
12. Heschel, *The prophets*, 4.
13. Heschel, *The prophets*, 19, 27.
14. J. Blenkinsopp, *A history of prophecy in Israel* (Louisville, KY: Westminster John Knox, 1983), 40–48.

15. S. M. Paul and S. D. Sperling, "Prophets and prophecy," in *Encyclopedia Judaica* 16 (2007): 567.
16. C. E. Hauer and W. A. Young, *An introduction to the Bible: a journey into three worlds*, 4th ed. (Upper Saddle River, NJ: Prentice Hall, 1998), 129.
17. H. C. Cryer, *Divination in ancient Israel and its near eastern environment: a socio-historical investigation* (New York: Continuum, 1994).
18. M. A. Sweeney, *The prophetic literature* (Nashville, TN: Abingdon, 2005), 24.
19. Paul and Sperling, "Prophets and prophecy," 567.
20. Paul and Sperling, "Prophets and prophecy," 567.
21. Hauer and Young, *An introduction to the Bible*, 131.
22. J. F. Wilson, *Religion: a preface* (Englewood Cliffs, NJ: Prentice Hall, 1982), 72–73.
23. See Sweeney, *The prophetic literature*, 127–164.
24. A. Berlin, "Reading Biblical Poetry," in A. Berlin and M. Z. Brettler, ed., *The Jewish study Bible* (New York: Oxford University Press, 2004), 2197.
25. R. Alter, *The art of biblical poetry* (New York: Basic, 1987), 140–141; and W. Brueggemann, *Finally comes the poet: daring speech for proclamation* (Minneapolis: Fortress, 1989), 5.
26. Alter, *The art of biblical poetry*, 141.
27. J. A. Davidson, *Toward a theology of beauty: a biblical perspective* (Lanham, MD: University Press of America, 2008), 190.
28. P. Friedrich, "The prophet Isaiah in Pushkin's 'prophet,'" in J.H. Leavitt, *ed. Poetry and prophecy: the anthropology of inspiration* (Ann Arbor: University of Michigan Press, 2007), 189.
29. Sendrey, *Music in ancient Israel*, 72.
30. See, for example, D. Weintraub, "Music and prophecy," *Journal of Synagogue Music* 301. 6:1 (1986): 34; Thiessen, *Selah*, 89; and Lockyer, Jr., *All the music of the Bible*, 94–95.
31. R. Orelli, *The prophecies of Isaiah* (Edinburgh: T. and T. Clark, 1889), 43.
32. F. W. Nietzsche, *On the genealogy of morality* (New York: Cambridge University Press, 2007), 73.
33. R. Otto, *The idea of the holy: an inquiry into the non-rational factor in the idea of the divine and its relation to the rational* (New York: Oxford University Press, 1950), 30.
34. Otto, *The idea of the holy*, 7.
35. Otto, *The idea of the holy*, 135.
36. Otto, *The idea of the holy*, 134.
37. Otto, *The idea of the holy*, 17.
38. Otto, *The idea of the holy*, 26.
39. *Hilkhot Yesodei ha-Torah*, 2:2.
40. Otto, *The idea of the holy*, 126.
41. Otto, *The idea of the holy*, 13.
42. Otto, *The idea of the holy*, 59.
43. van der Leeuw, *Sacred and profane beauty*, 231.
44. van der Leeuw, *Sacred and profane beauty*, 231.
45. W. James, *The varieties of religious experience* (London: Longmans, Green, 1905), 66.
46. W. Proudfoot, *Religious experience* (Berkeley: University of California Press, 1987), 132–133.
47. J. L. Friedmann, "A philosophy of Jewish sacred music," in J. L. Friedmann and B. Stetson, ed., *Jewish sacred music and Jewish identity: continuity and Fragmentation* (St. Paul: Paragon House, 2008), 5–6.
48. R. Viladesau, *Theology and the arts: encountering god through music, art and rhetoric* (New York: Paulist, 2000), 40.
49. J. A. Levine, *Synagogue song in America* (Crown Point, IN: White Cliffs, 1989), 79–106.
50. C. C. Judd, *Tonal structures in early music* (New York: Taylor and Francis, 2000), 270.

51. Viladesau, *Theology and the arts*, 40.
52. O. Söhngen, "Music and theology: a systematic approach," in J. Irwin, ed., *Sacred sound: music in religious thought and practice* (Chico, CA: Scholars, 1983), 8.
53. J. Glantz, "Introduction," in J. Glantz, ed., *The man who spoke to God* (Tel Aviv: The Tel Aviv Institute for Jewish Liturgical Music, 2008), 3.
54. A. Burgh, *Anecdotes of music: historical and biographical* (London: Longman, Hurst, Rees, Orme, and Brown, 1814), 23.
55. J. Opatoshu, *In Polish woods* (Philadelphia: Jewish Publication Society, 1921), 162.
56. E. Werner and I. Sonne, "The philosophy and theory of music in Judeo-Arabic literature," *Hebrew union college annual* 16 (1941): 251–319.
57. Gressman, *Musik und musikinstrumente im Alten Testament*, 16.
58. Z. Zevit, "First Kings," in A. Berlin and M. Z. Brettler, ed., *The Jewish study Bible* (New York: Oxford University Press, 2004), 717; and H. Hirschberg, "Elisha," in *Encyclopedia Judaica* 6 (2007): 350.
59. Zevit, "Elisha," 732.
60. F. W. Krummacher, *Elisha* (London: T. Nelson and Sons, 1870), 84.
61. Calmet et al., *Calmet's great dictionary of the holy Bible* (Boston: Crocker and Brewster, 1814), 100.
62. Shiloah, *Jewish Musical Traditions*, 43.
63. Braun, *Music in ancient Israel/Palestine*, 219.
64. J. W. Hilber, *Cultic prophecy in the Psalms* (Berlin: Walter de Gruyter, 2005), 184; S. A. Meier, *Themes and transformations in Old Testament prophecy* (Downers Grove, IL: InterVarsity, 2009), 85.
65. Sukk. 5:1.
66. G. L. Botterweck, "Kinnor," in G. J. Botterweck, H. Ringgren, and H. J. Fabry, ed., *Theological dictionary of the Old Testament*, vol. 7 (Grand Rapids: Wm. B. Eerdmans, 1995), 203.
67. G. A. Fatone, "Gamelan, techno-primitivism, and the San Francisco rave scene," in G. St John, ed., *Rave culture and religion* (New York: Routledge, 2004), 203.
68. M. F. Olmos and L. Paravsini-Gebert, *Creole religions of the Caribbean: an introduction from Vodou and Santería to Obeah and Espiritismo* (New York: NYU Press, 2003), 71–72.
69. W. R. Harper, *The Old Testament student*, vol. 8 (Chicago: Old Testament Book Exchange, 1889), 248; and S. Smith, *Prophetic song: gateway to glory* (Longwood, FL: Xulon, 2003), 30.
70. Ant. 9.28, 106.
71. Sendrey, *Music in ancient Israel*, 485.
72. J. G. Herder, *The spirit of Hebrew poetry*, vol. 2 (Burlington, VT: Edward Smith, 1833), 217; and Sendrey, *Music in ancient Israel*, 483.
73. Sachs, *The history of musical instruments*, 58–59.
74. M. Eliade, *The sacred and the profane: the nature of religion* (New York: Harcourt, 1959), 119.
75. Y. Kaufmann, *The religion of Israel: from its beginnings to the Babylonian exile* (New York: Schocken, 1960), 258.
76. Kaufmann, *The religion of Israel*, 96.
77. Hauer and Young, *An introduction to the Bible*, 145.
78. K. Craig, *Weight of the word: prophethood, biblical and quranic* (Sussex: Sussex Academic Press, 1999), 33.
79. N. Sarna, "Book of Psalms," in *Encyclopedia Judaica* 16 (2007): 670.
80. See, for example, E. Gerstenberger, "Jeremiah's complaints: observations on Jer. 15:10–21," *Journal of biblical literature* 82:4 (1963): 393–408; A. R. Diamond, *The confessions of Jeremiah in context: scenes of a prophetic drama* (Sheffield: Sheffield Academic Press, 1987), 124–25; and T. Longman and R. B. Dillard, *An introduction to the Old Testament* (Grand Rapids: Zondervan, 2006), 290.

Notes. Chapter 4

81. J.R. Lundbom, *Jeremiah 1–20: a new translation with introduction and commentary* (New York: Doubleday, 1999), 862; and Friedman, *Music and Jewish religious experience*, 108.

82. See Hutchinson, *Music of the Bible*, 42; Ryken, *Jeremiah and Lamentations*, 353; and Dempsey, *Jeremiah: preacher of grace, poet of truth*, 30.

83. J. A. Smith, "Musical aspects of Old Testament canticles in their biblical setting," 38–39; and J. D. Douglas and M. C. Tenney, *NIV compact dictionary of the Bible* (Grand Rapids: Zondervan, 1989), 395–397.

84. Sendrey, *Music in ancient Israel*, 159.

85. Langer, *Feeling and form*, 27.

86. M. Fishbane, *Text and texture: close readings of selected biblical texts* (New York: Schocken, 1979), 74.

87. Lundbom, *Jeremiah 1–20*, 863.

88. M. A. Sweeney, "Jeremiah," in A. Berlin and M. Z. Brettler, ed., *The Jewish study Bible* (New York: Oxford University Press, 2004), 966–967.

89. Rashi and Redak; see A. J. Rosenberg, *Jeremiah, volume 1: a new English translation of text, Rashi, and other commentaries* (New York: Judaica, 1985), 167.

90. Sweeney, "Jeremiah," 966.

91. J. R. Lundbom, *Jeremiah 1–20: a new translation with introduction and commentary* (New York: Doubleday, 1999), 859.

92. W. Baumgartner, *Jeremiah's poems of lament* (Sheffield: Sheffield Academic, 1988), 75.

93. Baumgartner, *Jeremiah's poems of lament*, 75.

94. I. Rabinowitz, "'Word' and literature in ancient Israel," *New literary history* 4:1 (1972): 130.

95. Sweeney, "Jeremiah," 966.

96. Lundbom, *Jeremiah 1–20*, 857.

97. Lundbom, *Jeremiah 1–20*, 857.

98. E. Fromm, *You shall be as gods: a radical interpretation of the Old Testament and its tradition* (New York: Holt, Rinehart, and Winston, 1966), 207.

99. H. W. Robinson, *Inspiration and revelation in the Old Testament* (Oxford: Clarendon, 1946), 263.

100. J. Silverman, *The undying flame: ballads and songs of the Holocaust* (Syracuse: Syracuse University Press, 2002), xv.

101. See L. B. Meyer, *Emotion and meaning in music* (Chicago: University of Chicago Press, 1958).

102. Werner and Sonne, "The philosophy and theory of music in Judeo-Arabic literature," 251–319.

103. M. A. Sweeney, *The prophetic literature* (Nashville: Abingdon, 2005), 198.

104. J. J. M. Roberts, *Nahum, Habakkuk, and Zephaniah: a commentary* (Louisville, KY: Westminster John Knox, 1991), 82; and Hauer and Young, *An introduction to the Bible*, 151.

105. Roberts, *Nahum, Habakkuk, and Zephaniah*, 84–85.

106. S. Mowinckel, *The Psalms in Israel's worship* (Grand Rapids: Wm. B. Eerdmans, 2004), 93.

107. See, for example, M. A. Sweeney, "Habakkuk," in J. L. Mays and J. Blenkinsopp, ed., *HarperCollins Bible commentary* (New York: HarperCollins, 2000), 668; R. D. Patterson, *Nahum, Habakkuk, Zephaniah: an exegetical commentary* (Dallas: Biblical Studies, 2003), 111; and M. O'Neal, *Interpreting Habakkuk as scripture: an application of the canonical approach of Brevard S. Childs* (New York: Peter Lang, 2007), 66.

108. R. D. Weiss, "Oracle," in D. N. Freedman, ed., *Anchor Bible dictionary*, vol. 5 (New York: Doubleday, 1992), 28–29.

109. Roberts, *Nahum, Habakkuk, and Zephaniah*, 85.

110. Sweeney, *The prophetic literature*, 198.

111. E. Ben Zvi, "Habakkuk," in A. Berlin and M. Z. Brettler, ed., *The Jewish study Bible* (New York: Oxford University Press, 2004), 1229.
112. O'Neal, *Interpreting Habakkuk as scripture*, 66.
113. T. Hiebert, "Theophany in the Old Testament," in D.N. Freedman, ed., *Anchor Bible dictionary* (New York: Doubleday, 1992), 509.
114. O'Neal, *Interpreting Habakkuk as scripture*, 66.
115. T. Hiebert, "Theophany in the Old Testament," 50.
116. W. A. Elwell and P. W. Comfort, *Tyndale Bible dictionary* (Carol Stream, IL: Tyndale House, 2001), 1194; and N. Sarna, "Book of Psalms," 674.
117. W. Wiersbe, *The Bible exposition commentary: Old Testament wisdom and poetry* (Colorado Springs: David C. Cook, 2004), 100.
118. T. Wallace, *Preaching and teaching outlines from the Psalms* (Murfreesboro: Sword of the Lord, 2001), vii.
119. See, for example, A. Calmet, *Dictionary of the holy Bible by Charles Taylor* (London: Holdsworth and Ball, 1832), 803; H. Lockyer, Sr., *Psalms: a devotional commentary* (Grand Rapids: Kregel, 1993), 184; and C. L. Carvalho, *Encountering ancient voices: a guide to reading the Old Testament* (Winona, MN: Saint Mary's, 2006), 225.
120. Nulman, *Concise encyclopedia of Jewish music*, 219.
121. BT Erub. 54a.
122. J. H. Hoffman, "Selah [forever]," in L. A. Hoffman, ed., *My people's prayer book: the amidah* (Woodstock, VT: Jewish Lights, 1998), 85.
123. Nulman, *Concise encyclopedia of Jewish music*, 219.
124. J. Steinberg, *Mishpat ha-urim* (Vilna: I. Piroschnikoff, 1902), 581.
125. J. Beimel, "Some Interpretations of the meaning of selah," *Jewish music forum bulletin* 4:1 (1943): 7.
126. See, for example, J. H. Hayes, *Introduction to the Bible* (Louisville, KY: Westminster John Knox, 1971), 16; R. J. Tournay, *Seeing and hearing God with the Psalms: the prophetic liturgy of the second temple in Jerusalem* (New York: Continuum, 1991), 62; and Braun, *Music in ancient Israel/Palestine*, 38.
127. Nulman, *Concise encyclopedia of Jewish music*, 147.
128. Sachs, *The history of musical instruments*, 125.
129. See, for example, W. F. Albright, *From the stone age to Christianity: monotheism and the historical process* (Baltimore: Johns Hopkins University Press, 1940), 231; Roberts, *Nahum, Habakkuk, and Zephaniah*, 86; and M. Z. Brettler, *How to read the Bible* (Philadelphia: Jewish Publication Society, 2005), 141.

Chapter 5

1. W. S. Pratt, "Religion and music," in J. H. Barrows, ed., *The world's parliament of religions*, vol. 2. (Chicago: Parliament, 1893), 1005.
2. Pratt, "Religion and music," 1005.
3. Pratt, "Religion and music," 1005.
4. BT Ber. 31a.
5. *Yad, Tefillah*, 6:16.
6. S. J. White, *Foundations of Christian worship* (Louisville, KY: Westminster John Knox, 2006), 41.
7. R. Wuthnow, *Producing the sacred: an essay on public religion* (Urbana: University of Illinois Press, 1994), 48–49.
8. E. R. Charles, *The voice of Christian life in song* (London: J. Nisbet, 1858), 2.
9. Pratt, "Religion and music," 1005.
10. J. R. Watson, *An annotated anthology of hymns* (New York: Oxford University Press, 2002), 6.
11. L. P. Glavich, *The Hebrew scriptures: called by the father* (Zurich: Benziger, 1992), 10.

12. R. Alter, *The book of Psalms: a translation with commentary* (New York: W.W. Norton, 2009), xviii.
13. King and Stager, *Life in biblical Israel*, 285; J. Day, *Psalms* (New York: Continuum, 2003), 16; and G. W. E. Nickelsburg and M. E. Stone, *Early Judaism: text and documents on faith and piety* (Minneapolis: Fortress, 2009), 56.
14. R. Kugler and P. Hartin, *An introduction to the Bible* (Grand Rapids: Wm. B. Eerdmans, 2009), 201.
15. H. Ringgren, *Sacrifice in the Bible* (London: United Society for Christian Literature, 1962), 7.
16. Boadt, *Reading the Old Testament*, 273.
17. Kaufmann, *The religion of Israel*, 111.
18. A. Rainey, "Sacrifice," in *Encyclopedia Judaica* 17 (2007): 644.
19. Boadt, *Reading the Old Testament*, 272.
20. Werner, *From generation to generation*, 6.
21. See Tam. 7:4.
22. Werner, *From generation to generation*, 7.
23. P. Birnbaum, *Encyclopedia of Jewish concepts* (New York: Hebrew, 1979), 550.
24. Birnbaum, *Encyclopedia of Jewish concepts*, 550.
25. S. D. Goitein, *A Mediterranean society* (Berkeley: University of California Press, 2000), 38.
26. J. L. Friedmann, *Music and Jewish religious experience: social and theological essays* (Saarbrücken: VDM Verlag, 2010), 24–37.
27. *De Musica* I. 3,4.
28. I. Reznikoff, "Intonation and modality in the music of oral tradition and antiquity," 542.
29. H. Antcliffe, "Music and religion," *The living age* 8:1 (1916): 157.
30. L. A. Hoffman, *The art of public prayer: not for clergy only* (Woodstock: VT: SkyLight Paths, 1999), 190.
31. Rubin and Baron, *Music in Jewish history and culture*, 25–26.
32. Aramaic Test. Levi, 4QTLevi.
33. Test. Reuben 6:7–8.
34. Joseph and Asenath 22:11–13.
35. Nulman, *Concise encyclopedia of Jewish music*, 152.
36. Zohar ii, 19a.
37. Edelman, *Discovering Jewish music*, 2.
38. BT Ar. 2:6.
39. E. Schleifer, "Jewish liturgical music from the Bible to Hasidism," in L. A. Hoffman, and J. R. Walton, ed., *Sacred sound and social change: liturgical music in Jewish and Christian experience* (Notre Dame: University of Notre Dame Press, 1992), 20.
40. *Shir Hashirim Rabbah*, ch. 3.
41. BT Ar. 11b; Jos., *Ant.* 20:218; and S. Safrai, "Temple," in *Encyclopedia Judaica* 19 (2007): 617.
42. Mid. 2:10.
43. BT Hul. 24a.
44. BT Hul. 24a.
45. BT Ar. 13b.
46. W. A. Elwell and P. W. Comfort, *Tyndale Bible dictionary* (Carol Stream, IL: Tyndale House, 2001), 1094.
47. BT Ar. 13b.
48. Safrai, "Temple," 621.
49. BT Tam. 5:4.
50. Idelsohn, *Jewish music*, 19.
51. BT Sot. 48a.
52. Idelsohn, *Jewish music*, 19.

Notes. Chapter 5

53. Werner, *From generation to generation*, 119.
54. Slobin, "Learning the lessons of studying Jewish music," 223.
55. A. Berlin and M. Z. Brettler, "Psalms," in A. Berlin and M. Z. Brettler, ed., *The Jewish study Bible* (Philadelphia: Jewish Publication Society, 2004), 1281.
56. Berlin and Brettler, "Psalms," 1280.
57. Berlin and Brettler, "Psalms," 1282.
58. Berlin and Brettler, "Psalms,"1439.
59. Sarna, "Book of Psalms," 667.
60. Berlin and Brettler, "Psalms," 1282.
61. B. K. Waltke et al., *The psalms as Christian worship: an historical commentary* (Grand Rapids: Wm. B. Eerdmans, 2010), 22.
62. F. E. Hibbard and D. D. Whedon, *The book of Psalms* (New York: Eaton and Mains, 1909), 10; Glavich, *The Hebrew scriptures*, 98; and Lockyer, Jr., *All the music of the Bible*, 88.
63. Sarna, "Book of Psalms," 668.
64. II QPsa col. 27.
65. R. Rendtorff, "The Psalms of David: David in the Psalms," in P. W. Flint and P. D. Miller, ed., *The book of Psalms: composition and reception* (Boston: Brill, 2005), 53.
66. Berlin and Brettler, "Psalms," 1283.
67. O. Eissfeldt, *The Old Testament: an introduction* (New York: Harper, 1965), 493.
68. R. E. Clements, "Wisdom," in D. A. Carson and H. G. M. Williamson, ed., *It is written: scripture citing scripture: essays in honour of Barnabas Lindars* (New York: Cambridge University Press, 1980), 80.
69. J. A. Loader, *Ecclesiastes: a practical commentary* (Grand Rapids: Wm. B. Eerdmans, 1986), 4.
70. B. S. Childs, *Introduction to the Old Testament as scripture* (London: SCM, 1979), 584.
71. R. A. Kassis, *The book of Proverbs and Arabic proverbial works* (Boston: Brill, 1999), 32.
72. Waltke et al., *The psalms as Christian worship*, 90.
73. H. F. Van Rooy, "The Psalms in early Syriac tradition," in P. W. Flint and P. D. Miller, ed., *The book of Psalms: composition and reception* (Leiden: Brill, 2005), 537–550.
74. A. Pietersma, "Septuagintal exegesis and the superscriptions of the Greek psalter," in P. W. Flint and P. D. Miller, ed., *The book of Psalms: composition and reception* (Leiden: Brill, 2005), 443–475.
75. H. J. Flanders et al., *People of the covenant: an introduction to the Old Testament* (New York: Oxford University Press, 1988), 407.
76. S. L. McKenzie, *King David: a biography* (New York: Oxford University Press, 2000), 38.
77. J. Goldingay, "Hermeneutics," in T. Longman and P. Enns, ed., *Dictionary of the Old Testament: wisdom, poetry and writings*, vol. 3 (Downers Grove, IL: InterVarsity, 2008) 1, 269.
78. B. K. Waltke and C. Yu, *An Old Testament theology: a canonical and thematic approach* (Grand Rapids: Zondervan, 2007), 872.
79. Lockyer, Jr., *All the music of the Bible*, 82.
80. Berlin and Brettler, "Psalms," 1283.
81. J. Calvin, *Commentary on the book of Psalms* 1 (Grand Rapids: Wm. B. Eerdmans, 1949), xxxvii.
82. M. Luther, *Luther's works, volume 35: word and sacrament* (Philadelphia: Fortress, 1960), 255–256.
83. H. Van Dyke, *The poetry of the Psalms* (New York: T.Y. Crowell, 1900), 1–24; R. Alter, *The art of biblical poetry* (New York: Basic, 1987), 111; and J. H. Eaton, *Meditating on the Psalms* (Louisville, KY: Westminster John Knox, 2005), 2–4.
84. A. Berlin, "Reading Biblical Poetry," in A. Berlin and M. Z. Brettler, ed., *The Jewish study Bible* (New York: Oxford University Press, 2004), 2101.
85. Eaton, *Meditating on the Psalms*, 14.

Notes. Chapter 5

86. Collins, *Introduction to the Hebrew Bible*, 470.
87. See, for example, Collins, *Introduction to the Hebrew Bible*, 470; and Brettler, *How to read the Bible*, 219.
88. Sendrey, *Music in ancient Israel*, 172.
89. W. S. Pratt, "Religion and the art of music," in J. L. Friedmann, comp., *The value of sacred music: an anthology of essential writings, 1801–1918* (Jefferson, NC: McFarland, 2009), 58.
90. BT Pes. 117a; JT Sukk. 3:12; and JT Meg. 1:9.
91. Eaton, *Meditating on the Psalms*, 5.
92. Sarna, "Book of Psalms," 673–675.
93. E. Foley and M. Paul, *Worship music: a concise dictionary* (Collegeville, MN: Liturgical Press, 2000), 18.
94. Sendrey, *Music in ancient Israel*, 166–167; and H. Gunkel, *Introduction to Psalms: the genres of the religious lyric of Israel* (Macon, GA: Mercer University Press, 1998), 311.
95. Gunkel, *Introduction to Psalms*, 311.
96. Gunkel, *Introduction to Psalms*, 311.
97. Mid. Teh. 118:14, 22; and BT Pes. 119a.
98. Sukk. 5:4; and Mid. 2:5.
99. Sarna, Book of Psalms," 673.
100. Sarna, "Book of Psalms," 670.
101. Mowinckel, *The Psalms in Israel's worship*, 61.
102. Mowinckel, *The Psalms in Israel's worship*, 106–192.
103. Sendrey, *Music in ancient Israel*, 175.
104. M. Tam. 7:4.
105. M. Tam. 7:3.
106. N. Sarna, *On the book of Psalms: exploring the prayers of ancient Israel* (New York: Schocken, 1995), 3.
107. Mid. Teh. 18:1.
108. L. C. Elson, "Ancient Jewish hymns," in J. L. Friedmann, comp. *The value of sacred music: an anthology of essential writings, 1801–1918* (Jefferson, NC: McFarland, 2009), 32.
109. Elson, "Ancient Jewish hymns," 31.
110. A. Robertson, *Christian music* (New York: Hawthorn, 1961), 29.
111. Irving quoted in Elson, "Ancient Jewish Hymns," 31.
112. Brueggemann, *The Psalms and the Life of Faith*, 193.
113. Thiessen, *Selah*, 87.
114. Friedmann, *Music and Jewish religious experience*, 38–49.
115. H. Gunkel, *The Psalms: a form-critical introduction* (Minneapolis: Fortress, 1967); P. D. Miller, *They cried to the lord: the form and theology of biblical prayer* (Minneapolis: Fortress, 1994), 206; and M. D. Goulder, *The Psalms of the return (book V, Psalms 107–150)* (New York: Continuum, 1998), 301.
116. E. G. Rust, *The music and dance of the world's religions: a comprehensive, annotated bibliography of materials in the English language* (Westport, CT: Greenwood, 1996), xv.
117. *In psalmum* 72.1.
118. *In psalmum* 99.4.
119. J. J. Collins, *Introduction to the Hebrew Bible*, 464.
120. Brueggemann, *The Psalms and the life of faith*, 192.
121. Brueggemann, *The Psalms and the life of faith*, 193.
122. Smith, *The wisdom literature and Psalms*, 196.
123. *Midrash Soher Tov*, 1:2.
124. Berlin and Brettler, "Psalms," 1281.
125. M. Davis, *Siddur for Sabbath and festivals* (New York: Mesorah, 2006), 296.
126. W. S. Prinsloo, "The Psalms," in J. D. G. Dunn and J. W. Rogerson, ed., *Eerdmans commentary on the Bible* (Grand Rapids: Wm. B. Eerdmans, 2003), 435.
127. Berlin and Brettler, "Psalms," 1446.

128. Berlin and Brettler, "Psalms," 1284.
129. A. J. Heschel, *The insecurity of freedom: essays on human existence* (New York: Farrar, Straus and Giroux, 1966), 245.
130. A. J. Rosenberg, *Mikraoth gedoloth: Psalms*, vol. 3 (New York: Judaica, 2001), 550.
131. O. P. Hiller, *God manifest* (Boston: Ottis Clapp, 1858), 100.
132. E. Davies, ed., *Great thoughts on great truths* (London: Ward, Lock, 1882), 423.
133. Davis, *Siddur for Sabbath and festivals*, 267.
134. *In psalmum* 99.4.
135. *In psalmum* 99.4.
136. J. L. Friedmann, ed., *Quotations on Jewish sacred music* (Lanham, MD: Hamilton, 2011), 37.
137. J. G. Conti and B. Stetson, "Can music be understood as a 'signal of transcendence'?" in J. L. Friedmann and B. Stetson, ed., *Jewish sacred music and Jewish identity: continuity and fragmentation* (St. Paul: Paragon House, 2008), xvi–xvii.
138. W. Cutter, "General introduction," in L. L. Arian, ed., *R'fuah sh'leimah: songs of Jewish healing* (New York: Transcontinental Music, 2005), 5.
139. Levitin, *The world in six songs*, 126.
140. F. Marshall and P. Cheevers, *Positive options for seasonal affective disorder (SAD): self-help and treatment* (Alameda, CA: Hunter House, 2003), 58.
141. S. Hallam, *Music psychology in education* (London: Institute of Education, 2006), 187.
142. S. Labowitz, *Miraculous living: a guided journey in kabbalah through the ten gates of the tree of life* (New York: Simon & Schuster, 1998), 197.
143. King and Stager, *Life in biblical Israel*, 5.
144. C. H. Spurgeon, *The treasury of David* (New York: Funk and Wagnalls, 1885), 32.
145. Brettler, *How to read the Bible*, 219.
146. W. Brueggemann, *An introduction to the Old Testament: the canon and Christian imagination* (Louisville, KY: Westminster John Knox, 2003), 277.
147. Levitin, *The world in six songs*, 42.
148. Levitin, *The world in six songs*, 50.
149. Berlin and Brettler, "Psalms," 1432.
150. Levitin, *The world in six songs*, 102.
151. Levitin, *The world in six songs*, 126.
152. Braun, *Music in ancient Israel/Palestine*, 10.
153. D. K. Stuart, *Hosea-Jonah* (Waco: Word Books, 1987), 317.
154. D. J. Harrington, *Why do we hope? images in the Psalms* (Collegeville, MN: Liturgical Press, 2008), iv.
155. Levitin, *The world in six songs*, 159–160.
156. Levitin, *The world in six songs*, 191.
157. J. W. Kleinig, *The lord's song: the basis, function and significance of choral music in chronicles* (New York: Continuum, 1993), 100.
158. J. F. D. Creach, "The Psalms and the cult," in D. G. Firth and P. Johnston, ed., *Interpreting the Psalms: issues and approaches* (Downers Grove, IL: InterVarsity, 2005), 132–137.
159. H. J. Kraus, *Psalms 1–59: a continental commentary* (Minneapolis: Fortress, 1993), 61–62.
160. Levitin, *The world in six songs*, 236.
161. S. Harvey, "Love," in A. A. Cohen and P. Mendes-Flohr, ed., *Contemporary Jewish religious thought: original essays on critical concepts, movements, and beliefs* (New York: Free Press, 1987), 561.
162. J. Pati, *Media and tribal development* (New Delhi: Concept, 2004), 112; O. Sacks, *Musicophilia: tales of music and the brain* (New York: Knopf, 2007), 244; and J. Jacobson, "Contrafaction," *Journal of synagogue music* 35 (2010): 212.
163. Levitin, *The world in six songs*, 3.

Bibliography

Albright, W.F. *From the stone age to Christianity: monotheism and the historical process.* Baltimore: Johns Hopkins University Press, 1940.
Alter, R. *The art of biblical poetry.* New York: Basic Books, 1987.
_____. *The book of Psalms: a translation with commentary.* New York: W.W. Norton, 2009.
Aluede, C.O., and D.B. Ekewenu. "Healing through music and dance in the Bible: its scope, competence and implication for the Nigerian music healers." *Studies on ethno-medicine* 3:2 (2009): 159–163.
Anderson, M.L., and H.F. Taylor. *Sociology: the essentials.* Belmont, CA: Wadsworth, 2010.
Antcliffe, H. *Music and religion. The living age* 8:1 (1916): 156–161.
Avenary, H. "Formal structure of psalms and canticles in early Jewish and Christian chant." *Musica disciplina* 7 (1953): 1–13.
Bacchiocchi, S. "Biblical principles of church music." *Endtime issues* 3:4 (2000): 1–32.
Bar-Efrat, S. "First Samuel." In A. Berlin and M.Z. Brettler, eds. *The Jewish study Bible.* New York: Oxford University Press, 2004. 558–618.
Barber, C.J. *Habakkuk and Zephaniah.* Chicago: Moody, 1985.
Barzilai, S. *Chassidic ecstasy in music.* Frankfurt am Main: Peter Lang, 2009.
Baumgartner, W. *Jeremiah's poems of lament.* Sheffield: Sheffield Academic, 1988.
Bayer, B., and A. Shiloah, "David, music." In *Encyclopedia Judaica,* 5 (2007): 457–458.
Beck, G.L. "Introduction." In G.L. Beck, ed. *Sacred sound: experiencing music in world religions.* Waterloo, ON: Wilfrid Laurier University Press, 2006. 1–27.
Befu, H. "Symbols of nationalism and nihonjinron." In R. Goodman and K. Refsing, eds. *Ideology and practice in modern Japan.* New York: Routledge. 1992. 26–46.
Beimel, J. "Divinity and music: a Jewish conception." *Jewish music* 1:1 (1934): 114–115.
_____. "Some Interpretations of the meaning of selah." *Jewish music forum bulletin* 4:1 (1943): 6–7.
Ben Zvi, E. "Habakkuk." In A. Berlin and M.Z. Brettler, eds. *The Jewish study Bible.* New York: Oxford University Press, 2004. 1226–1233.
Benjamin, D.C. *The Old Testament story: an introduction.* Minneapolis: Fortress, 2003.
Berlin, A. "Reading Biblical Poetry." In A. Berlin and M.Z. Brettler, eds. *The Jewish study Bible.* New York: Oxford University Press, 2004. 2097–2104.
Berlin, A., and M.Z. Brettler. "Psalms." In A. Berlin and M.Z. Brettler, eds. *The Jewish study Bible.* Philadelphia: Jewish Publication Society, 2004. 1280–1446.
Berliner, P. *The soul of mbira: music and traditions of the Shona people of Zimbabwe.* Chicago: University of Chicago Press, 1993.
Bilu, Y. "The taming of the deviants and beyond: an analysis of dybbuk possession and exorcism in Judaism." In M. Goldish, ed. *Spirit possession in Judaism: cases and contexts from the middle ages to the present.* Detroit: Wayne State University Press, 2003. 41–72.
Binder, A.W. *Biblical chant.* New York: Philosophical Library, 1959.
Birnbaum, P. *Encyclopedia of Jewish concepts.* New York: Hebrew, 1979.

Bibliography

Blenkinsopp, J. *A history of prophecy in Israel*. Louisville, KY: Westminster John Knox, 1983.
Boadt, L. *Reading the Old Testament: an introduction*. New York: Paulist, 1984.
Bock, K.A. "Harp music eases pain from lupus." *The harp therapy journal* 4:1 (1999).
Bohlman, P.V. *"The land where two streams flow": music in the German-Jewish community of Israel*. Urbana: University of Illinois Press, 1989.
Borowki, O. *Daily life in biblical times*. Atlanta: Society for Biblical Literature, 2003.
Botterweck, G.J. "Kinnor." In G.J. Botterweck, H. Ringgren, and H.J. Fabry, eds. *Theological dictionary of the Old Testament*, vol. 7. Grand Rapids: Wm. B. Eerdmans, 1995. 196–204.
Braun, J. *Music in ancient Israel/Palestine: archaeological, written and comparative sources*. Translated from the German by D.W. Scott. Grand Rapids: Wm. B. Eerdmans, 2002.
Brenner, A., and F. Van Dijk-Hemmes. *On gendering texts: female and male voices in the Hebrew Bible*. Boston: Brill, 1996.
Brettler, M.Z. *How to read the Bible*. Philadelphia: Jewish Publication Society, 2005.
Brewer, C. *Orchestrating learning skills*. Open ear (1996).
Brown, S. "'How does music work?' toward a pragmatics of musical communication." In S. Brown, and U. Volgsten, eds. *Music and manipulation: on the social uses and social control of music*. New York: Berghahn, 2006. 1–30.
Brueggemann, W. *Finally comes the poet: daring speech for proclamation*. Minneapolis: Fortress, 1989.
———. *An introduction to the Old Testament: the canon and Christian imagination*. Louisville, KY: Westminster John Knox, 2003.
———. *The Psalms and the life of faith*. Minneapolis: Fortress, 1995.
Brunson, A.C. *Psalm 118 in the gospel of John: an intertextual study on the new exodus pattern in the theology of John*. Tübingen: Mohr Siebeck, 2003.
Budd, M. *Music and emotions: the philosophical theories*. New York: Routledge and Kegan Paul, 1985.
Bunt, L. *Music therapy: an art beyond words*. Hove, UK: Psychology Press, 1994.
Burgh, A. *Anecdotes of music: historical and biographical*. London: Longman, Hurst, Rees, Orme, and Brown, 1814.
Burgh, T.W. *Listening to the artifacts: music in ancient Palestine*. New York: Continuum, 2006.
Calmet, A. *Dictionary of the holy Bible by Charles Taylor*. London: Holdsworth and Ball, 1832.
Calmet, A., C. Taylor, E. Wells, and S. Etheridge. *Calmet's great dictionary of the holy Bible*. Boston: Crocker and Brewster, 1814.
Calvin, J. *Commentary on the book of Psalms 1*. Grand Rapids: Wm. B. Eerdmans, 1949.
Campbell, D. *The Mozart effect: tapping the power of music to heal the body, strengthen the mind, and unlock the creative spirit*. New York: HarperCollins, 2001.
Carvalho, C.L. *Encountering ancient voices: a guide to reading the Old Testament*. Winona, MN: Saint Mary's, 2006.
Chadwick, N.K. *Poetry and prophecy*. New York: Cambridge University Press, 1942.
Chapman, J.L. *Singing and teaching singing: a holistic approach to classical voice*. San Diego: Plural, 2006.
Charles, E.R. *The voice of Christian life in song*. London: J. Nisbet, 1858.
Childs, B.S. *Introduction to the Old Testament as scripture*. London: SCM, 1979.
Clements, R.E. "Wisdom." In D.A. Carson, and H.G.M. Williamson, eds. *It is written: scripture citing scripture: essays in honour of Barnabas Lindars*. New York: Cambridge University Press, 1980. 67–86.
Clift, S.M., and G. Hancox. "The perceived benefits of singing: findings from preliminary surveys of a university college choral society." *Perspectives in public health* 12:4 (2001): 248–256.
Cobussen, M. *Thresholds: rethinking spirituality through music*. Burlington, VT: Ashgate, 2008.
Cohen, F.L. "Jewish music." In J.L. Friedmann, comp. *Music in Jewish thought: selected writings, 1890–1920*. Jefferson, NC: McFarland, 2009. 52–58.

Bibliography

Collins, J.J. *Introduction to the Hebrew Bible*. Minneapolis: Fortress, 2004.
_____. *A short introduction to the Hebrew Bible*. Minneapolis: Fortress, 2007.
Conti, J.G., and B. Stetson, 2008. "Can music be understood as a 'signal of transcendence'?" In J.L. Friedmann and B. Stetson, eds. *Jewish sacred music and Jewish identity: continuity and fragmentation*. St. Paul: Paragon House, 2007. xi–xvii.
Cornill, C.H. *The culture of ancient Israel*. Chicago: Open Court, 1914.
Crafts, W.F. *Trophies of song: Articles and incidents on the power of sacred music*. Boston: D. Lothrop, 1874.
Craig, K. *Weight of the word: prophethood, biblical and quranic*. Sussex: Sussex Academic Press, 1999.
Creach, J.F.D. "The Psalms and the cult." In D.G. Firth and P. Johnston, eds. *Interpreting the Psalms: issues and approaches*. Downers Grove, IL: InterVarsity, 2005. 119–137.
Cross, Jr., F.M., and D.N. Freedman. "The song of Miriam." *Journal of Near Eastern studies*, 14:4 (1955): 237–255.
Crowe, B.J. *Music and soulmaking: toward a new theory of music therapy*. Lanham, MD: Scarecrow, 2004.
Cryer, H.C. *Divination in ancient Israel and its near eastern environment: a socio-historical investigation*. New York: Continuum, 1994.
Cutter, W. "General introduction." In M. L. Arian, ed. *R'fuah sh'leimah: songs of Jewish healing*. New York: Transcontinental Music, 2000. 5–6.
Davidson, J.A. *Toward a theology of beauty: a biblical perspective*. Lanham, MD: University Press of America, 2008.
Davies, E., ed. *Great thoughts on great truths*. London: Ward, Lock, 1882.
Davis, C. "The effects of music and basic relaxation instruction on pain and anxiety of women undergoing in-office gynecological procedures." *Journal of music therapy*, 24:4 (1992): 202–216.
Davis, E.F. "Reading the song iconographically." In P.S. Hawkins and L.C. Stahlberg, eds. *Scrolls of love: Ruth and the Song of Songs*. New York: Fordham University Press, 2006. 172–184.
Davis, M. *Siddur for Sabbath and festivals*. New York: Mesorah, 2006.
Day, J. Psalms. New York: Continuum, 2003.
Dempsey, C.J. *Jeremiah: preacher of grace, poet of truth*. Collegeville, MN: Liturgical Press, 2007.
Diamond, A.R. *The confessions of Jeremiah in context: scenes of a prophetic drama*. Sheffield: Sheffield Academic Press, 1987.
Dickinson, E. "Oratorio performance in Europe and America." (In Hubbard, W.L., ed. *The American history and encyclopedia of music*. New York: Irving Squire, 1909. 1–10.
Dissanayake, E. "A review of the singing Neanderthals." *Evolutionary psychology* 3: (2005): 375–380.
Douglas, J.D., and M.C. Tenney. *NIV compact dictionary of the Bible*. Grand Rapids: Zondervan, 1989.
Douglas, M. *Purity and danger: an analysis of concepts of pollution and taboo*. New York: Routledge and Kegan Paul, 1966.
During, J. "Therapeutic dimensions of music in Islamic culture." In D. Koen, ed. *The Oxford handbook of medical ethnomusicology*. New York: Oxford University Press, 2008. 361–392.
Durkheim, E. *The elementary forms of religious life*. Translated from the French by Carol Cosman. New York: Oxford University Press, 2001.
_____. *Emile Durkheim on morality and society*. Robert Bellah, ed. Chicago: University of Chicago Press, 1973.
Eaton, J.H. *Meditating on the Psalms*. Louisville, KY: Westminster John Knox, 2005.
_____. *The Psalms: a historical and spiritual commentary with an introduction and new translation*. New York: Continuum, 2006.
Edelman, M.B. *Discovering Jewish music*. Philadelphia: Jewish Publication Society, 2003.

Edwards, D.M. "Joy." In J. Orr, ed. *The international standard Bible dictionary*, vol. 3. Chicago: Howard-Severance, 1915.
Edwards, J.M. "Women in music to ca. 1450." In K. Pendle, ed. *Women and music: a history*. Bloomington: Indiana University Press, 2001. 26–56.
Ehrenreich, A.B. *Dancing in the streets: a history of collective joy*. New York: Macmillan, 2007.
Eissfeldt, O. *The Old Testament: an introduction*. New York: Harper, 1965.
Eliade, M. *The sacred and the profane: the nature of religion*. New York: Harcourt, 1959.
Elson, L.C. "Ancient Jewish hymns." In J.L. Friedmann, comp. *The value of sacred music: an anthology of essential writings, 1801–1918*. Jefferson, NC: McFarland, 2009. 27–32.
Elwell, W.A., and P.W. Comfort. *Tyndale Bible dictionary*. Carol Stream, IL: Tyndale House, 2001.
Engel, C. *Music of the most ancient nations, particularly of the Assyrians, Egyptians, and Hebrews*. London: William Reeves, 1929.
Erlmann, V. "Trance and music in the Hausa Bòorii spirit possession cult in Niger." *Ethnomusicology*, 26:1 (1982): 49–58.
Farmer, H.G. "The influence of music from Arabic countries: a lecture delivered before the musical association." Lecture delivered before The Musical Association, 27 April 1926. London.
Fatone, G.A. "Gamelan, techno-primitivism, and the San Francisco rave scene." In St. John, G., ed. *Rave culture and religion*. New York: Routledge, 2004. 197–208.
Feldman, E. "Shirat hayam: a triumphant song of Jewish history." *Hayenu* 45:8 (2000): 5.
Finesinger, S.B. "The shofar." *Hebrew union college annual* (1931–32): 193–228.
Finkelstein, I., and N.A. Silberman. *The Bible unearthed: archaeology's new vision of ancient Israel and the origin of its sacred texts*. New York: Touchstone, 2012.
Fish, J.S. *Defending the Durkheimian tradition: religion, emotion and morality*. Burlington, VT: Ashgate, 2005.
Fishbane, M. *Text and texture: close readings of selected biblical texts*. New York: Schocken, 1979.
Flanders, H. J., R.W. Crapps, and D.A. Smith. *People of the covenant: an introduction to the Old Testament*. New York: Oxford University Press, 1988.
Foley, E., and M. Paul. *Worship music: a concise dictionary*. Collegeville, MN: Liturgical Press, 2000.
Foltz, T.G. "Drumming and re-enchantment: creating spiritual community." In L. Hume, and K. McPhillips, eds. *Popular spirituality: the politics of contemporary enchantment*. Burlington, VT: Ashgate, 2006. 131–146.
Forsyth, P. T. *Christ on Parnassus: lectures on art, ethic, and theology*. London: Independent, 1911.
Frankel, E. *The five books of Miriam: a woman's commentary on the Torah*. New York: HarperCollins, 1997.
Frazer, J.G. *The golden bough: a study in magic and religion*. London: Macmillan, 1919.
Freeman, L., M. Caserta, D. Lund, S. Rossa, A. Dowdy, and A. Partenheimer. "Music thanatology: prescriptive harp music as palliative care for the dying patient." *American journal of hospital palliative care*, 23:2 (2006): 100–104.
Friedmann, J.L. *Music and Jewish religious experience: social and theological essays*. Saarbrücken: VDM Verlag, 2010.
_____. "A philosophy of Jewish sacred music." In Friedmann, J.L. and Stetson, B. eds. *Jewish sacred music and Jewish identity: continuity and fragmentation*. St. Paul: Paragon House, 2008. 3–18.
_____, comp. *The value of sacred music: an anthology of essential writings, 1801–1918*. Jefferson, NC: McFarland, 2009.
_____, ed. *Quotations on Jewish sacred music*. Lanham, MD: Hamilton, 2011.
Friedrich, P. "The prophet Isaiah in Pushkin's 'prophet.'" In J.H. Leavitt, ed. *Poetry and prophecy: the anthropology of inspiration*. Ann Arbor: University of Michigan Press, 2007. 169–200.

Bibliography

Fromm, E. *You shall be as gods: a radical interpretation of the Old Testament and its tradition.* New York: Holt, Rinehart, and Winston, 1966.

Frymer-Kensky, T. *Studies in Bible and feminist criticism.* Philadelphia: Jewish Publication Society, 2006.

Fubini, E. *The history of music aesthetics.* Translated from the Italian by Michael Hartwell. London: Macmillan, 1990.

Gardiner, W. *The music of nature.* Boston: Ditson, 1832.

Gatewood, E.L. "The psychology of music in relation to anesthesia." *American journal of surgery, anesthesia supplement,* 35 (1921): 47–50.

Gendler, E.E. "Community." In A.A. Cohen and P. Mendes-Flohr, eds. *Contemporary Jewish religious thought: original essays on critical concepts, movements, and beliefs.* New York: Free Press, 1987. 81–86.

Gerstenberger, E. "Jeremiah's complaints: observations on Jer. 15:10–21." *Journal of biblical literature,* 82:4 (1963): 393–408.

Ginzberg, L. *The legends of the Jews,* vol. 3. Philadelphia: Jewish Publication Society, 1920.

Gioia, T. *Healing songs.* Durham: Duke University Press, 2006.

_____. *Work songs.* Durham: Duke University Press, 2006.

Glantz, J. "Introduction." In J. Glantz, ed. *The man who spoke to God.* Tel Aviv: The Tel Aviv Institute for Jewish Liturgical Music, 2008. 1–6.

Glavich, L.P. *The Hebrew scriptures: called by the father.* Zurich: Benziger, 1992.

Glavich, M.K. *The Catholic companion to the Psalms.* Chicago: ACTA, 2008.

Goitein, S.D. *A Mediterranean society.* Berkeley: University of California Press, 2000.

Goldingay, J. "Hermeneutics." In T. Longman and P. Enns, eds. *Dictionary of the Old Testament: wisdom, poetry and writings,* vol. 3. Downers Grove, IL: InterVarsity, 2008. 267–280.

Gorfinkle, J.I. *The eight chapters of Maimonides on ethics.* New York: Columbia University Press, 1912.

Goulder, M.D. *The Psalms of the return (book V, Psalms 107–150).* New York: Continuum, 1998.

Gressman, H. *Musik und musikinstrumente im Alten Testament.* Giessen: J. Rickler, 1903.

Grunlan, S.A., and M.K. Mayers. *Cultural anthropology: a Christian perspective.* Grand Rapids: Zondervan, 1988.

Gunkel, H. *Introduction to Psalms: the genres of the religious lyric of Israel.* Macon, GA: Mercer University Press, 1998.

_____. *The Psalms: a form-critical introduction.* Minneapolis: Fortress, 1967.

Ha'am, A. *Selected essays.* Philadelphia: Jewish Publication Society, 1912.

Hallam, S. *Music psychology in education.* London: Institute of Education, 2006.

Hang, X. *Encyclopedia of national anthems.* Lanham, MD: Scarecrow, 2003.

Hanna, J.L. *To dance is human: a theory of nonverbal communication.* Chicago: University of Chicago Press, 1997.

Hanser, S.B. *Music therapy and stress reduction research. Journal of music therapy,* 12:4 (1985): 193–206.

Harper, W.R. *The Old Testament student,* vol. 8. Chicago: Old Testament Book Exchange, 1889.

Harrington, D.J. *Why do we hope? images in the Psalms.* Collegeville, MN: Liturgical Press, 2008.

Hartman, G. "Imagination." In A.A. Cohen and P. Mendes-Flohr, eds. *Contemporary Jewish religious thought: original essays on critical concepts, movements, and beliefs.* New York: Free Press, 1988. 451–472.

Harvey, S. "Love." In A.A. Cohen and P. Mendes-Flohr, eds. *Contemporary Jewish religious thought: original essays on critical concepts, movements, and beliefs.* New York: Free Press, 1987. 557–563.

Hast, D.E., J.R. Cowdery, and S.A. Scott. *Exploring the world of music: an introduction to music from a world music perspective.* Dubuque: Kendall/Hunt, 1999.

Bibliography

Hauer, C.E., and W.A. Young. *An introduction to the Bible: a journey into three worlds*, 4th ed. Upper Saddle River, NJ: Prentice Hall, 1998.
Haviland, W.A., E.L. Prins, and B. Mcbride. *Cultural anthropology: the human challenge*, 11th ed. Belmont, CA: Thomson Wadsworth, 2005.
Haweis, H.R. "Music, emotions, and morals." In J.L. Friedmann, comp. *The value of sacred music: an anthology of essential writings, 1801–1918.* Jefferson, NC: McFarland, 2009. 99–102.
Hayes, J.H. *Introduction to the Bible.* Louisville, KY: Westminster John Knox, 1971.
Herder, J.G. *The spirit of Hebrew poetry*, vol. 2. Translated from the German by James Marsh. Burlington, VT: Edward Smith, 1833.
Herzog, G. "Music's dialects: a non-universal language." *Independent journal of Columbia University* 6:10 (1939): 1–2.
Heschel, A.J. *The insecurity of freedom: essays on human existence.* New York: Farrar, Straus and Giroux, 1966.
_____. *The prophets: an introduction.* New York: Harper, 1962.
Heskes, I. *Passport to Jewish music: its history, traditions, and culture.* New York: Tara, 1994.
Hibbard, F.E., and D.D. Whedon. *The book of Psalms.* New York: Eaton and Mains, 1909.
Hiebert, T. "Theophany in the Old Testament." In D.N. Freedman, ed. *Anchor Bible dictionary.* New York: Doubleday. 1992.
Hilber, J.W. *Cultic prophecy in the Psalms.* Berlin: Walter de Gruyter, 2005.
Hiller, O.P. *God manifest.* Boston: Ottis Clapp, 1858.
Hirschberg, H.Z. "Elisha." In *Encyclopedia Judaica*, 6 (2007): 350–351.
Hoffman, J.H. "Selah [forever]." In L.A. Hoffman, ed. *My people's prayer book: the Amidah.* Woodstock, VT: Jewish Lights, 1998.
Hoffman, L.A. *The art of public prayer: not for clergy only.* Woodstock: VT: SkyLight Paths, 1999.
Hofman, S. *Miqra'ey musica: a collection of biblical references to music in Hebrew, English, French and Spanish.* Tel Aviv: Israel Music Institute, 1974.
Honeycutt, J.M., and M.E. Eidenmuller. "Communication and attribution: an exploration of the effects of music and mood on intimate couples' verbal and non-verbal conflict resolution behaviors." In V.L. Manusov and J.H. Harvey, eds. *Attribution, communication behavior, and close relationships.* New York: Cambridge University Press, 2001. 21–37.
Houtman, C. *Exodus.* Leuven: Peeters, 1996.
Hutchinson, E. *Music of the Bible: or, explanatory notes upon those passages in the sacred scriptures which relate to music.* Boston: Guild and Lincoln, 1864.
Idelsohn, A.Z. *Jewish music in its historical development.* New York: Henry Holt, 1929.
Imber, N.H. *Music of the Psalms. Music: a monthly magazine* 6 (1894): 568–588.
Jaaniste, J. "Cultural meaning and the art therapies in recovery." *Synergy* 2:1 (2006): 5–7.
Jacobson, J. "Contrafaction." *Journal of synagogue music* 35 (2010): 211–228.
Jacox, F. *Bible music: being variations, in many keys, on musical themes from scripture.* London: Hodder and Stoughton, 1871.
James, W. *The varieties of religious experience.* London: Longmans, Green, 1905.
Jankowsky, R.C. "Music, spirit possession and the in-between: ethnomusicological inquiry and the challenge of trance." *Ethnomusicology forum* 16:2 (2007): 185–208.
Johnson, A.G. *The Blackwell dictionary of sociology: a user's guide to sociological language.* Malden, MA: Blackwell, 2000.
JPS Hebrew-English Tanakh. Philadelphia: Jewish Publication Society, 1999.
Judd, C.C. *Tonal structures in early music.* New York: Taylor and Francis, 2000.
Kadden, B., and B.B. Kadden. *Teaching tefillah: insights and activities on prayer.* West Orange, NJ: Behrman House, 1990.
Kamil, J. *The ancient Egyptians: life in the old kingdom.* Cairo: American University in Cairo Press, 1996.
Karpf, A. *The human voice: how this extraordinary instrument reveals essential clues about who we are.* New York: Bloomsbury, 2006.

Bibliography

Kassis, R.A. *The book of Proverbs and Arabic proverbial works*. Boston: Brill, 1999.
Kaufmann, Y. *The religion of Israel: from its beginnings to the Babylonian exile. Translated from the Hebrew by Moshe Greenberg*. New York: Schocken, 1960.
King, P.J., and L.E. Stager. *Life in biblical Israel*. Louisville, KY: Westminster John Knox, 2001.
Kirsch, J. *King David: the real life of the man who ruled Israel*. New York: Ballantine, 2000.
Kivy, P. *Music alone: philosophical reflections on the purely musical experience*. Ithaca: Cornell University Press, 1990.
Kleinig, J.W. *The lord's song: the basis, function and significance of choral music in chronicles*. New York: Continuum, 1993.
Kolyada, Y. *A compendium of musical instruments and instrumental terminology in the Bible*. London: Equinox, 2009.
Komter, A.E. *Social solidarity and the gift*. New York: Cambridge University Press, 2005.
Kottak, C.P. *Cultural anthropology*. New York: McGraw-Hill, 2004.
Kovach, A. "Shamanism and guided imagery and music: a comparison." *Journal of music therapy*, 22:3 (1985): 154–165.
Kraus, H.J. *Psalms 1–59: a continental commentary*. Minneapolis: Fortress, 1993.
Krummacher, F.W. *Elisha*. London: T. Nelson and Sons, 1870.
Kugel, J.L. *The idea of biblical poetry: parallelism and its history*. New Haven, CT: Yale University Press, 1981.
Kugler, R., and P. Hartin. *An introduction to the Bible*. Grand Rapids: Wm. B. Eerdmans, 2009.
Kunej, D., and I. Turk. "New perspectives on the beginnings of music: archaeological and musicological analysis of a middle Paleolithic bone 'flute.'" In N.L. Wallin, B. Merker, and S. Brown, eds. *The origins of music*. Cambridge: MIT Press. 2001. 235–268.
Labowitz, S. *Miraculous living: a guided journey in kabbalah through the ten gates of the tree of life*. New York: Simon & Schuster, 1998.
Lachmann, R. *Jewish cantillation and song in the isle of Djerba*. Jerusalem: Hebrew University, 1940.
Lack, R. *Twenty four frames under: a buried history of film music*. London: Quartet, 1997.
Langer, S.K. *Feeling and form: a theory of art developed from philosophy in a new key*. New York: Charles Scribner's Sons, 1953.
Larrick, G. *Musical references and song texts in the Bible*. Lewiston, NY: Edwin Mellen, 1990.
Lasor, W.S., D.A. Hubbard, and F.W. Bush. *Old Testament survey: the message, form, and background of the Old Testament*. Grand Rapids: Wm. B. Eerdmans, 1996.
Latham, W., and C. Eagle, "Music for the severely disabled child." *Music education journal*, 38:49 (1982): 30–31.
Lavenda, R.H., and E.A. Schultz. *Core concepts in cultural anthropology*, 2d ed. New York: McGraw-Hill, 2003.
Lemche, N.P. "David's rise." *Journal for the study of the Old Testament*, 4:10 (1979): 2–25.
_____. *The Old Testament between theology and history: a critical survey*. Louisville, KY: Westminster John Knox, 2008.
Lemmelijn, B. "'Genesis' creation narrative: the literary model for the so-called plague tradition?" In A. Wénin, ed. *Studies in the book of Genesis: literature, redaction and history*. Leuven: Peeters, 2001. 407–420.
Levine, J.A. *Synagogue song in America*. Crown Point, IN: White Cliffs, 1989.
Levitin, D.J. *The world in six songs: how the musical brain created human nature*. New York: Dutton, 2008.
Loader, J.A. *Ecclesiastes: a practical commentary*. Grand Rapids: W.B. Eerdmans, 1986.
Lockyer, Jr., H. *All the music in the Bible: an exploration of musical expression in scripture and church hymnody*. Peabody, MA: Hendrickson, 2004.
Lockyer, Sr., H. *Psalms: a devotional commentary*. Grand Rapids: Kregel, 1993.
Longfellow, H.W. *The prose works of Henry Wadsworth Longfellow*. London: David Bogue, 1851.

Longman, T., and R.B. Dillard. *An introduction to the Old Testament.* Grand Rapids: Zondervan, 2006.
Lundbom, J.R. *Jeremiah 1–20: a new translation with introduction and commentary.* New York: Doubleday, 1999.
Luther, M. *Luther's works, volume 35: word and sacrament.* Philadelphia: Fortress, 1960.
Mach, Z. "National anthems: the case of Chopin as a national composer." In Stokes, M., ed. *Ethnicity, identity, and music: the musical construction of place.* New York: Berg, 1997. 61–70.
Malefijt, A.D.W. *Religion and culture: an introduction to anthropology of religion.* Prospect Heights, IL: Waveland, 1968.
Manasseh, S. "A song to heal your wounds: traditional lullabies in the repertoire of the Jews of Iraq." *Musica Judaica* 7 (1991–92): 1–29.
Marshall, F., and P. Cheevers. *Positive options for seasonal affective disorder (SAD): self-help and treatment.* Alameda, CA: Hunter House, 2008.
Marttila, M. *Collective reinterpretation in the Psalms: a study of the redaction history of the Psalter.* Tübingen: Mohr Siebeck, 2006.
Matthews, D.A., and C. Clark. *The faith factor: proof of the healing power of prayer.* New York: Viking, 1998.
May, L. *The socially responsive self: social theory and professional ethics.* Chicago: University of Chicago Press, 1996.
McDermott, J.J. *Reading the Pentateuch: a historical introduction.* New York: Paulist, 2002.
McKenzie, S.L. *King David: a biography.* New York: Oxford University Press, 2000.
McNeill, W.H. *Keeping together in time: dance and drill in human history.* Cambridge: Harvard University Press, 1995.
Meier, S.A. *Themes and transformations in Old Testament prophecy.* Downers Grove, IL: InterVarsity, 2009.
Mellor, P.A. "Sacred contagion and social vitality: collective effervescence in *Les formes élémentaires de la vie religieuse.*"(In W. S. F. Pickering, ed. *Émile Durkheim: critical assessments of leading sociologists,* vol. 2. New York: Routledge, 2001. 167–88.
Meremi, A.E. "Traditional African concept of sound/motion: its implication for and application in music therapy." *British journal of music therapy,* 11:10 (1997) 66–72.
Merriam, A.P. *The anthropology of music.* Evanston, IL: Northwestern University Press, 1964.
Meyer, L.B. *Emotion and meaning in music.* Chicago: University of Chicago Press, 1958.
Miller, J.M., and J. H. Hayes. *A history of ancient Israel and Judah.* Louisville, KY: Westminster John Knox, 1986.
Miller, P.D. *They cried to the lord: the form and theology of biblical prayer.* Minneapolis: Fortress, 1994.
Miller, T.E., and A.C. Shahriari. *World music: a global journey.* New York: Routledge, 2008.
Miller, W.T. *The book of Exodus: question by question.* New York: Paulist, 2009.
Mills, W.E., and R.A. Bullard, eds. *Mercer dictionary of the Bible.* Macon, GA: Mercer University Press, 1990.
Miscall, P.D. *The workings of Old Testament narrative.* Minneapolis: Fortress, 1983.
Mithen, S. *The singing Neanderthals: the origins of music, language, mind and body.* London: Weidenfeld and Nicolson, 2005.
Montagu, J. *Musical instruments in the Bible.* Lanham, MD: Scarecrow, 2002.
Moreno, J.J. "The music therapist: creative arts therapist and contemporary shaman." In D. Campbell, ed. *Music: physician for times to come.* Wheaton, IL: Quest, 1991. 167–186.
Moery, C., ed. *MacMillan on music: essays on music by Sir Ernest MacMillan.* Toronto: Dundurn, 1997.
Mowinckel, S. *The Psalms in Israel's worship.* Translated from the Norwegian by D.R. Ap-Thomas. Grand Rapids: Wm. B. Eerdmans, 2004.
Muchimba, F. *Liberating the African soul: comparing African and western Christian music and worship styles.* Colorado Springs: Biblica, 2008.

Bibliography

Munro, S., and B. Mount. "Music therapy in palliative care." *Canadian medical association journal*, 199:9 (1978): 1029–1032.

Mursil, A. *The manners and customs of the Rwala Bedouins*. New York: American Geographical Society, 1928.

Myers, H., ed. *Ethnomusicology: historical and regional studies*. New York: W.W. Norton, 1993.

Nattiez, J.J. *Music and discourse: toward a semiology of music*. Translated from the French by Carolyn Abbate. Princeton: Princeton University Press, 1990.

Nettl, B. *The study of ethnomusicology: thirty-one issues and concepts*. Urbana and Chicago: University of Illinois Press, 2005.

Neusner, J. *Judaism*: the basics. New York: Routledge, 2006.

Neusner, J., and W.S. Green. *Dictionary of Judaism in the biblical period*, vols. 1 and 2. New York: Macmillan, 1996.

Nickelsburg, G.W.E., and M.E. Stone. *Early Judaism: text and documents on faith and piety*. Minneapolis: Fortress, 2009.

Nietzsche, F.W. *On the genealogy of morality*. Keith Ansell-Pearson, ed. New York: Cambridge University Press, 2007.

Nulman, M. *Concise encyclopedia of Jewish music*. New York: McGraw-Hill, 1975.

_____. "The Shirah melody in the Ashkenazi and Sephardic traditions." *Journal of Jewish music and liturgy* 7 (1984): 12–21.

Oldfield, A., and M. Adams. "The effects of music therapy on a group of profoundly mentally handicapped adults." *Journal of mental deficiency research* 28 (1990): 37–40.

Olmos, M.F., and L. Paravsini-Gebert. *Creole religions of the Caribbean: an introduction from Vodou and Santería to Obeah and Espiritismo*. New York: New York University Press, 2003.

Olsen, D.A. "Shamanism, music, and healing in two contrasting South American cultural areas." In D. Koen, ed. *The Oxford handbook of medical ethnomusicology*. New York: Oxford University Press, 2008. 331–360.

O'Neal, M. *Interpreting Habakkuk as scripture: an application of the canonical approach of Brevard S. Childs*. New York: Peter Lang, 2007.

Opatoshu, J. *In Polish woods*. Translated from the Polish by Isaac Goldberg. Philadelphia: Jewish Publication Society, 1921.

Orelli, C. *The prophecies of Isaiah*. Edinburgh: T. and T. Clark, 1889.

Osherow, M. *Biblical women's voices in early modern England*. Burlington, VT: Ashgate, 2009.

Otto, R. *The idea of the holy: an inquiry into the non-rational factor in the idea of the divine and its relation to the rational*. Translated from the German by John W. Harvey. New York: Oxford University Press, 1950.

Pasture, G.P.H. *Powwow*. Cody, WY: Buffalo Bill Historical Center, 1989.

Pati, J. *Media and tribal development*. New Delhi: Concept, 2004.

Patterson, R.D. *Nahum, Habakkuk, Zephaniah: an exegetical commentary*. Dallas: Biblical Studies, 2003.

Paul, S.M., and S.D. Sperling. "Prophets and prophecy." In *Encyclopedia Judaica*, 16 (2007): 566–580.

Pegg, C., H. Myers, P.V. Bohlman, and M. Stokes. "Ethnomusicology." In S. Sadie, ed. *The new grove dictionary of music and musicians*, 2d ed., vol. 8. New York: Grove's Dictionaries. 2001. 367–403.

Peters, J.S. *Music therapy: an introduction*. Springfield, IL: C.C. Thomas, 2000.

Pfeiffer, R.H. *Introduction to the Old Testament*. New York: Harper, 1941.

Pietersma, A. "Septuagintal exegesis and the superscriptions of the Greek psalter." In P.W. Flint and P.D. Miller, eds. *The book of Psalms: composition and reception*. Leiden: Brill, 2005. 443–475.

Pratt, W.S. "Religion and music." In J.H. Barrows, ed. *The world's parliament of religions*, vol. 2. Chicago: Parliament, 1893. 1005–1008.

_____. "Religion and the art of music." In J.L. Friedmann, comp. *The value of sacred music: an anthology of essential writings, 1801–1918*. Jefferson, NC: McFarland, 2009. 51–66.

Prinsley, D.M. "Music therapy in geriatric care." *Australian nurses journal* 15:9 (1986): 48–49.
Prinsloo, W.S. "The Psalms." In J.D.G. Dunn and J.W. Rogerson, eds. *Eerdmans commentary on the Bible*. Grand Rapids: Wm. B. Eerdmans, 2003. 369–436.
Proudfoot, W. *Religious experience*. Berkeley: University of California Press, 1987.
Rabinowitz, I. "'Word' and literature in ancient Israel." *New literary history* 4:1 (1972): 119–139.
Radano, R.M. *Lying up a nation: race and black music*. Chicago: Chicago University Press, 2003.
Radcliffe-Brown, A. *Structure and function in primitive society: essays and addresses*. New York: The Free Press, 1952.
Rainey, A. "Sacrifice." In *Encyclopedia Judaica*, 17 (2007): 639–644.
Ramey, L. *Slave songs and the birth of African American poetry*. New York: Macmillan, 2008.
Randel, D.M. *The Harvard dictionary of music*. New York: W.W. Norton, 2003.
Rappaport, R.A. *Ritual and religion in the making of humanity*. New York: Cambridge University Press, 1999.
Rendtorff, R. "The Psalms of David: David in the Psalms." In P.W. Flint and P.D. Miller, eds. *The book of Psalms: composition and reception*. Boston: Brill, 2005. 53–64.
Reznikoff, I. "Intonation and modality in the music of oral tradition and antiquity." In T.A. Sebeok and J. Umiker-Sebeok, eds. *The semiotic web 1986: a yearbook of semiotics*. New York: Walter de Gruyter, 1987. 567–569.
Richards, L.O. *Bible reader's companion*. Colorado Springs: David C. Cook, 2002.
Ringgren, H. *Sacrifice in the Bible*. London: United Society for Christian Literature, 1962.
Roberts, J.J.M. *Nahum, Habakkuk, and Zephaniah: a commentary*. Louisville, KY: Westminster John Knox, 1991.
Robertson, A. *Christian music*. New York: Hawthorn, 1961.
Robinson, H.W. *Inspiration and revelation in the Old Testament*. Oxford: Clarendon, 1946.
Robinson, R., and A. Winold. *The choral experience: literature, materials, and methods*. New York: Harper's College, 1976.
Rosenberg, A.J. *Jeremiah, volume 1: a new English translation of text, Rashi, and other commentaries*. New York: Judaica, 1985.
_____. *Mikraoth gedoloth: Psalms*, vol. 3. New York: Judaica, 2001.
Rosner, F. *Moses Maimonides' three treatises on health*. Haifa: Maimonides Research Institute, 1990.
_____. "Moses Maimonides on music therapy and his responsum on music." In M. Nulman, ed. *Essays of Jewish music and prayer*. New York: Yeshiva University Press, 2005. 119–134.
Rothschild, S., and S. Sheridan, eds. *Taking up the timbrel: the challenge of creating ritual for Jewish women today*. London: SCM, 2000.
Rouget, G. *Music and trance: a theory of the relations between music and possession*. Chicago: University of Chicago Press, 1985.
Rowell, L. *Thinking about music: an introduction to the philosophy of music*. Amherst: University of Massachusetts Press, 1984.
Rubin, E., and J.H. Baron. *Music in Jewish history and culture*. Detroit: Harmonie Park, 2006.
Russell, B.D. *The song of the sea: the date of composition and influence of Exodus 15:1-21*. New York: Peter Lang, 2007.
Rust, E.G. *The music and dance of the world's religions: a comprehensive, annotated bibliography of materials in the English language*. Westport, CT: Greenwood, 1996.
Ryken, L., J. Wilhoit, and T. Longman. *Dictionary of biblical imagery*. Downers Grove, IL: InterVarsity Press, 1998.
Ryken, P.G. *Jeremiah and Lamentations: from sorrow to hope*. Wheaton, IL: Crossway, 2001.
Sachs, C. *The history of musical instruments*. New York: Norton, 1940.
_____. *World history of the dance*. New York: Seven Arts, 1952.

Bibliography

Sacks, O. *Musicophilia: tales of music and the brain.* New York: Knopf, 2007.
Safrai, S. "Temple." In *Encyclopedia Judaica,* 19 (2007): 611–625.
Sairam, T.V. "Therapeutic usefulness of music." *Music therapy today* 7:1 (2006): 115–119.
Saliers, D.E. *Music and theology.* Nashville: Abingdon, 2007.
Salzman, L. "To figure or not to figure: the iconoclastic proscription and its theoretical legacy." In C.M. Soussloft, ed. *Jewish identity and modern art history.* Berkeley: University of California Press, 1999. 67–86.
Samuel, M. *Haggadah of Passover.* New York: Hebrew, 1942.
Sanders, J.A. *The Dead Sea Psalms scroll.* Ithaca: Cornell University Press, 1967.
Sankaran, R. "Homeopathic healing in music." In D. Koen, ed. *The Oxford handbook of medical ethnomusicology.* New York: Oxford University Press, 2008. 393–409.
Sarna, N.M. *Songs of the heart: an introduction to the book of Psalms.* New York: Schocken, 1993.
_____. *On the book of Psalms: exploring the prayers of ancient Israel.* New York: Schocken, 1995.
_____. "Book of Psalms." In *Encyclopedia Judaica,* 16 (2007): 663–675.
Schleifer, E. "Jewish liturgical music from the Bible to Hasidism." In L.A. Hoffman and J.R. Walton, eds. *Sacred sound and social change: liturgical music in Jewish and Christian experience.* Notre Dame: University of Notre Dame Press, 1992. 13–58.
Schmidt, R.S. *Exploring religion,* 2d ed. Belmont, CA: Wadsworth, 1988.
Schrock, K. "Why music moves us." *Scientific American mind,* 20 (2009): 32–37.
Schueller, H.M. *The idea of music: an introduction to musical aesthetics in antiquity and the middle ages.* Kalamazoo: Medieval Institute, Western Michigan University, 1988.
Seemann, B. "Proceedings of the society." *Journal of anthropology* 1 (1870): clv–clvi.
Seidel, J. "Possession and exorcism in the magical texts of the Cairo Geniza." In M. Goldish, ed. *Spirit possession in Judaism: cases and contexts from the middle ages to the present.* Detroit: Wayne State University Press, 2003. 73–98.
Sendrey, A. *Music in ancient Israel.* New York: Philosophical Library, 1969.
Sendrey, A., and M. Norton. *David's harp: the story of music in biblical times.* New York: New American Library, 1963.
Shelemay, K.K. *Soundscapes: exploring music in a changing world.* New York: W.W. Norton, 2001.
Shiloah, A. *Jewish musical traditions.* Detroit: Wayne State University Press, 1995.
Silverman, J. *The undying flame: ballads and songs of the Holocaust.* Syracuse: Syracuse University Press, 2002.
Slater, P.J.B. "Birdsong repertoires: their origins and use." In N.L. Wallin, B. Merker and S. Brown, eds. *The origins of music.* Cambridge: MIT Press, 2001. 49–64.
Slobin, M. "Learning the lessons of studying Jewish music." *Judaism: a quarterly journal of Jewish life and thought* 4:2 (1995): 220–225.
Smith, J.A. "Musical aspects of Old Testament canticles in their biblical setting." In I. Fenlow, ed. *Early music history,* vol. 17. New York: University of Cambridge Press, 1998. 221–264.
Smith, J.E. *The wisdom literature and Psalms.* Joplin, MO: College, 2007.
Smith, S. *Prophetic song: gateway to glory.* Longwood, FL: Xulon, 2003.
Söhngen, O. "Music and theology: a systematic approach." In J. Irwin, ed. *Sacred sound: music in religious thought and practice.* Chico, CA: Scholars, 1983. 1–20.
Sosis, R., and C. Alcorta. "Signaling, solidarity, and the sacred: the evolution of religious behavior." *Evolutionary anthropology,* 12:6 (2003): 264–274.
Spencer, F.S. *Dancing girls, loose ladies, and women of the cloth: the women in Jesus' life.* New York: Continuum, 2004.
Spina, F.A. "1 Samuel 17." In R. Van Harn, ed. *The lectionary commentary: the Old Testament and Acts.* Grand Rapids: William B. Eerdmans. 2001. 185–188.
Spurgeon, C.H. *The treasury of David.* New York: Funk and Wagnalls, 1885.
Stafford, W.C. *A history of music.* London: Constable, 1830.

Bibliography

Stainer, J. *The music of the Bible: with some account of the development of modern musical instruments from ancient types.* London: Novello, 1914.

Stein, F., and S.K. Cutler. *Psychosocial occupational therapy: a holistic approach.* Florence, KY: Cengage Learning, 2002.

Steinberg, J. *Mishpat ha-urim.* Vilna: I. Piroschnikoff, 1902.

Stern, C. *Gates of prayer: the new union of prayer.* New York: Central Conference of American Rabbis, 1975.

Stokes, M. *Ethnicity, identity, and music: the musical construction of place.* New York: Berg, 1997.

Stuart, D.K. Hosea-Jonah. Waco: Word Books, 1987.

Sullivan, J.W.N. "Beethoven: his spiritual development." In R. Katz and C. Dahlhaus, eds. *Contemplating music: source readings in the aesthetics of music.* Hillsdale, NY: Pendragon. 1993. 55–64.

Sweeney, M.A. "Habakkuk." In J.L. Mays and J. Blenkinsopp, eds. *HarperCollins Bible commentary.* New York: HarperCollins, 2000. 668–670.

_____. "Jeremiah." In A. Berlin and M.Z. Brettler, eds. *The Jewish study Bible.* New York: Oxford University Press, 2004. 917–1041.

_____. *The prophetic literature.* Nashville: Abingdon, 2005.

Thielemann, S. *The spirituality of music.* New Delhi: APH, 2001.

Thiessen, D. *Selah: a guide to music in the Bible.* Chicago: Cornerstone, 2002.

Tigay, J.H. "Exodus: introduction and annotations." In A. Berlin and M.Z. Brettler, eds. *The Jewish study Bible.* New York: Oxford University Press, 2004. 102–202.

Tiryakian, E.A. "Durkheim, solidarity, and September 11." In J.C. Alexander and P.D. Smith, eds. *The Cambridge companion to Durkheim.* New York: Cambridge University Press, 2005. 305–321.

Titon, J.T., L. Fujie, D. Locke, T. Cooley, D.P. Mcallester, A.K. Rasmussen, and D.B.B. Reck. *Worlds of music: an introduction to the music of the world's people.* Belmont, CA: Wadsworth, 2005.

Tole, L.A. "Durkheim on religion and moral community in modernity." *Sociological inquiry* 63:1 (1993): 1–29.

Tournay, R.J. *Seeing and hearing God with the Psalms: the prophetic liturgy of the second temple in Jerusalem.* New York: Continuum, 1991.

Trigger, B.G., B.J. Kemp, D. O'connor, and A.B. Lloyd. *Ancient Egypt: a social history.* New York: Cambridge University Press, 1983.

Updike, P. "Music therapy results for ICU patients." *Dimensions of critical care nursing,* 9:1 (1990): 39–45.

Van Der Leeuw, G. *Sacred and profane beauty: the holy in art.* 2d ed. Translated by David E. Green. New York: Oxford University Press, 2006.

Van Dyke, H. *The poetry of the Psalms.* New York: T.Y. Crowell, 1900.

Van Rooy, H.F. "The Psalms in early Syriac tradition." In P.W. Flint and P.D. Miller, eds. *The book of Psalms: composition and reception.* Leiden: Brill, 2005. 537–550.

Viladesau, R. *Theology and the arts: encountering god through music, art and rhetoric.* New York: Paulist, 2000.

Von Rad, G. *Old Testament theology: the theology of Israel's historical traditions.* Louisville, KY: Westminster John Knox, 2001.

Wade-Matthews, M. *Music: an illustrated history.* London: Hermes House, 2002.

Wallace, T. *Preaching and teaching outlines from the Psalms.* Murfreesboro: Sword of the Lord, 2001.

Waltke, B.K., J.M. Houston, and E. Moore. *The psalms as Christian worship: an historical commentary.* Grand Rapids: Wm. B. Eerdmans, 2010.

Waltke, B.K., and C. Yu. *An Old Testament theology: a canonical and thematic approach.* Grand Rapids: Zondervan, 2007.

Watson, J.R. *An annotated anthology of hymns.* New York: Oxford University Press, 2002.

Wegner, P.D. *Journey from texts to translations: the origin and development of the Bible.* Grand Rapids: Baker Academic, 2004.

Bibliography

Weintraub, D. "Music and prophecy." *Journal of Synagogue Music* 16:1 (1986): 30–35.

Weiss, R.D. "Oracle." In D.N. Freedman, ed. *Anchor Bible dictionary*, vol. 5. New York: Doubleday, 1992. 28–29.

Weitzman, S. *Song and story in biblical narrative: the history of a literary convention in Ancient Israel*. Bloomington: Indiana University Press, 1997.

Werner, E. *From generation to generation: studies on Jewish musical tradition*. New York: American Conference of Cantors, 1967.

Werner, E., and I. Sonne. "The philosophy and theory of music in Judeo-Arabic literature." *Hebrew union college annual* 16 (1941): 251–319.

West, T., and G. Ironson. "Effects of music on human health and wellness: psychological measurements and research design." In B. Koen, ed. *The Oxford handbook of medical ethnomusicology*. New York: Oxford University Press, 2008. 410–443.

White, S.J. *Foundations of Christian worship*. Louisville, KY: Westminster John Knox, 2006.

Whyte, R.B. "Religion and music." *Music educators journal* 32:6 (1946): 18–19, 21.

Wiersbe, W. *The Bible exposition commentary: Old Testament wisdom and poetry*. Colorado Springs: David C. Cook, 2004.

Wigram, T., J. De Baker, and J. Van Camp. "Music therapy training: a process to develop the musical and therapeutic identity of the music therapist." In T. Wigram and J. De Baker, eds. *Clinical applications of music therapy in developmental disability, paediatrics and neurology*. Philadelphia: Jessica Kingsley, 1999. 282–297.

Wigram, T., I.N. Pedersen, and L.O. Bonde. *A comprehensive guide to music therapy: theory, clinical practice, research, and training*, vol. 1. Philadelphia: Jessica Kingsley, 2002.

Williams, S. "Patients with Parkinson's disease find relief with harp music." *The harp therapy journal* 6:1 (2001): 6–7.

Wilson, J.F. *Religion: a preface*. Englewood Cliffs, NJ: Prentice Hall, 1982.

Wilson-Dickson, A. *The story of Christian music: from Gregorian chant to black gospel*. Minneapolis: Fortress, 1992.

Wine, S. T. *A provocative people: a secular history of the Jews*. Farmington Hills, MI: IISHJ and Milan, 2012.

Wolfe, R. *The twelve religions of the Bible*. Lewiston, NY: Edwin Mellen, 1982.

Wuthnow, R. *Producing the sacred: an essay on public religion*. Urbana: University of Illinois Press, 1994.

Zeltner, P.M. *John Dewey's aesthetic philosophy*. Amsterdam, PA: John Benjamins, 1975.

Zevit, Z. "First Kings." In A. Berlin and M.Z. Brettler, eds. *The Jewish study Bible*. New York: Oxford University Press, 2004. 668–726.

Zimmerman, L.M., M.A. Pierson, and J. Markei. "Effect of music and patient anxiety in coronary care units." *Heart lung* 17:5 (1988): 560–566.

Zornberg, A.G. *The particulars of rapture: reflections on Exodus*. New York: Doubleday, 2001.

Zwettler, M. *The oral tradition of classical Arabic poetry: its character and implications*. Columbus: Ohio University Press, 1978.

Index

Aaron 38, 47, 55, 123, 134, 136
Abel 62, 118
Abiathar 102
Abraham 68, 118
Academy for Jewish Religion, California 4
Adam 68
Africa 50, 53, 77, 99
Agag 76
Ahab 88, 98
Ahijah 88
Akhenaten 16
Akkadian 110, 111, 129
Al Alamot 133
Al Ayyelet ha-Shahar 133
Al ha-Gittit 133
Al ha-Sheminit 133
Al Mahalat 133
Al Malik Al Afdal 61
Al Shoshanim 133
Al Tashhet 133
Aleppo 15
allopathic music 96, 107
Alter, Robert 89
Altshuler, Ira 79
Amalekites 76
Ambrose 137
America 21, 50, 51, 79
Amos 37, 86, 88, 95, 104, 120, 128, 136
Anathoth 101
Antcliffe, Herbert 122
Anthropological Society of London 20
Apollo 60
Arabs 51, 70, 85
Aram 87
Aramaic 129
Arch of Titus 34
archaeology 8, 17, 25, 69, 70, 155
archaeomusicology 16

Ark 54, 68, 100, 118, 123, 124, 130, 135
Asaph 68, 95, 99, 112, 124, 130, 148
Ashkenazi Jews 94
Assyria 34, 69, 85, 98
Augustine 121, 139, 142

Babylonia 34, 69, 71, 102, 104, 107, 117, 124, 135
Bar Kokhba revolt 69
Baumgartner, Walter 104
Bedouins 85
Beersheva 101
Beimel, Jacob 26–27, 111
Ben Arza 55
Benjamin 102
Benjamin, Don C. 77
Beth-Shemesh 118
Bethel 101
Bethlehem 65
Binder, Abraham W. 26
Bochim 118
Bohlman, Philip V. 37
"Bolero" 79
Braun, Joachim 8
Brill-Loewe, Joel 70
Brueggemann, Walter 89, 137, 139

Caesarea-Mazaca 74
Cain 34, 62, 118
California State University, Long Beach 4
call-and-response 46–51
Calvin, John 131
Canaan 49, 70, 84, 87, 100, 118, 123, 129
Canaanites 41, 48
Caribbean 99
Carpathian 22
ceremony 13, 32, 35–36, 99, 134, 148–149
Chaldeans 107–108, 109

Index

chariots 41, 48
Childs, Brevard S. 128
China 60, 111
choirs 9, 33, 37, 47, 51, 102, 111, 124–125, 130, 133–134
Christianity 3, 8, 25, 26, 27, 42, 60, 68, 120, 136, 137, 152
Chronicler 56, 124
church 28, 38, 29, 60, 69, 94, 116, 137
Clark, Connie 60–61
collective effervescence 40, 57
community 3, 29, 32–41, 46, 52, 95, 115–116, 122, 131, 135, 145, 149, 151, 162
Cornill, Carl Heinrich 71
courtiers 58–59, 63, 68, 80, 161
Crafts, Wilber Fisk 27–28
cymbals 37, 54, 55, 56, 67, 99, 112, 124, 125, 130, 134, 138, 140

Dance 19, 21, 22, 24, 30, 36, 37, 43, 46, 51–53, 54, 56, 67–68, 84, 96, 99–100, 113, 138, 140, 157, 158
Daniel 70, 108
David 1, 7, 8, 9–10, 11, 13, 24, 27, 28, 29, 33, 37, 42, 47, 54, 56, 58–82, 88, 98, 100, 110, 112, 122, 124, 127, 128–130, 135, 137, 140, 154, 155, 158, 160, 161
Deborah 13, 42, 47, 56, 67
Diaspora 15, 16, 50, 126
dirge 66, 87
doxology 88, 139–140
drinking songs 37, 87
drums 50, 52–54, 69, 79, 99, 111, 157
Durkheim, Émile 7, 32, 38–41, 43, 57, 91, 135

Ecclesiasticus 55
Edomites 41
Edwards, D. Miall 72
Egypt 2, 9, 31, 41–42, 44, 45–46, 49–50, 55, 56, 61, 69, 70, 87, 102, 107, 117, 121, 129, 153, 157
Elegúa 99
Eliade, Mircea 101
Eliezer b. Jacob 125
Elijah 96–97, 100, 101
Elisha 27, 84, 86, 96–101
Elkanah 115
Elohim 127
England 22, 44
Esau 62
Esther 13
Ethan 124, 130

Ethiopian Orthodoxy 56
ethnomusicology 5, 12, 13, 20, 24, 37, 163
Europe 20–21
Evans, Peggy 4
exile 37, 56, 84, 102, 124, 134
exodus 9, 10, 16, 31, 45, 52, 154, 155
Ezekiel 83, 89, 95

feast 24, 29, 46, 53, 62, 71, 96, 119–120, 135, 149, 157, 161
Fertile Crescent 15
festival 29, 36, 71, 99, 135–136, 139, 149, 162
flute 18, 50, 69, 99, 112, 133, 153
Forsyth, P.T. 35
Freud, Sigmund 91
Friedmann, Elvia 4
Frymer-Kensky, Tikva 18
funerals 33, 36, 157

Gardiner, William 20
Gatewood, Esther 79
Genesis 11, 34, 92, 140
Gereboff, Joel 4
Germany 15
Gibeah 101
Gilgal 76, 101, 118
Glantz, Leib 95
"God Save the Emperor" 44
Goliath 64–65
Greek language 70, 78, 129, 132
Greek mythology 60, 98
Greenwich School of Theology 4
Gressman, Hugo 96
guild 67, 100, 125, 148
Gunkel, Hermann 134

Ha'am, Ahad 10, 11
Habakkuk 86, 96, 104, 107–112
Haggai 13
Halevi, Judah 141
Hallel 126
hallelujah 127, 138–139, 145
Hannah 57, 115–116
harp 37, 50, 54, 56, 59, 67, 70, 99, 112, 124–125, 134, 138, 140
Hassidism 56, 142
hazzan 95
Hebron 101
Heman 56, 68, 95, 99, 112, 124, 130
Herzog, George 21
Heschel, Abraham Joshua 85, 141
Hezekiah 34, 124

Index

higgayon 133
High Priest 55, 102, 136
Hinduism 60
Hofman, Shlomo 33
homeopathic music 96, 107
Horeb 96
Hosea 88, 121
hozeh 95
Huldah 88
hymn 22, 28, 31, 42, 43, 45, 47, 50, 87, 90, 110, 116, 129, 130, 132, 138–139, 141, 145, 147, 151, 158, 159
"Hymn of Aten" 16

Ibn Ezra, Abraham 70, 110
iconoclasm 35
Idelsohn, Abraham Z. 14–15, 26, 70, 126
idolatry 35
igbodu 99
Imber, Naphtali Herz 68
India 60, 85, 111
Indies 21
instruments 1, 5, 6, 8, 13, 21, 24, 27, 33, 34, 50, 54, 57, 61, 67, 68–72, 74, 84, 99, 100, 110, 111, 124, 126, 133, 138, 140, 151, 153, 154, 160, 161
Iraq 33
Irving, Edward 137
Isaac 62, 118
Isaiah 47, 71, 89–90, 96, 120, 162
Ishmael 62
Ishtar 16
Islam 68, 85
iso principle 75–80

Jabal 34,
Jacob 62, 86, 92, 118, 123
James, William 93
Jeduthun 68, 95, 99, 112
Jehoahaz 97
Jehoiakim 104
Jehoram 97, 98, 101
Jehoshaphat 88, 97–98
Jehu 88, 97
Jephthah 56
Jeremiah 83, 86, 89, 96, 101–107, 108, 112, 120, 128
Jericho 74
Jeroboam 88
Jerusalem 9, 14, 15, 16, 23, 34, 37, 50, 51, 54, 64, 68, 102, 104, 107, 116, 118, 124, 126, 134, 136, 139, 143, 149, 159

Jesse 62–63, 64, 140
Jezebel 96, 98
Joash 97, 124
Job 76, 162
Jonah 13, 89
Jonah ben Abitai 98
Jonathan 66
Joseph 49, 63
Josephus 70, 71, 100
Josiah 88, 102
Jubal 27, 34, 57, 71
jubilus 142
Judah 84, 87, 97, 102, 105, 107–108, 109, 141, 145
Judaism 3, 10, 12, 14–15, 26, 27, 33, 35, 36, 41, 50, 53, 60, 61, 68, 95, 103, 110, 123, 126, 132, 136–137, 140, 143

Kabbalah 27
Kabbalat Shabbat 137
Katchko, Adolph 26
Kaufmann, Yehezkel 117
kavvanah 115–116
Kenites 76
Kershaw Chadwick, N. 85
King, Paul J. 17
Korahites 68, 130, 148
Krummacher, Friedrich Wilhelm 98

la-menazze'ah 110, 111, 133
Lamentations 128
Laodicea 74
Latter Prophets 56, 83–84, 113
Leah 123
Levites 9, 15, 33, 55, 56, 67, 68, 71, 99, 100, 103, 108, 110, 112, 117, 122, 123–126, 134, 136, 145, 148, 151, 152, 159
Levitin, Daniel J. 7, 117, 144–150, 151, 152, 161
Lockyer, Herbert, Jr. 47
Longfellow, Henry Wadsworth 22
Lundbom, Robert 102
Luther, Martin 131
lyre (*kinnor*) 1, 10, 11, 27, 29, 34, 37, 50, 54, 56, 58, 69, 61, 62, 63–64, 65, 66, 67, 68–75, 78, 80, 81, 82, 90, 99, 102, 124, 125, 134, 138, 140, 153, 155, 156, 158, 161

Maccabean era 127, 128
Mach, Zdzisław 44
Maimonides, Moses 61, 62, 92, 115
Malachi 13
Malkizedek 68

Index

marching 9, 33, 45, 124, 152
Marduk 135
Marx, Karl 91
Matthews, Dale A. 60–61
Mediterranean 51
Meremi, A.E. 77
Merriam, Alan P. 21–22
Mesopotamia 2, 16, 87, 153
Micah 13, 105, 120
Micaiah 88
Middle Eastern dance 53
military music 19, 33, 45, 51, 56, 65, 152, 154
Minor Prophets 83, 89
miracle 31, 42, 87, 97, 101, 155
Miriam 9, 38, 42, 46–48, 51–53, 55–56, 100, 112, 151
Mishnah 55, 69, 135, 136
Mithen, Steven 18
mizmor 132
Mizpah 101, 118
Moabites 41, 49, 97, 98
monarchy 1, 8, 23, 24, 36, 97, 98, 128, 155, 158, 160
monastic orders 28
Mongolia 21
Moses 9, 10, 31, 38, 41, 42, 45, 47, 55, 61, 65, 68, 103, 112, 118, 123, 130, 140, 151
Mowinckel, Sigmund 136–137
musaf 126
music therapy 3, 7, 18, 58–61, 75–80, 81, 143, 147, 152, 158, 161
mysterium fascinans 91
mysterium tremendum 91, 93

nabi 111–112
Nachman of Breslov 27, 143
Nahum 13, 94
Naples 22
Nathan 88
national anthem 43–46
Native American dance 52–53
Nazirites 88
Neanderthals 18
Near East 2, 18, 34, 53, 65, 69, 74, 87, 153
Nebuchadnezzar 108
Nettle, Bruno 21–22
New Year 134–135
Nietzsche, Friedrich 91
niggun 142, 143
Noah 118
Nob 118
North-West University, Potchefstroom 4

Norton, Mildred 71
Nulman, Macy 70
numinous 7, 86, 91–94

Obadiah 13
Opatoshu, Joseph 95
Ophrah 118
oracle 87, 97, 108
orchestra 33, 37, 56, 93, 124–125
orisha 99–100
oro cantado 99
oro del eyá 99
oro seco 99
Orpheus 60
Otto, Rudolf 7, 32, 38–41, 43, 57, 91, 135

Paleolithic caves 1, 18
Passhur 104, 105
Passover 9, 31, 46
Pasture, George Horse 52–53
Peninah 115
Persians 74
Petrenko, Ester 4
Pfeiffer, Robert Henry 73
Pharaoh 9, 16, 31, 42, 48, 57
Philistine 41, 48, 62, 76
Phinehas 123
pilgrimage 33, 115
Pinchos of Koretz 27
pipe 34, 71, 125, 133, 138, 140
plagues 31, 45
poetry 2, 5, 7, 11, 13, 15, 20, 22, 24, 25, 29, 31, 42, 66, 81, 83, 85, 89–90, 95, 108, 128, 131–132, 141, 154, 155, 158, 160
Portaleone, Abraham 70
Pratt, Waldo S. 114, 116
priesthood 8, 23, 24, 123, 160
priestly blessing 136
prophecy 1, 7, 8, 11, 13, 23, 24, 71, 82, 83–113, 152, 154, 155, 158, 160, 161
Proudfoot, Wayne 93
Proverbs 128
psalmist 37, 43, 105, 107, 128–130, 132, 140, 146, 148
psalmos 132
Psalms (Psalter) 1, 6, 7, 9, 10, 11, 13, 15, 25, 27, 28, 29, 33, 37–38, 67, 68, 102, 103, 104, 106–107, 110–111, 114–152, 155, 159, 161

Quakers 28
Qumran 68, 129

Index

Rabbi Amni 74
Rabbi Judah 70
Rabbi Nehemiah 47
ragas 60
Ramah 118
Ravel, Maurice 79
Red Sea 7, 8, 24, 28, 31, 32, 42, 44, 45, 48, 49–51, 53, 54, 100, 151, 158, 160
responsorial singing 9, 43, 46–51, 103, 157
Reuben 63
Ringgren, Helmer 117
Rochester, Kathleen 4
Rome 34, 69
Rouget, Gilbert 77–78
Rowell, Lewis 61–62
royal court 17, 58–59, 63, 66, 68, 80, 88, 121, 161
Ruth 13
Rwala 85

Sabbath 9, 136, 137
Sachs, Curt 60, 70, 77
sacrifice 9, 76, 117–122, 125, 126
Samuel 62, 64, 76, 88, 100–101, 115
sanctuary 42, 49, 56, 138, 141
Santería 99–100
Sarna, Nahum M. 135
Saul 1, 7, 27, 56, 58–82, 88, 98, 100, 118, 127, 158, 161
Scotland 22
Second Commandment 35
Seemann, Berthold 20
Sefer Tehillim 132
selah 110, 111, 133
Sendrey, Alfred 2, 33, 64, 71, 100, 103, 136
Sennacharib 34
Septuagin 129
sermon 87
shaman 59, 60, 67, 87
Sharlin, William 4
Shechem 101
Shema 47
shigionoth 110
Shiloh 101, 115, 118
shir 133
Shirah 45
Shnuer Zalman of Liadi 142
shofar 74
Shushan 13
Sicily 22
Simon son of Onias 55
slavery 9, 32, 38, 45, 42, 46, 49, 50, 51, 57, 97, 157, 158

Slobin, Mark 15
Smith, John Arthur 9, 47
Socrates 85
Solomon 10, 102, 118, 124, 128–129, 130, 136
Song of Ascents 127, 135
Song of the Sea 1, 7, 8–9, 11, 23, 24, 28, 29, 31–57, 67, 155, 157, 160
Sonne, Isaiah 96, 107
Spain 22
speech-melody 13, 30, 90
Spencer, Herbert 52
Spurgeon, Charles H. 144
Stager, Lawrence E. 17
Steinberg, J. 111
Stokes, Martin 37
Stone, Jon R. 4
Sumaria 101, 129
Sweden 143
Sweeney, Marvin 4, 103
Switzerland 22
synagogue 3, 26, 38, 45, 47, 94, 116–117, 126
Syria 70, 129
Syriac Peshitta 129

Talmud 9, 47, 69, 71, 74, 111, 125
tamid 119, 126
Tannaitic period 129
te'amim 45
Temple (Jerusalem) 7, 9, 14, 15, 16, 18, 23, 24, 27, 33, 36, 38, 41, 50, 51, 53, 54–56, 61, 71, 95, 100, 102–103, 104, 106, 108, 110, 111, 116–117, 118–121, 122, 123–126, 127–128, 132–136, 139–141, 144, 148, 149, 150, 151, 152, 157, 159, 160, 161
theosophy 88, 109
Thiessen, Donald 45, 66
tikkun hak'lali 143–144
timbrel 47, 51, 53, 54, 56, 99, 112, 138, 140
Torah (Pentateuch) 9, 11–13, 44, 89, 126, 139–140
trumpet 12, 34, 45, 50, 54–55, 124–125, 133, 153
Tubal-Cain 34
Tyrol 22

Ugaritic 129

van der Leeuw, Gerardus 93
van Rooy, Herrie 4
Venice 22
victory 2, 13, 28, 34, 37, 42, 44–45, 51, 54,

Index

56, 57, 64, 67, 71, 90, 98, 134, 146, 157, 160
Viladesau, Richard 94

Wagner, Richard 44
Waltke, Bruce 129
weddings 33, 36, 61
Werner, Eric 96, 107, 119–120
Western culture 1, 4, 20, 21, 60, 86, 94
wine 37, 55, 117, 118
Wine, Sherwin T. 9

women 55–56
wonderworker 87, 97, 100
work songs 2, 22, 152, 157
World Wars 60

Yemen 14, 33

Zadok 102
Zedekiah 102
Zohar 124

www.ingramcontent.com/pod-product-compliance
Lightning Source LLC
Chambersburg PA
CBHW032059300426
44116CB00007B/818